THELONIOUS MONK QUARTET FEATURING
JOHN COLTRANE AT CARNEGIE HALL

OXFORD STUDIES IN RECORDED JAZZ
Series Editor JEREMY BARHAM

Louis Armstrong's Hot Five and Hot Seven Recordings
Brian Harker

The Studio Recordings of the Miles Davis Quintet, 1963–68
Keith Waters

Benny Goodman's Famous 1938 Carnegie Hall Jazz Concert
Catherine Tackley

Keith Jarrett's The Köln Concert
Peter Elsdon

Thelonious Monk Quartet Featuring John Coltrane at Carnegie Hall
Gabriel Solis

THELONIOUS MONK QUARTET FEATURING JOHN COLTRANE AT CARNEGIE HALL

GABRIEL SOLIS

Oxford University Press is a department of the University of Oxford.
It furthers the University's objective of excellence in research,
scholarship, and education by publishing worldwide.

Oxford   New York
Auckland   Cape Town   Dar es Salaam   Hong Kong   Karachi
Kuala Lumpur   Madrid   Melbourne   Mexico City   Nairobi
New Delhi   Shanghai   Taipei   Toronto

With offices in
Argentina   Austria   Brazil   Chile   Czech Republic   France   Greece
Guatemala   Hungary   Italy   Japan   Poland   Portugal   Singapore
South Korea   Switzerland   Thailand   Turkey   Ukraine   Vietnam

Oxford is a registered trade mark of Oxford University Press in the UK and certain other countries.

Published in the United States of America by
Oxford University Press
198 Madison Avenue, New York, NY 10016

© Oxford University Press 2014

All rights reserved. No part of this publication may be reproduced,
stored in a retrieval system, or transmitted, in any form or by any means,
without the prior permission in writing of Oxford University Press,
or as expressly permitted by law, by license, or under terms agreed with the
appropriate reproduction rights organization. Inquiries concerning
reproduction outside the scope of the above should be sent to the
Rights Department, Oxford University Press, at the address above.

You must not circulate this work in any other form
and you must impose this same condition on any acquirer.

Library of Congress Cataloging-in-Publication Data
Solis, Gabriel, 1972–
Thelonious Monk Quartet featuring John Coltrane at Carnegie Hall / Gabriel Solis.
pages   cm.—(Oxford studies in recorded jazz)
Includes bibliographical references and index.
ISBN 978-0-19-974435-0 (hardback : alk. paper)—ISBN 978-0-19-974436-7 (pbk. : alk. paper)
1. Monk, Thelonious—Criticism and interpretation.   2. Coltrane, John, 1926–1967—Criticism and
interpretation.   3. Thelonious Monk Quartet—Performances—New York (State)—New York.
4. Jazz—History and criticism.   I. Title.
ML417.M846S56 2013
785'.35165—dc23   2013016796

3 5 7 9 8 6 4 2
Printed in the United States of America
on acid-free paper

FOR MEL WILLIAMS, MY JAZZ GURU—DJ, ACTIVIST, AND TENOR SAXOPHONIST EXTRAORDINAIRE, WHO TAUGHT ME TO LOVE MONK AND TRANE WHEN I WAS A KID

SERIES PREFACE

THE OXFORD STUDIES in Recorded Jazz series offers detailed historical, cultural, and technical analysis of jazz recordings across a broad spectrum of styles, periods, performing media, and nationalities. Each volume, authored by a leading scholar in the field, addresses either a single jazz album or a set of related recordings by one artist/group, placing the recordings fully in their historical and musical context, and thereby enriching our understanding of their cultural and creative significance.

With access to the latest scholarship and with an innovative and balanced approach to its subject matter, the series offers fresh perspectives on both well-known and neglected jazz repertoire. It sets out to renew musical debate in jazz scholarship, and to develop the subtle critical languages and vocabularies necessary to do full justice to the complex expressive, structural, and cultural dimensions of recorded jazz performance.

JEREMY BARHAM
UNIVERSITY OF SURREY
SERIES EDITOR

ACKNOWLEDGMENTS

THIS BOOK COULD not have been completed without the intellectual, personal, and financial support of many. I offer my deep thanks to all who made it possible and saw me through the process.

I wish to recognize the Illinois Program for Research in the Humanities first. The fellowship year away from teaching and the community of scholars they provided me in 2009–10 was crucial in the initial stage of conceptualizing the project. I am also grateful to the University of Illinois Research Board, which supported research assistants for the preparation of the manuscript at two critical junctures. I thank Gary McPherson and the University of Melbourne, whose invitation to deliver a workshop series on improvisation pedagogy in 2011 gave me a chance to work through some of the questions about intergenerational learning this book raises. And I offer sincere thanks to Yu Wakao and the membership of the Japanese Association for the Study of Musical Improvisation, whose invitation to deliver a keynote address at their conference in 2012 helped me sharpen the conceptual framework for the book.

My deepest, warmest thanks go to my research assistants, Bryan Felix and Euan Edmonds, doctoral students in jazz studies at the University of Illinois, without whose enormous help I might never have completed the book.

I have had the pleasure of talking with and getting feedback on drafts of this project from a brilliant community of ethnomusicologists and music historians. I owe them a great deal. My colleagues at the University of Illinois in musicology and composition: Christina Bashford,

Donna Buchanan, Bill Kinderman, Erik Lund, Gayle Magee, Jeff Magee, Bruno Nettl, Katherine Syer, Steve Taylor, and Tom Turino; jazz scholars John Howland, Travis Jackson, and Lara Pellegrinelli; ethnomusicologists Tomie Hahn and Sean Williams; and no doubt many, many more. I am indebted to Robert Snarrenberg, whose classes at Washington University opened my eyes and ears to what music theory and analysis can be. And special thanks go to my teacher, tireless mentor, and friend, Ingrid Monson.

My friends and family deserve all the thanks I can give, and more, for bearing with me through this project, encouraging my enthusiasm, and stoking my fires when they flagged. There are far too many to name here, but I say this: Ellen, Andrea, Coleman, and Bella, you have been my inspiration, and you have kept me at least a little humble.

Thanks.

CONTENTS

INTRODUCTION 3

1 Monk with Coltrane: The Story of a Collaborative Relationship 23

2 Jazz in the Concert Hall: The Morningside Community Center Benefit and the Jazz Concert as an Institution to 1957 38

3 Playing Ballads: "Monk's Mood" and "Crepuscule with Nellie" 54

4 Up-tempo Tunes, Convention, and Innovation: "Evidence" and "Nutty" 69

5 Scripting the Sound of Surprise: "Bye-Ya" and "Sweet and Lovely" 93

6 Abiding Favorites: "Blue Monk" and "Epistrophy" 125

7 Together at Last, Together Forever: Monk and Coltrane on Record in 2005 146

NOTES 165

REFERENCES 171

INDEX 177

THELONIOUS MONK QUARTET FEATURING
JOHN COLTRANE AT CARNEGIE HALL

INTRODUCTION

FOR A SCANT six months in 1957, John Coltrane played in Thelonious Monk's band. Filling the tenor spot previously held by Sonny Rollins, he added a searing, sprinting foil to Monk's understated, ambling piano. Coltrane was a young player, his most enduring work still to come, but he brought with him impressive technique and a considerable playing history, most recently with Miles Davis. Monk was from an older generation, but only finally coming into his own as a recording artist and bandleader at the time. In the 1950s, Monk's decision to hire Coltrane was barely noted, but in retrospect it has come to be seen as one of the most important partnerships in the history of modern jazz. The quartet, including Monk, Coltrane, bassists Wilbur Ware and Ahmed Abdul-Malik, and drummer Shadow Wilson, appeared regularly at the Five Spot Café in the Bowery, just on the edge of Greenwich Village, but was documented in only a limited way at the time. They made a handfull of studio recordings, some of which were not released until a number of years later, due to contractual problems, and Blue Note issued a scratchy live bootleg in 1993, recorded during a one-night engagement Coltrane had with Monk's band in 1958. The recording, captured by Coltrane's wife, Naima, on a portable tape recorder, is the essence of lo-fi; as much bar noise as music, the balance obscures some of Coltrane's playing and the band sounds tinny and far away (Sheridan 2001, 88–89). Even after remastering for release as part of the complete Thelonious Monk on Blue Note box set, the Five Spot recording has remained largely a collector's piece.

Early in 2005 Larry Appelbaum, a sound archivist at the Library of Congress, made what has to be one of the biggest finds in the history of jazz recordings. Unnoticed for decades in the library's archives, in a plain folder with little to identify it, Appelbaum unearthed reel-to-reel tapes containing a November 29, 1957, Morningside Community Center benefit concert, which the Voice of America recorded in Carnegie Hall but never broadcast. The tapes caught Monk and Coltrane at creative peaks, clearly digging one another's playing, working with a representative set list and best of all, recorded with a state-of-the-art system. The recording sounded good: Monk and Coltrane's playing came through clearly, and the rhythm players, Ahmed Abdul-Malik and Shadow Wilson, were clearly audible—more than can be said even for many studio recordings of the time.

From these tapes, which included nearly all of the night's multi-artist lineup, the sets featuring the Monk/Coltrane quartet were released as the album *Thelonious Monk Quartet with John Coltrane at Carnegie Hall* in 2005 on Blue Note records. The album's release was a major event, undoubtedly one of the most widely covered jazz releases of the recent past in the American and European press. Malcolm Jones, writing breathlessly in *Newsweek*, called it "The musical equivalent of discovering a new Mount Everest," and the *Washington Post* said, "for jazz fans, this discovery is almost like coming across the Holy Grail" (Jones 2005, 58; Schudel 2005, N01). In addition to critical success, the album has sold well, handily overshadowing any other jazz release at the time.

The story of this recording is of fundamental interest to jazz history, for a number of reasons. First, the concert is interesting because of the fact that as an event it was somewhere between an everyday club date and a monumental undertaking. The grouping of performers was quite good, and the night was remarked upon in the *Times*, but it was not a one-of-a-kind event. There was no "conceptual" program, no special compositions or arrangements on the bill, and it was not initiated as an opportunity to record a live album. Still, it was at Carnegie Hall and was intended for broadcast. What we now hear on the tapes is something common for its time, but absolutely, remarkably, special. It is a window onto a moment, a working musical partnership that is otherwise gone. Moreover, in addition to this distinction at the time, it is also unusual because it has such a thin subsequent history. Unlike Monk's live recordings from Europe through the late-1950s and early-1960s, or Coltrane's recordings at the Village Vanguard or Birdland, which have become familiar, well worn, carefully listened to, and closely studied by generations of fans and jazz musicians, *Thelonious Monk Quartet with John Coltrane at Carnegie Hall* quite simply did not exist in the jazz world between the night it was recorded and 2005.[1]

This book, in line with the rest of the volumes in the series, focuses extensively on analytical close readings of the pieces on the album *Thelonious Monk Quartet with John Coltrane at Carnegie Hall*. However, those close readings serve also to motivate historical questions about changes in jazz over the course of the twentieth century, and critical questions about the place of jazz in American culture. Beyond this, by focusing on the recording as a cultural object with significance in itself, rather than simply as a document of music making, this book raises issues that place contemporary jazz in relation to the field of media studies.

The late 1950s, when the recording was made, were a period of legendary intensity in jazz history. Miles Davis seemed to reach a new peak every year, with the albums *Cookin'*, *Steamin'*, *Relaxin'*, and *Workin'*—guidebooks to classic hard bop style—all recorded within a few months in 1956 and released in 1957, following up on *'Round About Midnight*, and followed by a series of fine albums culminating in 1959's landmark *Kind of Blue*. Sonny Rollins recorded something, as a leader or sideman, virtually every month between 1956 and 1959, producing the grand eponymous albums for Blue Note and the irreverent and ultimately hard-swinging *Way Out West* for Contemporary. Sonny Stitt and Dizzy Gillespie, Benny Golson and Hank Mobley, Art Blakey and the Jazz Messengers, Max Roach, the Modern Jazz Quartet, Milt Jackson, Hank Jones, Horace Silver, Lennie Tristano, and Gerry Mulligan all wrote and played and recorded songs and albums that would challenge their contemporaries and become standards in time. A language that had been worked out in rehearsal, on stage, and in countless jam sessions in large and small venues throughout the country in the previous decade was well and truly in flower on the recordings these musicians and many others made at the time.

Beyond this, as David Rosenthal notes in his book *Hard Bop*, the period has been seen as a final golden age, a resurgence, a time when jazz thrived in dialogue with a large, appreciative audience. Not just an elite music for a relatively small cadre of aficionados—America's Classical Music, as it would come to be dubbed, for better and for worse—jazz in the late 1950s was a cutting-edge popular music. The hard bop years were, as Rosenthal sees it, quoting Andrew Hill, the time "before the music got separated"—separated from its audience, fully separated from pop, separated at least in jazz criticism into the myriad warring camps of the 1960s (1992, 69).

Finally, the 1950s were an exceptional moment for live jazz recordings. There had, of course, been live recordings stretching back for decades, thanks in large measure to the broadcast wires that were built into many concert halls to produce the syndicated shows that were the staple of radio in the 1930s (McDonough 2006, 36). However, postwar innovations in recording technology—the drive to create ever smaller devices capable of capturing sound with ever greater fidelity—meant that by the late 1950s any record company could (and many did) produce high-quality recordings in situ at essentially any major jazz venue, most importantly the small nightclubs that had risen to prominence in the late 1930s and 1940s as the best spaces for modern jazz.

Given the wealth of documentation of jazz—live and in the studio—from this seminal moment in the music's history, it may seem odd to focus an entire volume on an obscure live recording that was never intended for release, and was in fact not released until nearly fifty years after the fact. This recording of Monk and Coltrane is, however, singular and rewards extended consideration. In a way, the recording should not be particularly interesting: the repertoire for the two sets is entirely made up of work the band played night after night, and there are relatively few moments that break out of the well-established modern jazz formal frame. The group plays the heads in unison, followed by a series of solos that maintain the form of the heads in relatively straightforward ways, and finally end in closing choruses in which the band restates the head, again in unison. Within this framework, the performances are remarkable. Most importantly, the recording is a document of truly brilliant musicians creating something—hammering, forging, molding, willing something new into being—something that is both a compendium of what was possible within jazz conventions of the day and a glimpse of how those conventions could be pushed forward.

Beyond the music itself, the recording is an unparalleled document of a micro-moment in jazz history, or perhaps a moment in jazz's microhistory. Monk's decision to hire Coltrane for his quartet was a small thing in each of the musicians' lives, at least at the moment, yet it came to have remarkably far-reaching consequences for the shape of jazz to come, so to speak. Coltrane's work, even more than Monk's, was profoundly changed by the experience of playing in the group—more, perhaps, than any of the many other tenor players who played with him over the years. Some, like Johnny Griffin, served as foils to Monk's style but were relatively unchanged by it; others, like Charlie Rouse, were deeply committed to Monk's demands as a bandleader but seem already to have absorbed Monk's language by the time they worked with him. Coltrane came to Monk's band at a fortuitous time in his career, as though looking for the key to new directions he was seeking, and was attuned to the possibilities suggested by Monk's music.

Finally, this recording's peculiar history, from the initial conditions of its production to its ultimate, belated release, offers a unique lens through which to understand postwar jazz recordings as things in themselves. With care, it can be heard to speak to the political economy of jazz in the 1950s, the meaning of style and genre, the place of performance and recording and the contexts of jazz as a business and a job, as well as, of course, an art, and it can be heard to speak eloquently to the same questions and issues in jazz at the start of the twenty-first century. Because of the long gap between recording and release, it was unusual and special in 2005 and could be invested with all the fantasies and frustrations of the jazz community in a time of extensive nostalgia.

CONCEPTUALIZATIONS OF IMPROVISATION, INTERACTION, MUSICAL WORKS, AND THE JAZZ RECORDING

The questions within jazz scholarship this book most directly asks revolve around how to understand musical repetition of many sorts as it relates to conceptualizations of improvisation, composition, and the making of musical works. This constellation of theoretical concerns will be present in shifting patterns throughout the rest of this book, though not always explicitly. It will be useful, then, before moving forward with the details of the recording, to unpack the remarkable complexity that improvisation, composition, and repetition represent in jazz performances and on jazz recordings, as can be heard in these tracks. Starting with improvisation, composition, and repetition in the music itself—the details, "on the ground," of jazz—these concerns move analysis to larger and larger frames of reference, including questions about aesthetics, the circulation of ideas in social networks, the cultural life of music in the twentieth and twenty-first centuries, and the political economy of jazz and the American recording industry.

I start with repetition, because it is elemental. In being elemental, its meanings are also broad, diffuse, and fluid. Many aesthetic theorists have spoken about repetition, and, at least as importantly, it has been the subject of regular vernacular theory among both musicians and audiences. Repetition is central to recent cognition-based music theories, being fundamental to the creation of comprehensibility in music. Eugene Narmour's study of musical expectation describes repetition as basic not only to music but to the human organism: we are "similarity automatons regardless of domain, level, or operation" (2000, 395). As such, when we make music we make a repetitive, patterned set of sounds because such a set of sounds is central to our modes of perception and cognition. According to this theory, we yearn to hear repetition and to interpret what we hear as pattern. Adam Ockelford begins from this position to propose a "zygonic" theory of music, which in a sense argues that all meaning comes from relationships of imitation, which as he points out, amount to repetition (2005, 2–3).[2] Although his analyses generally tend to consider zygonic relationships, or repetitions, within a work, he points to a much larger sphere in which we perceive and understand such relationships: "the single concept of a zygon bequeaths a vast perceptual legacy with many potential manifestations; between, for example, pitches, timbres, processes and forms the same; over different periods of time; and within the same and between different pieces, performances and hearings" (22). Michael Tenzer's recent goal of establishing a unified musical theory that holds true for any of the world's musics starts from similar ground, taking periodicity—"repetition or restatement, literal or transformed, of all kinds"—as the fundamental object of consideration. He says, "Music is nothing if not iteration and pattern; periodicity is music's ultimate organizer on many levels.... The absence of periodicity in *any* music is a challenge to imagine. Even if one could invent such music algorithmically, we, as aware listeners, would impose or construct pattern, as that is the nature of mind relating to world" (2006, 22–23). Repetition in jazz, specifically, has been a subject of fascination, snap judgment, and dismissive off-hand pronouncement since the genre's earliest emergence into the public eye.

In spite of this attention, the subject of repetition has hardly been exhausted in the study of midcentury jazz, much less music in general. An important starting point is to consider distinct kinds of repetition and their effects in jazz. What is repeated, and how does the passage of time between iterations impact how we experience repetition? Ingrid Monson's article "Riffs, Repetition, and Theories of Globalization" creates a framework for asking these questions. As she notes, jazz incorporates repetition as a structural principle at essentially every meaningful level, from the smallest details of musical form, the moment-to-moment sonic events that make up a performance, to the largest order—pieces and styles (1999, 32). I follow up some of the implications of Monson's work here, adding particularly a diachronic dimension to the highest-order conceptualization of the way repetition functions in the music, focusing on how it allows us to understand personal temporalities, at the level of biography and the musical career, and communal temporalities, at the level of history and cultural memory.

Jazz performances are made up of cyclic repetitions in nesting orders of magnitude. At the most immediate level are the cycles of extremely short duration, the rhythmic cycles that, taken together, produce the ongoing sense of groove within the performance. Here I mean both the pulsing figure of the beat and its subdivision into two or three or more components, the regular, recurrent patterns of stress and release through which music pushes forward in time. I also mean the succession of beats in a 4/4 measure, with a backbeat, again a succession of stressed and unstressed pulses in time that give a sense of movement to the music. And finally, I mean the characteristic patterns of the rhythm section— the ride cymbal and hi-hat, for instance, and the walking bass lines that incorporate both repetition and variation. Monson has written eloquently about this phenomenon, calling it "a rhythmic relation or feeling existing *between* two or more musical parts and or individuals" (1996, 68, original emphasis). She quotes clarinetist Don Byron, describing a groove as a kind of "euphoria that comes from playing good time *with* somebody" (ibid., original emphasis). Laurent de Wild, discussing Monk's music in particular, has also written about it, under the rubric of "time," and taking the notion of euphoria further, in an explicitly spiritual and romantic sense: "Why does it always take at least two people to make time?... When you are two together, it's the beginning of a shared experience, a faith expressing itself, faith in a god which is the original pulse and which is worshipped in a church that is the music itself. Creating time is a truly mystical and communal experience.... It's an act of love, as opposed to masturbation" (1997, 34). None of this necessarily deals with the way repetition functions as the central figure in the production of a groove or time in jazz, though it is implicit. I focus explicitly on repetition in this process in order to make clear that it is the first point on the continuum from small to large, the lowest-level ongoing repetition, felt at the level of beat and meter. Charles Keil's theory of "Participatory Discrepancies" is predicated on this in a way, and the fleshing out of that idea has certainly looked at repetition as a musical force (1987). That said, Keil and others have tended to celebrate the minute variations within repetition—the "discrepancies" that invite participation—while I wish to highlight for a moment the massive level of repetition itself. Of course both repetition and variation are important, but I would simply reiterate that the predictable repetition of a number of musical figures is absolutely central to the enjoyment of most jazz.

At the next level, within most jazz chorus forms there are patterns of melodic, rhythmic, and harmonic repetition that are partially cyclical, that serve to mark out the flow of time into regular, recurrent units. If the groove is felt largely at the level of beat and meter, these secondary cycles involve repetitions—often only partial—that usually mark off binary units of musical time: two measures, four measures, eight measures, sixteen measures. The common thirty-two-bar song forms are massively cyclical, with periods usually operating at all of the binary divisions of thirty-two measures. An AABA song form incorporates cyclical repetition of eight-measure sections, at the very least, and its drama plays out through the dynamic of repetition and contrast. The four sections can be thought of as A/statement, A/reiteration with or without alteration, B/ contrast, and A/reiteration with or without alteration. This patterning generally happens melodically, rhythmically, and harmonically and can, of course, be overlain by longer-scale tonal processes, such as the common structural move from IV to V over the course of the B section, which tie the whole thirty-two-bar structure into one linear process as well. Blues forms also work through periodicity, with the most common pattern being twelve bars divided into three equal four-bar sections, commonly labeled aab or aa'b. These four bars most often also involve a drama of repetition and contrast: a/statement, a'/altered repetition, b/ contrast. Although Monk composed forms that are irregular, in their number of measures and subdivisions, the majority of his work and all of the standards he played include regular periodicity of this sort. Much of the formal interest in the solos on this recording come from the musicians working creatively at times to project, and at times to undermine, the impact of precisely these kinds of repetitive structures.

Finally, normatively speaking, jazz performances in most (but not all) styles are characterized by the cyclical repetition of the chorus form. This, also, is implicit in most theoretical/analytical discussion of jazz, but its consequences in terms of musical experience are not always fleshed out explicitly. Musicians actually treat the regular repetition of the chorus structure quite differently from one another, and from one piece to the next. Monk tended to treat the individual choruses of his solos as independent units to some degree, routinely highlighting their divisions from one another, and building larger-scale forms by piecing together choruses like building blocks. Coltrane, on the other hand, often (though by no means always) phrased in such a way as to obscure chorus structure, creating larger-order form through redefining the length of sections within his solo. In either case, of course, their accompanists helped define the cyclical repetition of the chorus and create larger-scale form, either through reiteration of the formal moves the soloists made or by contrast. This is the level of repetition that I address most directly in the analyses that make up Chapters 3 through 6.

Beyond these types of cyclical repetition, jazz performances incorporate noncyclical repetition at essentially every level. From the creation of musical figures and phrases through the use of motivic repetition, to the kinds of repetition that create intermusical reference, noncyclical repetition is a key tool in creating musical meaning.[3] In relation to the recording of Monk's band with John Coltrane at the Morningside Heights benefit, the repetition of pieces of music is the most compelling on this level. On the bill that evening, Monk chose pieces he had played over and over, many of them since the very beginning of his career, with essentially every band he led over the course of a bit more than twenty years by that time. For Coltrane the tunes may not have been quite as deeply ingrained in his fingers and imagination, but they were still pieces he had played with Monk's band for months, day in and day out. In fact, a primary difference between this recording and the studio recordings Monk and Coltrane made some months prior is a result of that repetition. The audience that evening would, of course, have had varying levels of familiarity with the pieces, but the musicians would have had an intimate knowledge of the tunes, a knowledge honed over many repetitions, night after night.

The literature on jazz has only begun to view this intertextual repetition of whole pieces in performance as an object of musical analysis, but it holds significant potential as an area of investigation. Tom Perchard has developed an extensive and very interesting analysis of how Monk's solos function as improvisatory composition—I would like to call it "improvosing" or "comprovisation"—by looking at a number of performances he recorded of "Lulu's Back in Town" in Paris in 1966 (2011). This sort of analysis—like my own analysis of two solos by Johnny Griffin on the song "Evidence," from 1958—makes the case that jazz improvisation is a process that involves memory, engages musicians in ongoing evaluation of their own work, and connects repetitions of a single piece not only as discrete musical instances but in fact as nodes in networks of creative activity (Solis 2004). Likewise, Monk did not play a "simulacrum" of improvisation on "Lulu's Back in Town," as French critic Michel-Claude

Jalard worried in 1964. Rather, he was, as Perchard says, "working to a kind of composition, at least, improvising according to a largely fixed formal plan" (2011, 83). Nor was it by happenstance that Griffin played two structurally related solos on "Evidence" the two nights it was being recorded in the late fifties when he was playing with Monk. Rather, the two recordings captured the larger fact that while he was in Monk's band, Griffin was working out the musical ideas suggested to him by the song, creating his own way of saying something with it.[4] The terms "improvised" and "composed" are stretched to their limits in looking at Monk's playing, as Perchard clearly recognizes, when he describes Monk's style being defined by a tendency to "interpolate licks which have been so expanded that they appear not to link ideas, or cross from chord to chord or bar to bar, but instead function as blocks of 'composed' music dropped into an otherwise 'improvised' solo" (ibid.). The difficulty Perchard has at the moment of conclusion, of situating Monk's solos in terms of the dialectic of improvisation and composition is, in fact, the heart of his article's contribution and is not limited to Monk, although it is exceptionally clear in Monk's playing.[5] In neither Monk's nor Griffin's case is this evidence of a creative lack, but rather of the structural presence of repetition that often characterizes good improvisation, and of how jazz music making confounds the basic premise on which a categorical distinction between improvisation and composition rests. In the case of this recording, the similarities and differences in Monk's approach to repertoire over time is an important interpretive wedge, as is the linking of particular items of repertoire to one another in various performances and recordings to make musical experiences that extend beyond the individual work.

A focus on musical repetition in this context inevitably leads one to look at the broader, somewhat ahistorical discussion of black aesthetics as a way of understanding formal processes in jazz. This is not a book about race as such, nor even a book in which the primary argument is about racialization in music, but the recording's context of midtwentieth- and early twenty-first-century America makes race an inevitable component of the book's primary focus on socially grounded aesthetics. In the final chapter I take up a discussion of race as a component of the marketing of jazz in the 1990s and 2000s—the branding of the "Young Lions"—and various iterations of nostalgia in jazz. I have written in a number of contexts about Monk's music as "Afro-modern," borrowing a term from Houston A. Baker, particularly trying to excavate what might be the ways in which his musical choices are informed by and reflect black aesthetics. Perchard has critiqued my work in this vein, arguing that an overemphasis on the African American context has similarly trapped analyses of Monk's music in an essential, uniform paradigm, when Monk actually breaks the paradigm not only of Western formalism but also of African American contextualism (2011, 75). Perchard is quite right when he argues that Monk thought "textually"—which is to say that he appears to have had a strong work concept in mind for many of his pieces, both in how he wanted the heads played and in how he improvised on them. Moreover, he is correct in saying that at times Monk appears to play solos that engage in only a limited way in what many would think of simply as improvisation. Rather, his penchant to draw on large blocks of what Perchard calls "quasi-textual formalization" in his solos confounds any simple view of improvisation as something made up from nothing in the moment (82). This does not, however, in any way reduce the value of looking at Monk's playing as interactive, as Perchard suggests it does, or of reading that interactivity as a musical value nurtured and prized in African American traditions.[6] My argument is that the black, Afro-modern context for Monk's work offered models for and fostered both spontaneous, interactive innovation and studied, precise repetition. The only thing that would make this seem like a contradiction is a limited view of the history of black musical life in America.

The sort of repetition that governs the creation of work concepts and relative "fixity" in jazz performances is not, incidentally, the kind of "intermusicality" nurtured in African American musical forms that has occupied many jazz scholars, myself included, over the past decade or so, starting with Paul Berliner's *Thinking in Jazz* (1994) and Ingrid Monson's *Saying Something* (1996), but it is not incompatible with a discussion of that kind of noncyclical repetition. Of course, references of all sorts—to other jazz solos and songs, to bits of pop culture, to classical compositions, and so on—can be embedded in the recurrent structures of "improvosed" solos, but the more spontaneous, momentary references that Monson, in particular, discusses, are a different kind of repetition and have a different effect (1996, 44–45, 146–52). The repetition of musical structures that I highlight above may begin as spontaneous musical utterances, but they take on a kind of fixity over time that comes from their regular, if not cyclical, repetition. References often stand out, in contrast, as single-instance occurrences that may gain their power by virtue of breaking the frame of cyclicity and fixity. They work because they are repetitions of materials that audiences have heard, elsewhere, at other times, and in other contexts; but they tend to be most successful if they are unanticipated by listeners and sound spontaneous. This may even be incorporated into a musician's "comprovisational" thinking.

Repetition, at all of the levels I have identified, is central to most of the issues raised by the album *Thelonious Monk Quartet with John Coltrane,* as a document of performance and as a part of jazz history and American cultural life. Most immediately, it plays a fundamental role in the conceptual organization of musical creativity into improvisation and composition, and the emergent concept of the thing created, the musical work. Improvisation—defined for the moment loosely as the (often interactive) creation of new versions of pieces of music in the act of performance—has been, since at least the 1940s, the hallmark of jazz. It is one musical feature that jazz's proponents often point to in order to separate jazz from other popular musics and from the Western classical tradition; it is the musical feature that has been the focal point and key to ideas about the basic hero myth in the music, incorporating skill, genius, and musical progress in jazz; and it is the musical feature around which a sense of the music's mystery, often couched as spiritual transcendence, coalesces. At times it has also been an aspect of jazz that commentators (and performers) used to link that music to other performance traditions from the African Diaspora, the Middle East, and India. Composition, by contrast, has been a term imbued with a different cultural value when used in jazz, drawing on the prestige of the Western classical tradition and its practice of celebrating a relatively fixed body of canonical works (Lydia Goehr's "Imaginary Museum" 1992). As I have argued elsewhere, a small number of jazz musicians have been lionized as "true" composers—Duke Ellington, Charles Mingus, Thelonious Monk—a term that I believe has obscured as much about their creative work and that of their bands as it has clarified (Solis 2008, 120).

My use of the terms "comprovisation" and "improvosed" above is intended to suggest a more nuanced, or perhaps simply a troubled, theory of the kinds of creativity at play in jazz. I propose that a thoughtful consideration of repetition, of all types and at all levels, in the performances that make up *Thelonious Monk Quartet with John Coltrane* necessarily leads to a somewhat tempered understanding of the divide between improvisation and composition and the making of musical works in jazz. Writing in 1974, Bruno Nettl already proposed a theory of composition and improvisation that ran counter to established, commonsense notions. Rather than view the two as antitheses—Apollonian and Dionysian modes of musical creativity, the one a measured, intellectual process that incorporates evaluation and revision and the other an ecstatic outpouring, musical stream of unconscious, something very near glossalalia—Nettl described the two terms as fundamentally "part of the same idea"

(1974, 6). He retained the terms to describe these two parts but built an influential theory suggesting that the process—the idea—that both are part of is neither more nor less than musical performance itself. In his words, "The conclusion that recurs again and again in our thoughts is...that all performers improvise to some extent. What the pianist playing Bach and Beethoven does with his models—the scores and accumulated tradition of performance practice—is only in degree and not in nature, different from what the Indian playing an *alap* in *Rag Yaman* and the Persian singing the *Dastgah of Shur* do with theirs" (19). More recent work, much of it drawn from ethnographic studies of jazz, but also from studies of American folk music performance, Indonesian gamelan styles, Iranian and Indian mode-based classical music performance, and composition in common-practice Western classical music before 1850, have added further layers to understanding the questions raised by any straightforward use of the terms (Atre 2007; Monson 2008, 2009; Nooshin 2003; Parikh 2007; Ravikiran 2007; Sutton 1998; Turino 2009). I suggest here, ultimately, that in jazz we might be principally attentive to moments of formal regularity—repetition from performance to performance—and how repetition facilitates evaluation and self-awareness. Ultimately, I am less invested in changing the terminology to describe jazz performance than I am in understanding the nature of the creative activity it represents.

If the terms improvisation and composition remain useful for jazz studies, it is because they reflect commonsense distinctions between creative activities undertaken in different contexts and with different immediate goals in mind. They are, however, by no means radically separate in practice. Quite the contrary: for the most part, they represent multiply interlocking activities. Repetition of various sorts is clearly implicated in both the activities of composition and improvisation and in how we think about their musical products. The interconnection between the two modes might be set out as follows: jazz composition is most normatively found in the writing of "heads." These short, generally at least partially stereotypical, song forms usually incorporate "catchy" melodies and harmonic progressions, so that they remain appealing on multiple repetitions—neither too complex to satisfy casual listening nor too simple to repay close attention. Unlike composition in other contemporary forms, however, jazz heads are also created with the express purpose in mind of providing inviting frameworks for improvisation. This is a key point to understanding repertoire in jazz, as it is perhaps the single most important thing that sets new jazz composition apart from repertoire initially written for other genres (Solis 2009, 99–100). Improvisation, then, is central to jazz composition, providing a primary source of aesthetic purpose. Improvisation, as a distinct musical practice, is also interlaced with composition, in part due to this reciprocal relationship (that is, because most—but not all—jazz improvisation involves the creation of new musical utterances in the context of the repetition of precomposed structures; Berliner 1994, 221–27). Equally important, though, is the idea that compositional thinking in the act of performance—that is, thinking in terms of the creation of repeatable forms—and the repetition of units of various sizes from one improvisation on a given piece to the next is common in mainstream jazz practice.

This is not the case just for the small number of jazz musicians who become known as "compositional" in their outlook, but in fact for many, if not most, players. There is an unfortunate lack of credible direct evidence of this except in the recordings themselves. In the voluminous body of interviews with jazz musicians conducted mostly by journalists, but increasingly by scholars, this topic has come up relatively seldom and often tangentially. For the most part, the newness of improvisation—the "sound of surprise" that is taken to be constitutive of jazz—has been a foregone conclusion, a background assumption, and as a result has not been deeply interrogated. On the other hand, indirect evidence abounds. Charles H. Garrett's discussion of Louis Armstrong's work in the 1920s, particularly the largely similar tunes "S.O.L. Blues" and "Gully Low Blues" from 1927, treats the subject in an early context (2008, 117–120). Garrett focuses on the reasons for the release of "Gully Low" at the time and the decision not to release "S.O.L.," noting differences in the lyrics, and the fact that "Gully Low" has by far the more musically successful ending. On "S.O.L." the band is ragged—unprofessional sounding by contemporary standards—and on "Gully Low" they are tight. My own article on the reissue of Monk's live recordings from the Five Spot—the immediate successors to the live recording with John Coltrane that is the subject of this book—makes a very similar case regarding the difference between the originally released sets and those that Monk did not want released at the time (Solis 2004). The musical issues at stake for Armstrong, Monk, and their producers in selecting recordings for release appear to have been ones that specifically inhabit the ground in which improvisational and compositional concepts blend.

Thomas Owens's now-classic study of Charlie Parker's repeated use of what would become stock riffs (in his playing and in bebop more generally) might be seen as another source of indirect evidence of this phenomenon (1974). Although he does not use the language of folklore in the dissertation, the basic approach, which searches for formulas and looks at how Parker used them in specific harmonic contexts, owes a debt to Albert Lord and Millman Perry's studies of "oral-formulaic composition." For the most part Owens's argument in "Charlie Parker: Techniques of Improvisation"—and the use it has been put to by studies drawing on it—has leaned on the "oral-formulaic" aspect of improvisation; but it is interesting to stress the word "composition" as well. Henry Martin does this, though using the term "thematic improvisation" rather than "composition" in his book on the Parker (1996). The point of Owens's analysis was to demonstrate conclusively the extent to which Parker's fluidity, wit, and grace operated within a regularized framework. The considerable transcriptions accompanying the dissertation also shows hints of a musical process at work that involved evaluation, revision, and other features more often associated with composition. Martin, objecting to Owens's argument that "[Parker's] solos are normally organized without reference to the theme of the piece being performed," argues instead that "Parker would often absorb the *underlying* foreground motives and voice-leading structures of the themes, then fashion his solos in light of that larger-scale thematic material," a kind of "compositional" thought, as I see it (Owens 1974 v.1, 269; Martin 1996, 3).

A study of repetition in jazz at all of these levels not only is of use in understanding how a performance works but also bears on aesthetic questions of cultural significance within jazz scenes. One of the most compelling issues in aesthetic scholarship since the late 1990s that has some bearing in attempting to understand how the jazz community understands music has been the question of aesthetic ontology, and particularly the idea of the musical work, growing out of Germanic studies of *musikalische Werkbegriff*. A number of scholars have looked at what constitutes a musical work, when the idea of the musical work entered into Western aesthetics, and whether the phenomenon is unique to the Western classical tradition. A study such as this, which focuses attention directly on a musical object (the album) itself made up of a number of discrete musical objects (the album's tracks), clearly invites some further discussion of the topic. The status of musical works, as the concept emerged in the Western classical tradition, is in an oppositional relationship to improvisation, broadly understood. Lydia Goehr sees the concept of the musical work coalescing around 1800, in all the major repertoires of classical composition except opera—orchestral music, chamber music, and solo piano repertoire—significantly in tandem with changes in ideas about the extent to which interpretation in these repertoires should involve improvisation (1992, 8, 108–9, 234). William Kinderman has offered a compelling argument revising aspects of Goehr's analysis, suggesting a more extensive period of emergence for the work concept in Western classical music (2009, 307-8). More importantly, however, his argument challenges Goehr's presupposition that the conception of the musical work in the nineteenth century sets up an oppositional relationship between improvisation and composition, instead seeing them as "part of the same idea," following Nettl. Tellingly, Goehr predicates her argument on an opposition between classical music, which has musical works, and African American vernacular traditions—including jazz—which she says does not (1992, v, 249-53).

Common sense suggests otherwise. Relatively little has been written on what kinds of things might constitute musical works in jazz, but in fact this album points in a coherent direction for an aesthetic ontology of jazz. On the one hand, both album and tracks constitute, in their production and use, some kind of musical works. They are, following Albin Zak's and Theodore Gracyk's analyses of rock recordings as musical works, autographic (Gracyk 1992, 32-33; Zak 2001). They are mechanically reproducible but "carry with them the physical traces of their making," and they cannot be reproduced exactly in performance (2001, 21-22). The precise series of waveforms that was electronically registered and then transferred to sound reproduction devices (CD, digital file) is unique and maximally thick in terms of what parameters are given. This, to me, at least, is primarily interesting in terms of the production of the work as a musical commodity. On the other hand, the pieces that were performed by Monk's quartet with Coltrane on the evening this recording was made are also works, but allographic ones. That is, they are works that can be realized in any performance, and they are "equally authentic so long as they 'comply' with the score" (or better, with the precomposed, fixed elements of their musical syntax; Zak 2001, 22). At stake in an analysis of these performances, then, are not only questions about creativity in the moment, "in the course of performance," but also about conceptualizations of songs as works in jazz. These works are clearly less thick than the recordings themselves, but they are not without worklike qualities. In fact, their repetition over time, within particular social relationships—playing networks, and the performer-audience relationships, themselves mediated by the industry, all of which, despite significant fluidity, are nonetheless a real part of making the jazz community—gives them a particular ontological status that is, in fact, peculiar to and definitive of jazz.

Each of these aesthetic issues—the various kinds of repetition in the moment of performance, the various registers of repetition and variation through which we conceptualize creativity, and the ways repetition and variation bear on the ontology of the musical work—has been the subject of sociocultural critique within American music-cultures of the twentieth and early twenty-first centuries. Not surprisingly, given music's complicated status as an art with deep cultural significance and a commodity circulating within a large, powerful industry in the West, the conceptual trajectories that lead from musical repetition to aesthetic systems of the various Western musical modernities have a significant role in the political economies of music in the second half of the twentieth century and the beginning of the twenty-first. For any number of writers, musicians, and a wide body of listeners, the pleasures of musical repetition, for instance, have signified racial solidarity, racial boundary crossing, class consciousness, gender identity, and the "generation gap." The contested recognition and interpretation of improvisational and compositional creativity has signaled similar fault lines in the American culture wars. For instance, a belief in the lack of musical works in jazz—the idea that even though jazz may have songs, tunes, pieces, and so forth, it does not really have works—can reasonably be seen as a significant component of the fact that no jazz musician won a Pulitzer Prize in music until Wynton Marsalis was awarded one for his semiclassical oratorio, *Blood on the Fields*, in 1997—not Duke Ellington, not Thelonious Monk, not Charlie Parker or Dizzy Gillespie or John Coltrane or Miles Davis.[7]

Each of these layers, from the minutia of note-to-note patterns of repetition to the middle range of songs and their versions, to the ways jazz has fit into the cultural politics of the 1950s and the early 2000s, serves as a framework for understanding Monk and Coltrane's work and its place in jazz history. As with the consideration of any great art, the analysis of this music also offers an opportunity to more clearly understand its aesthetic and social context as well. This becomes clear particularly when looking at the recording not only as music in the abstract and not only as a document of a performance from 1957, but also as a commercial recording released in 2005.

CHAPTER OUTLINE

My approach to this book divides into three large sections. I begin with a historical set of chapters placing the performance into its context in the late 1950s; I then move to a longer section dedicated to close analyses of the recording's tracks; and finally I finish with a brief section tracing out the recording's place in the 2000s.

PART 1: "MONK AND COLTRANE" AND "THE MORNINGSIDE HEIGHTS BENEFIT AND JAZZ CONCERTS TO 1957"

This section considers two important contexts for the production of the original tapes that were used for *Thelonious Monk Quartet with John Coltrane at Carnegie Hall*. Chapter 1 looks at Monk and Coltrane's careers up to this point, setting the stage for a concert that might not have been seen as momentous at the time but nevertheless happened to come at an important moment in each career. The collaboration between Monk and Coltrane is now widely seen as one of the most important in modern jazz history; it has been considered largely in books and articles on one or the other, but not in this kind of synthesis. The most striking point to emerge from this is the extent to which jazz collaborations can have a definitive impact on both older and younger musicians, even if they do not always do so. Jazz's status as a music that, rather famously, is thought to incorporate in a symbolic or metaphorical sense American ideas about democracy is perhaps best thought about in collaborations such as this. It clarifies both the openness and democratic qualities of the music and the uneven ground on which that business is worked out.

Chapter 2 looks at the Morningside Heights Community Center benefit concert in general, arguing that this recording is a document of an important kind of jazz concert—a type that has not been widely discussed in the writing about jazz concerts more generally. The concert—not offering any high concept, but simply a range of the best performers on the scene at the time—is an interesting glimpse into the jazz world of its day. Perhaps the most important thing about this concert is the range of performers who appeared on the bill, including representatives of a spectrum from pop to the avant-garde edges of mainstream jazz in 1957. There is some writing on benefit concerts in the 1960s, which note this as typical, but at least in the 1950s this breadth characterized not only benefit concerts but other kinds of performance opportunities as well. Indeed, it represents in an important way the play of distinction and integration that defined the place of jazz in American culture at the time. That is, it shows how modern jazz strove to distinguish itself as a special art, but at the same time how it was still viewed as compatible with other popular genres and listened to at least casually by general audiences.

PART 2: FOUR CHAPTERS, EACH ON TWO TRACKS FROM THE ALBUM

Chapters 3 through 6 consider the pieces on the album analytically, looking both at Monk's compositions and at the group's approach to playing them and improvising. The breadth of material and playing make it worth looking at each piece in detail. The recording is notable for jazz scholars because it represents the Monk quartet with Coltrane at the peak of the band's creative powers. The night's set is representative of what the group was playing at the Five Spot, and suggestive of what Coltrane and Monk would have liked about playing with each other and with the rhythm section of Ahmed Abdul-Malik and Shadow Wilson. The sets seem chosen specifically to showcase what was distinctive and interesting about that group, in general and in relation to the rest of the acts performing that evening. They highlight Monk's compositional ability; the soloing power of Coltrane's developing "sheets of sound" style; the spare, compelling approach Monk took as well as his occasional virtuoso flourishes; and the sensitive interaction of which the band was capable.

The analyses in these chapters focus on the most compelling aspects of the particular performances and thus are to some extent *sui generis*. Chapter 3 focuses on the first set's two ballads, "Monk's Mood" and "Crepuscule with Nellie" (the first and third pieces from the set, respectively). Because the group played no solo improvisations on these two pieces, the chapter's analyses are mainly oriented toward understanding how the interpretations on that night's concert compared with other recorded versions. Chapter 4 considers two up-tempo pieces on the first set, "Evidence," and "Nutty." Bearing in mind the live aspect of this recording, a key element of the analyses is a discussion of how these pieces pair with and flow from the ballads that they follow. Chapter 5 looks at the first two numbers from the second set, "Bye-Ya" and "Sweet and Lovely." This set was composed of an original in song form, a standard, and a blues, plus the closing theme song, "Epistrophy," and a focus of this chapter and the chapter that follows is looking at how Monk, Coltrane, and the rhythm section approach these types of pieces. "Bye-Ya" is the performance that most clearly shows Coltrane working with "sheets of sound," while "Sweet and Lovely" gives the band an opportunity to play a somewhat extensively arranged piece in a classic hard bop style. Chapter 6 deals with the last full piece of the second set, "Blue Monk," and the performances of "Epistrophy" ending each set.

PART 3: MONK AND COLTRANE, TOGETHER AT LAST, TOGETHER FOREVER; THE RECORDING IN 2005

The last chapter stands apart in a way from the previous ones, considering the album in the context of its production *as an album*. Though the

Voice of America recorded the concert for broadcast, there is no reason to think that anyone involved would have considered it material for a commercially produced LP. In 2005, by contrast, the recording had unequaled value, as a previously unreleased complete concert recording of Monk and Coltrane together at the peak of their collaboration. This album, perhaps better than any release in the 2000s, speaks volumes about the changes in jazz between 1957 and 2005. Obviously, both Monk and Coltrane went on to be revered (literally beatified, in Coltrane's case), but there is more to it. In this album we can see in stark relief the increasing cultural prestige of jazz, and the widening distance from other parts of popular culture; we can see the rising fascination of jazz with a golden age; we can see in an interesting way the impact of the institutionalization of jazz education; and we can see how jazz has participated in the heightened media sophistication of the music industry in the second half of the twentieth century.

A NOTE ON TRANSCRIPTIONS

Where useful, the analyses that make up the bulk of this book are supported with transcriptions. I have endeavored to produce transcriptions that give as much detail as necessary to clarify the analytical points they support, without introducing extraneous information. In most cases issues of pitch and rhythm in the musicians' playing are relatively straightforward to capture in standard notation, and in the interest of readability, I have not introduced unusual notations. Of course there are myriad aspects of the performance—timbre, micro-timing, and pitch inflection, among others—that are not represented in the examples. I expect most readers will look at the notation as an aid to listening, and thus I chose to leave these elements to the reader's ear, since they are easy to hear but difficult to notate. I have not included full score transcriptions, in order to streamline presentation and hone in on individual moments in one part or another. Nevertheless, my analyses generally look at the musical decisions the band is making as significantly interactive. Finally, because the heads are readily available in a legal "fake book," published by Hal Leonard (2002), I have included only transcriptions of solos and their accompaniment in this volume.

CHAPTER 1
MONK WITH COLTRANE
The Story of a Collaborative Relationship

THE COLLABORATION BETWEEN Monk and Coltrane documented on this album was one among numerous creative partnerships that each musician sought out in the late 1950s, but it was a particularly important one. This chapter places Monk and Coltrane's work together in the context of their musical biographies, in order to see the recording as part of two personal trajectories, intersecting at a crucial moment. For Coltrane, in particular, working with Monk had a profound impact. As a developing young musician, he had the most dramatic musical change in front of him, and significantly it is possible to hear echoes of Monk's approach to jazz in Coltrane's mature style. Yet Coltrane also came to the band as an artist with a compelling vision, and it is possible to see the months they worked together as important ones in Monk's career as well. As for the rhythm section, neither Shadow Wilson nor Ahmed Abdul-Malik went on to lead a band, and neither one's career has been substantially documented as Monk's and Coltrane's have; but both brought considerable playing histories to the performance, and without their contribution Monk and Coltrane would not have sounded the way they did. Although this chapter focuses on the two better-known musicians, Wilson and Abdul-Malik were major contributors to the overall shape of the performance, as will be seen in later chapters.

The most significant thing, for a critically informed jazz scholarship, about Coltrane and Monk's work together is not simply its place in each performer's career trajectory, but rather its impact on their creativity, on how composition and improvisation intertwined in their approaches not only to soloing but to every aspect of their approach to jazz. Each one was a major presence as a performer, and both wrote pieces. Monk is more celebrated as a composer now, and Coltrane more lauded for his brilliance as a player; but the two registers of creativity were necessarily intertwined. Monk wrote pieces not in the abstract but as vehicles for himself and his side men; and when he played them, alone and in ensembles, they became works in a much larger sense. Coltrane was certainly one of the most technically compelling saxophonists of his or any age, but his performance was more than that. Feeding ideas from Monk's music into improvised frameworks, Coltrane was fully engaged with the creation of new versions of old pieces that represented a kind of collaborative poiesis, or work-making in the act of performance. How much Coltrane drew on these experiences in writing new heads is beyond the scope of this book; but it should be noted that some of his songs, at least—"Giant Steps," in the most extreme instance—can be seen as a result of precisely this kind of composition-in-action process.

MONK AND HIS SIDEMEN, 1940–1957

Monk's earliest recordings as a leader, which he made for the Blue Note label from 1947 to 1952, surrounded him with a variety of sidemen, not all equal to the task of interpreting his music.[1] Idrees Sulieman, Danny Quebec West, and Sahib Shihab were all interesting young players, but Milt Jackson stands out as the strongest of these sessions, as a musician with a bluesy sensibility that meshed well with Monk's own approach to the compositions. Still, other musical relationships from this period may have had more lasting significance for Monk. He played in Coleman Hawkins's band in 1944—before his Blue Note recordings—and the connection clearly made a deep impression (Kelley 2009, 95–96). More than a decade later, in 1957, Monk returned the favor and hired Hawkins (along with Coltrane, Gigi Gryce, and Ray Copeland) for what would be a seminal Riverside album, *Monk's Music*. Beyond the personal connection between Monk and Hawkins, the two had a compositional affinity for one another. Both musicians were fond of tritone substitution and had a penchant for using whole-tone-based material in solos. Monk's 1947 composition "I Mean You," which he originally called "Stickball," was first recorded by Hawkins (ibid., 120).

In the early 1950s, his star on the rise, Monk signed with Prestige records and was able, at that point, to work extensively with Sonny Rollins, who would play with Monk on and off until early 1957. Monk had performed and recorded in a number of formats at this point, including solo, trios, quintets, and sextets, but his work with Rollins—as both a leader and a sideman—pointed to the piano-tenor combination as one of his defining sounds. Additionally, Monk's work with and without Rollins during this period found him working not only with a tenor but also with a particularly hard-swinging rhythm section. Monk routinely recorded at this point with either Art Blakey or Max Roach on drums and a range of bassists, notably Percy Heath and Al McKibbon. Blakey and Roach were quite different as drummers, but they shared the distinction at the time of being intense, in-the-pocket modern drummers.

By 1957 Monk was in a position to hire a stable band, despite strangely mixed fortunes. Having lost his cabaret card, and with it the right to take engagements in any of Manhattan's jazz clubs, Monk was forced to play shorter, less remunerative gigs in Brooklyn and outside New York.[2] This did not slow down his recording career, however. Up to this point, Monk's work at Blue Note and Prestige had been small-scale, as neither company had a significant marketing budget or was in a position to push Monk's career. Blue Note was known for recordings of boogie-woogie and traditional jazz, with its most important recordings to that point coming from Meade Lux Lewis, Albert Ammons, and Sidney Bechet. But it was also known as a musician's label, with an "uncommercial" attitude and interest in recording the best possible music at hand. As one of Alfred Lion's earliest press releases, dated 1939, said, "Blue Note records are designed simply to serve the uncompromising expression of hot jazz and swing, in general" (Cook 2003, 12). To that end, Lion's approach led him, for instance, to give Ammons extra time in the studio, and to release his sides as twelve-inch singles, rather than the industry-standard ten-inch. Nonetheless, in 1948 Blue Note's biggest successes were still to come. The iconic hard bop that really made the company's name—eventually making the label a prime bit of property for consolidation into Sony Music Co., and making its sound and album cover art a primary point of reference for hip hop musicians in the 1990s—was largely a product of

Rudy Van Gelder's work with musicians such as Horace Silver and Art Blakey in the mid-1950s. The Monk recordings were, in fact, very nearly Blue Note's first foray into modern jazz.

In 1952, Prestige was in a similar position to Blue Note in many respects. It was a small label with relatively little ability to produce hit records, much less market the ones it made in a concerted way. Bob Weinstock, president and founder of Prestige, may have been a more capable businessman than Lion and Wolff—he had gotten into the business early, selling jazz records out of his house via mail order as an adolescent—but his focus on small group jazz necessarily made his business a niche affair. The company became known for producing records in the shortest possible time; one well-known quip goes "The difference between Blue Note and Prestige is two days of rehearsal" (Cook 2003, 57). Although he was quite pleased to join the label, and in spite of having the opportunity to record primarily his own compositions with sympathetic sidemen, over time Monk became increasingly unhappy at Prestige. In part his growing dissatisfaction seems to have come from a sense that he was not being promoted or otherwise treated as well as the label's other stars, Miles Davis and Milt Jackson (Kelley 2009, 182–83). Beyond this, he may simply have wanted a label where he felt more valued. Prestige had Monk in a long-term contract, but his records were not selling, and the company was happy to let him go (185).

Regardless of Monk's feelings about working under the conditions Weinstock created at Prestige, he was able to make some truly excellent recordings there. He worked with Art Blakey and Max Roach on drums, and Percy Heath and Gary Mapp on bass for the recordings released on an album titled *Thelonious Monk Trio*, and with Sonny Rollins for recordings under each of their names. The trio album was a significant change from Monk's Blue Note recordings. There may have been less rehearsal, but the record, made over the course of three sessions—two in 1952 and one in 1954—showcases Monk well. He chose interesting work for the three sessions: each of those from 1952 includes three of his own compositions and one standard ("Sweet and Lovely" and "These Foolish Things"), and the final one produced two recordings, "Blue Monk" and "Just a Gigolo." With this range of material and a stellar, but comfortable, rhythm section, Monk excelled.

The version of "Blue Monk" on this session is a testament to the importance of a good connection between musicians in any jazz performance, as well as to how subtle changes can have a determining effect in the qualitative difference between two versions of a piece, without in fact changing its essential features as a musical work. Tempo is a key aspect

FIGURE 1.1. "Blue Monk," Percy Heath's Bass Line, Monk's Second Chorus

in differentiating particular versions of "Blue Monk," but one that receives only limited attention in discussions of it (or any jazz recording). Ben Riley, Monk's drummer in the mid-1960s and later a champion of his music through the group Sphere, has noted the importance of Monk's approach to the tempos of his songs. Rather than having just a few tempos he preferred for "in-the-pocket" playing, Monk asked Riley to play his pieces at a wide variety of speeds, including at times asking him to play "Blue Monk" at a tempo Riley found excruciatingly slow.[3] On the Prestige recording, the band plays at a fully comfortable, walking blues tempo, around 135–140 bpm. The tempo is, of course, only one aspect of the performance's pacing. There is an intensity and propulsion to this version that is a result largely of Heath's unfalteringly steady walking bass lines (Fig. 1.1). His note choice, generally conventional blues patterns, outlining the major harmonies, and especially giving energy to the swooping shifts to the IV chord, is important, but even more significant is his solid, almost equally weighted quarter note rhythm.

Art Blakey, while also keeping a clear sense of time moving forward in the performance, was freed up by Heath's time keeping to serve as a foil for Monk's solo work, underscoring and giving weight to the ways Monk shapes a multichorus solo. Monk played fifteen choruses on the recording, which break down roughly into four sections: two choruses of introduction, an eight-chorus main section, three choruses of an extended climax, which transitions over the course of the thirteenth chorus to a two-chorus coda, the end of which transitions to Heath's bass solo. The introductory section is characterized by Monk's use of single-note lines that clearly articulate the four-measure periods of the blues form. Blakey allows Monk to gradually build up this section, remaining in a background supporting role by playing only time, with essentially no fills. Monk's main gambit throughout the long main section is to play a single riff for each chorus, transforming it through the chord changes of the blues form, and often breaking away from it during the last four measures, in line with the standard aab poetic form of the blues. These riff choruses do not follow a clear trajectory (of rising intensity, for instance), but Blakey helps shape the succession of choruses by varying his level of activity, from playing time only to playing extensive response figures and polyrhythmic patterns. He initiates this by introducing a polyrhythmic figure in the turnaround of chorus 3, which he then repeats at the end of choruses 4 and 5 (Fig. 1.2). In chorus 6 he reduces his activity, and in the seventh chorus, while Monk plays more melodic material than he had for the past four choruses, Blakey keeps time. While Monk strongly separates sections and choruses, Blakey uses a polyrhythmic comping pattern to connect the end of chorus 8 to chorus 9, driving the form forward as the solo begins to get long (Fig. 1.3). In chorus 10, which serves as a transition to the climactic choruses 11 through 13, Blakey does not play the polyrhythmic groove but does introduce response fills in the second four-measure section. Monk creates a climax by playing shout choruses in a "locked hands" style for three measures. In response to Monk's growing intensity, Blakey holds back his own activity somewhat, supporting Monk with strong time-keeping patterns in choruses 11 and 12. Monk allows the energy of the climactic shout choruses to dwindle in the thirteenth chorus, and Blakey correspondingly picks up, playing fills where Monk leaves space. Monk uses the last two choruses of his solo as a conclusion, gradually fading out, and Blakey supports him, playing steady time, letting the energy dissipate in advance of the next solo.

Prestige also placed Monk in some unusual combinations: he had Julius Watkins on French horn, along with Sonny Rollins on tenor and Percy Heath and Willie Jones on bass and drums for one date; Frank Foster on tenor and Ray Copeland on trumpet with Curly Russell and Art Blakey on bass and drums for another; and he was back with Milt Jackson on vibes on a date led by Miles Davis, along with Percy Heath on bass—again—and Kenny Clarke, with whom Monk had played extensively in the 1940s at Minton's, on drums. These recordings, all from 1953 and 1954, still seem somehow not quite to capture Monk in full stride. Interestingly, Monk's own piano playing does seem fully comfortable

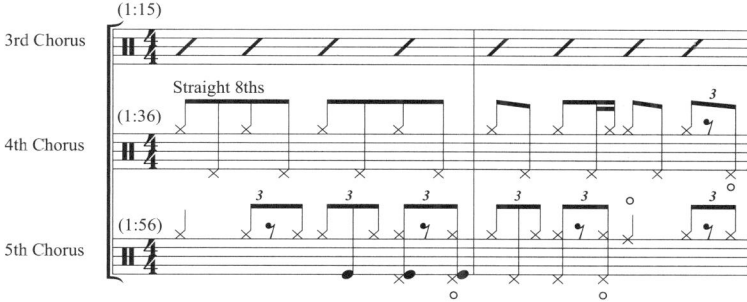

FIGURE 1.2. "Blue Monk," Art Blakey's Drum Fills in Turnaround of Third to Fifth Choruses

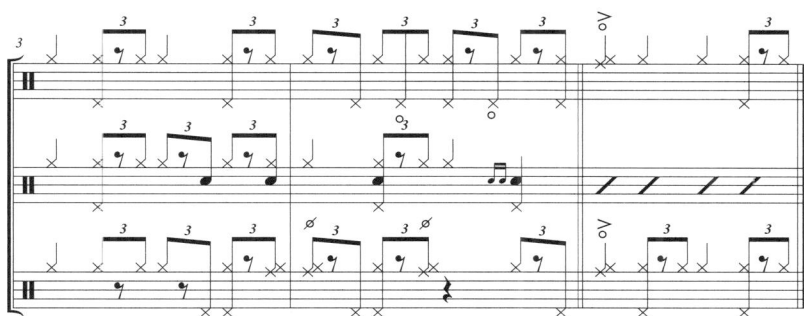

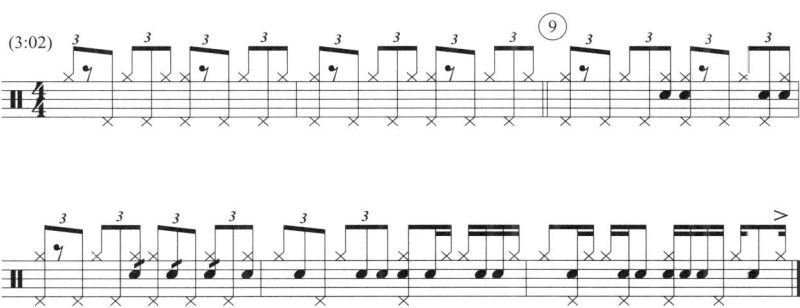

FIGURE 1.3. "Blue Monk," Art Blakey's Playing from mm. 11–12 of Monk's Eighth Solo Chorus into Ninth Chorus

here. These are rough recordings in certain respects that, for better or worse, do capture the "first take" energy Weinstock was known to like, and they are engaging for that reason, but Monk does not seem to have hit his stride as a bandleader on the dates. The horn players Monk worked with, in particular, though excellent players, and ones similar in some important ways to the sorts of musicians he would work with in the ensuing years, do not sound as though they share Monk's vision—or at times any vision—for what the performances are intended to be.

If "Blue Monk" is exemplary of what Monk was able to do with Blakey and Heath, much of the larger ensemble work he recorded with Prestige gives examples of what could happen with musicians who were not yet fully engaged in the project of developing a vision for Monk's compositions in themselves. "Locomotive," for example, is an unusual composition, which obsessively develops a single riff (appropriately, somewhat train-whistle-like in its dissonant clusters). Each soloist plays well on the recording—Monk developing a set of riffs, and both Ray Copeland and Frank Foster playing with bluesy materials—but the performance as a whole is disjointed precisely because of the significant differences in how Monk and his accompanists approach the material.

In 1955 Orrin Keepnews bought out Monk's contract from Prestige (famously for $108.27), signed him at Riverside, produced a series of brilliant recordings, and marketed Monk with remarkable success. The recordings, made over the course of four years and a few months, stand as one of the most remarkable artistic canons in any kind of music, including jazz. Monk's power and vision as a musician, and also as a person—captured in stories, interviews, photographs, and later film, as well as in his compositions and playing—are palpable and can overshadow the presence of others working on these projects. They are, nonetheless, clearly the result of collaborations: between Monk and his bands, and between musicians and producer. There is a balance here between consistency and variety in both band types and band mates. Monk appears regularly in tenor, piano, bass, and drum quartets, but he also works in quintet, sextet, septet, and (small) jazz orchestral settings. The rhythm sections shift over time, but Wilbur Ware, Sam Jones, and Ahmed Abdul-Malik appear repeatedly on bass, and Art Blakey, Shadow Wilson, and Art Taylor each appear on multiple dates on drums. Moreover, the Riverside recordings give a fair representation of the musicians Monk was playing with in concert at the time.

When Monk got his cabaret card reinstated in the spring of 1957, he was highly visible. His first gig, a six-month engagement at the Five Spot

Café, was popular and treated among New York's bohemians with all attendant pomp as the homecoming event of the year. In a sense, the period 1957–1959, when Monk worked consistently, moving from Coltrane to Johnny Griffin and then Charlie Rouse in relatively quick succession, was a key turning point in his career. How much of the turn can be attributed to collaborative relationships with these tenor players is debatable, but at least one aspect is likely to have stemmed from his experiences in this period. The period that followed, in which he played consistently with Rouse, showed Monk as a bandleader who ably got his groups to play his music compatibly with his vision and sound, while still developing their own distinct voices. That kind of mature musical leadership must have come at least in part from working so closely and extensively with strong, yet sensitive, sidemen like Coltrane.

COLTRANE, 1946–1957

If Monk came to the collaboration with Coltrane as a veteran musician at a crucial time of reemergence, in 1957 John Coltrane was still emerging as an artist.[4] His youth in South Philadelphia and a stint in U.S. Navy bands gave him a strong background in the pop of the day, as well as in the African American R&B/gospel/jazz continuum that he mined extensively after returning to civilian life in 1946. Louis Porter describes his early jazz recordings, such as those he made with service mates in Hawai'i in 1946 after being discharged (while waiting to be sent home) as awkward, noting that his ideas were "ahead of his fingers" (Porter 2000, 50). Porter clearly shows that Coltrane did not develop in isolation, nor come into the musical world fully formed; rather he was "a normal person growing and developing in a fortunately inspired circle of musicians," and "few of [his] Philadelphia colleagues remember him as having that touch of genius" (44). As he says, Coltrane was, as a youth, "a fine young player with lots of room for growth" (45). And yet grow Coltrane did, in ways and at a pace that were more or less unrivaled by his compatriots. Porter documents how, with a few years of "maniacally" intense study (with Mike Guerra through the Ornstein School and then Dennis Sandole through the Granoff Studios, as well as on the bandstand), Coltrane was becoming differentiated from the rest of his contemporaries (50, 53).

Coltrane had a number of early jobs playing R&B but particularly remembered work with King Kolax's group, playing a mix of things, including modern jazz, as truly his "school" (Porter 2000, 56–57). His early career seems to have moved from success to success, including time in and around Philadelphia playing in Jimmy Heath's band, an extended job in Eddie "Cleanhead" Vinson's band, and finally a position on the roster with Dizzy Gillespie's big band. Moreover, throughout this time he had already embarked on a program of formal, explicit experimentation, using everything at hand to develop and extend his already solid grasp of the intricacies of harmony. This success was sidelined in the early 1950s for four years, partly because his heroin addiction became less manageable, and partly because he seems to have been content to play middle-of-the-road jobs with whatever bandleader wanted to hire him. He was, in a word, making a living (88).

A return to cutting-edge music making, and the beginning of Coltrane's mature career, came with a job in Miles Davis's band starting in 1955. Working with Davis and the legendary rhythm section of Red Garland on piano, Paul Chambers on bass, and Philly Joe Jones on drums, Coltrane quickly developed a distinctive, but still workmanlike, hard bop style, nicely showcased on the albums *Workin'*, *Cookin'*, *Relaxin'*, and *Steamin'* (all recorded in two days for Prestige in 1956, but released one at a time). Here Davis mostly eschews complicated arrangements of the sort Horace Silver was crafting with the Jazz Messengers, opting instead for a more straight-ahead blowing session sound: five musicians playing standards and new jazz heads, with extensive improvised solos, as they might on a club date. To achieve this, each of the tracks that make up the four Prestige albums was recorded in a single take.

CONVERGENCE: COLTRANE AND MONK TOGETHER IN 1957

Coltrane and Davis rather famously split because of the saxophonist's drug problems, and as a result Coltrane was otherwise unattached in 1957 when Monk was looking for a tenor player to round out his group. Monk had recorded in solo, trio, and quintet settings under contract to Riverside and had been gigging, albeit sporadically, mostly with quartets. He had played with Sonny Rollins throughout much of 1954, with Charlie Rouse and Johnny Griffin, each briefly in 1955, and with Ernie Henry on alto saxophone for two weeks in 1956. Coltrane began working with Monk informally over the course of some weeks in early 1957. This relationship started with Monk teaching Coltrane "Monk's Mood" one night in the apartment of the baroness and jazz maven Pannonica de Koenigswarter in the Algonquin hotel, and it continued with the saxophonist visiting Monk's home almost daily (Kelley 2009, 218). As though commemorating the beginning of this musical connection, Coltrane played one tune, a majestic interpretation of "Monk's Mood," on the April 1957 recording date that produced *Thelonious Himself*. In July, two weeks after Monk began his extended residency at New York's Five Spot, Coltrane joined the band on a regularized basis. Over the course of the months from July to December 1957, the two played together nearly every week, six nights per week, at the Five Spot, along with bassist Wilbur Ware and drummer Shadow Wilson, with whom Monk had played previously (the band had a day off every Monday). This means the band played roughly one hundred shows together, which is enough to become intimately familiar with one another's sound, style, and approach, under any circumstances.

Coltrane remembered his time with Monk as a formative experience, particularly one that forced him to think more extensively about how he projected form in his playing. Monk's approach to accompaniment, often remaining silent for much of the band's solos, left Coltrane's lines exposed, particularly compared to the support he got from Red Garland or Kenny Drew on previous albums. Coltrane famously described playing with Monk as being "like stepping into an elevator shaft," and he described being "thrown" by Monk's playing; but he also specifically noted the fun he had in exploring Monk's compositions with Ware.[5]

COLLABORATION: AN ACCOUNTING FOR THE RIVERSIDE RECORDINGS

Not counting the live at Carnegie Hall release, Monk and Coltrane's playing together was documented on three studio releases with Riverside—one track on *Thelonious Himself*, and the albums *Monk's Music* and *Monk and Coltrane*—plus one bootleg recording from the Five Spot recorded by Coltrane's then-wife, Naima Coltrane. The first of these recordings was of the song "Monk's Mood," for which Monk added tenor to what was otherwise a solo date. The recording is striking, even in the context of an album that is consistently introspective: a nearly eight-minute rendition of the song, at the very end of the B side, that consists of two-and-a-half slow renditions of the head—the first chorus is Monk solo and Coltrane plays on the rest—separated by a substantial cadenza at the tenor's entrance.

The first full session featuring Coltrane actually came in June 1957, a month before Monk secured the return of his cabaret card and was in a position to hire Coltrane on as his regular tenor player. These sessions, which produced the album *Monk's Music*, were with a septet. Gigi Gryce's arrangements for the date were straightforward and particularly allowed the contrast between the young Coltrane and the established Coleman

Hawkins to shine. After playing together for a scant few weeks in July and early August, Monk and Coltrane made their only studio recordings together in a quartet setting, recording three tracks at Reeves Sound Studios in New York: "Nutty," "Ruby, My Dear," and "Trinkle Tinkle." The three tracks were not released at the time, and Chris Sheridan notes that they "have always been held to be inferior to the level of music-making heard in the second half of [the quartet's] tenure at the Five Spot" (Sheridan 2001, 77). That said, when they were finally released in 1961, on the Riverside subsidiary Jazzland, the recordings were greeted with strongly positive reviews. The last session by the quartet to be recorded was the live show at the Five Spot in 1958, months after Coltrane had left Monk's band to work as a leader under his own name. The impetus to record seems to have been either Coltrane's or his wife, Naima's. Personal, in situ recording was still uncommon at that point, although portable recording equipment had been widely available since the 1940s (thus the existence of Jerry Newman's recordings from Minton's, recorded direct to 78 rpm disc, or Dean Benedetti's 1948 recordings of Charlie Parker, recorded on reel-to-reel tape). The interest in making the recording at the Five Spot must have come from the fact that Coltrane already thought of his time with Monk as a turning point, and was disappointed with how little the quartet had recorded (Sheridan 2001, 88–89). A one-night engagement, substituting for Charlie Rouse, provided a singular opportunity to get one last glimpse of the two of them together.

That the collaboration between Monk and Coltrane was a turning point for the tenor player is easily heard from the recordings he made, both with Monk and on his own at the time. As Porter notes, Coltrane was in the studio ten times during the months he worked with Monk (mostly in others' bands, but occasionally as a leader, as well) so his transformation is well documented. Coltrane himself also clearly saw the experience as a transformation, and he said as much in interviews. In an extended interview with August Blume, a Baltimore area jazz aficionado, Coltrane said, "I learned a lot with [Monk]. I learned little things, you know, I learned to watch the little things" (DeVito 2010, 21). Coltrane thought that the critics at the time were too fixated on the details of what he was playing and missed the biggest point: his delight at being able to learn, from night to night on the bandstand, from his experiences at the time. As he said to François Postif in 1961, "The critics, at that time, were all wrapped up in what we were doing, but you know, for a musician it's really difficult to take a stand on that; really, the only thing that mattered for me wasn't so much what I played but being able to play, and with Monk as well!" (DeVito 2010, 132)[6]

That said, the critics were generally quite positive about his work with Monk. Coltrane had made a name with Miles Davis, even if their relationship was rocky; and Monk's engagement at the Five Spot was widely heralded as a significant milestone in jazz, even if his playing remained controversial and drew scorn as well as admiration. As Ben Ratliff put it, "Had the group been able to make a proper record—or had the Carnegie Hall concert been released then—it might have proved a peak achievement for both musicians. But it seems fair to assume that it wouldn't have appreciably altered the course of public opinion about either musician" (Ratliff 2008, 40).

CONCLUSION: WHAT MAKES THIS COLLABORATION SO IMPORTANT?

The period Monk and Coltrane spent working together is typically addressed because of its impact on Coltrane. Again, Ratliff says, "It is tempting to try to figure out exactly, down to the atom—in terms of harmony and rhythm and melody—what John Coltrane got from Thelonious Monk, since that year has often been described as Coltrane's turning point" (2008, 35–36). Ratliff does not satisfy his temptation but instead focuses on the larger sense of personal and artistic growth that Coltrane described from his time with Monk. As Coltrane sad to Don DeMichael, "I felt I learned from [Monk] in every way—through the senses, theoretically, technically... I could watch him play and find out the things I wanted to know. Also, I could see a lot of things that I didn't know about at all" (DeMichael 1960, quoted in Ratliff 2008, 36). Ratliff rightly senses that Coltrane "wasn't so much after the specific phrases and changes... but much larger areas of music-making that he hadn't considered" (36). Monk gave Coltrane space and freedom—literally, quite famously by leaving him alone on the bandstand to play hugely long solos, but also figuratively, pushing him to overcome obstacles of conventional thought and imagine finding a new musical language.

I suggest, however, there is also a more mundane answer: not, perhaps, a new harmonic concept that Coltrane learned from Monk, nor a new rhythmic conception, but still a specific musical concept that Coltrane developed during his time with Monk. I think Coltrane's work with Monk shows the development of a more sophisticated conception of form in solos, and one that can be tied to Monk's example. Monk did indeed give Coltrane space, but he also gave him musical direction. Coltrane's solos on *Monk's Music* are often interesting, but they show no particular attention to architectonic form. He described his time playing at the Five Spot as a kind of working through musical exercises on the bandstand. "[Monk] ... got me into the habit of playing long solos on his pieces," he told Don DeMichael, "playing the same piece for a long time to find new conceptions of solos. It got so I would go as far as possible on one phrase until I ran out of ideas" (DeMichael 1960, quoted in Porter 2000, 111). This seems to characterize precisely the kind of performance captured on the live recordings from the Five Spot, but much less so the concert at Carnegie Hall. As will become clear in the following chapters, Coltrane's solos on the Carnegie Hall concert are relatively short—mostly no more than two or three choruses—while his solos at the Five Spot were much longer—ten choruses or more at times. In either case, though, after months playing until he "ran out of ideas," there is a clear sense of architectonics to Coltrane's playing, and one that he carried with him into his work as a leader. Moreover, Coltrane seemed to learn from Monk the idea of building the architectonics of a solo from the materials of the head, creating a kind of unification to the whole performance that was often not heard in modern jazz. This is, of course, one of Monk's hallmarks, and though it is not always part of Coltrane's later playing, in certain instances (*A Love Supreme*, perhaps most strikingly) a nearly obsessive motivic logic came to be central to his work.

It is harder to pinpoint the impact of the collaboration on Monk, if there was one. Monk was a mature musician by the time he hired Coltrane, and from the start he had been doggedly singular in his artistic vision. He clearly liked having his work interpreted by a soloist who understood what he was looking for but also brought a distinct sound and approach to the music, and in this sense Coltrane was a perfect collaborator. Robin Kelley sees the time at the Five Spot as a turning point in Monk's career—and surely it was—but not necessarily a turning point for his music: "With the assistance of brothers Coltrane, Wilson, Ware, and Abdul-Malik, Monk had turned the Five Spot into the hippest monastery in the Western world. But it worked both ways: this tiny little bar in the East Village gave him the boost he needed. It raised his spirit, helped provide sustenance, and positioned him in a community that truly dug his music" (Kelley 2009, 239). I would argue that it was not just the gig at the Five Spot that gave Monk this sustenance, but the opportunity to work, night after night, with a group that heard and respected his ideas. It may also have been deeply gratifying for Monk to have a real pupil, in John Coltrane. We know that Coltrane spent whole days with Monk, learning everything from Monk's still obscure pieces to how to play multiphonics on the saxophone, and also taking walks to see the city from Monk's point of view and eat ice cream (Monk's favorite). We know from Coltrane that the experience was deeply satisfying to the young saxophonist. It must also have been valuable to Monk, because although he was generous to young aspiring musicians (Steve Lacy described similar experiences under Monk's tutelage), he was not always so free with his time. We might wish there was more of a record of the few months when Monk's quartet featured John Coltrane, but the two sets from Carnegie Hall in November 1957 captured on a recording meant for the Voice of America, but destined to sit in the Library of Congress until 2005, give ample evidence of the value and pleasure the two musicians found in their time together.

CHAPTER 2

Jazz in the Concert Hall
The Morningside Community Center Benefit and the Jazz Concert as an Institution to 1957

THE COLLABORATION BETWEEN Monk and Coltrane may have taken time to gel, but when, in November, the band had the opportunity to play the Morningside Community Center benefit at Carnegie Hall, they had been playing together for twenty-two weeks, six nights a week, aside from brief vacations, and the band was tight. Coltrane said that though Monk's tunes were difficult, the months he spent learning them in Monk's apartment and on the bandstand had made them familiar (DeVito 2010, 17–18). Moreover, although Monk's habit of "strolling" (getting up from the piano and leaving it to the bass and drums to provide accompaniment) during Coltrane's solos at the Five Spot could be unnerving, it also gave him a chance to build an easy rapport with Shadow Wilson and the bass players Wilbur Ware and Ahmed Abdul-Malik, who supported him on his musical journeys. Nights at the Five Spot had been a working lab for this band, allowing them to try out material and become comfortable with one another's ideas for a specialist and highly appreciative audience, but the stage of Carnegie Hall would be an opportunity to share their music in a much more compact form with a more general, if still highly enthusiastic, audience. Monk's quartet was one of six sharing a bill that night that seems strikingly diverse now but was not particularly unusual at the time, including cutting-edge modern jazz small groups, one of the only truly popular modern jazz big bands, genre-spanning vocalists, and a rising R&B star.

The "jazz concert" phenomenon, presenting jazz on stage in a concert hall for a seated audience, had a reasonably long history by 1957, going back at least thirty years to Paul Whiteman's "Experiment in Modern Music" at Aeolian Hall.[1] The Carnegie Hall concert's setting might still have occasioned note at the time, though it was a good twenty years after Benny Goodman's seminal Carnegie Hall concert, because jazz was seen in the public eye as lowbrow music, more appropriate to night clubs, taverns, and dance halls than the auditorium.[2] If so, the concert's noteworthiness would have been more a matter of perception than reality. An important point that has largely escaped notice in the literature on jazz concerts is just how common, if not commonplace, an evening of this sort had become by the late fifties. A perusal of advertisements and concert listings in the *New York Times* from 1956 to 1959, for instance, shows jazz concerts as a weekly, if not daily, event. Writers dealing with the jazz concert have focused primarily on notable events—the Whiteman and Goodman concerts, Monk's Town Hall concert from 1958, the Jazz at the Philharmonic series—which were musically or historically distinctive, or both. Concerts such as the Morningside Community Center benefit are under the radar of this history precisely because they were common.[3] In fact, this particular concert would not have been notable at all, and would not be remembered now, were it not for the accident of history through which it happened to produce one of a small handful of recordings of Monk and Coltrane playing together.

That said, as a normal event the concert is still worthy of scholarly attention. In particular, the lineup is interesting. Only Monk and Coltrane's sets from the night are commercially available, but it should be borne in mind that they fit into the larger evening, for an audience who, after all, had paid to see the whole concert. The concert lineup ran the gamut in a way that was not atypical for the time (though it would be unlikely today): a sampling of avant-garde and more conservative styles, pre-bop and post-bop, "hot" and "cool," East Coast and West Coast, obscure and accessible, and, importantly, jazz, pop, and R&B. All of these conceptual sets have come to be interpreted as not only opposite but antithetical in jazz criticism, an aesthetic judgment that continues to shape jazz scholarship subtly and not so subtly (Ake 2001; Gendron 1995; Gioia 1998; Porter 2012; Rosenthal 1992). This concert helps us see all of this music, instead, as part of a complex musical ecology, with multiple points of contact and overlapping communities of musicians and audiences.[4]

This chapter looks at jazz concerts as a particular kind of social, artistic, and economic event, placing the Morningside Community Center benefit in a context to understand why it took the shape it did, how it fit into the jazz scene of the late 1950s, and what people thought of it at the time. Ultimately, understanding the conventions and expectations of jazz concerts as they developed over the decades leading up to 1957 helps explain the Monk quartet's musical choices, from repertoire to improvisational approach. The phenomenon of the jazz concert started as an unusual, special event, and importantly it remained so into the 1950s and 1960s. It tended to entail a higher degree of formality, and often more eclecticism, than nightclub or dance hall settings. Both of these features have made such events appealing to wide audiences, but they have also potentially tainted them for a segment of the primary jazz audience, for whom spontaneity may be opposed to formality and authenticity opposed to eclecticism. However, even though it is easy to think about live and mechanically reproduced music as somehow diametrically opposed, in fact in jazz there is a broader continuum. Musical events, on stage and in studios, can encapsulate elements of spontaneity and originality, while also involving critical reflection and revision, without being starkly divided into live versus not live.

In order to explore the issues raised by this recording as a document of one segment of a jazz concert in the late 1950s, this chapter places it in a broader context. I look at jazz concerts as a particular genre of musical event, with a history dating back virtually to the beginnings of jazz itself, and one that has changed significantly in form and both musical and cultural expectations over time. I then consider the social and economic considerations central to concert organization in the 1950s, as important influences impacting the Carnegie Hall concert in particular. Finally, I look at the tepid critical response to this concert, which diverges radically and importantly from the critical response to the recording when it was released nearly fifty years later.

THE JAZZ CONCERT AS A GENRE

Two basic formats dominated in the presentation of jazz on the concert stage by the 1950s. The first of these was the nonprogrammatic long-form concert featuring the music of a single ensemble, of which Monk's concert at Town Hall in February 1959 is an example. Its program featured performances of Monk's compositions orchestrated by Hall Overton for the purpose of the concert, played by a specially constituted ensemble. The ten-piece group, which included tuba and French horn, in addition to more common jazz winds and rhythm section, rehearsed extensively, working with Monk and Overton on the pieces. The core of the group, however, was Monk, Charlie Rouse—his newly hired tenor saxophonist—bassist Sam Jones, and drummer Art Taylor. The concert was a special event, by all means, as befits its location in what Orrin Keepnews, who recorded the concert for Riverside records, has described as "the second most prestigious concert hall in the city at that time," but it had no extramusical program ("Orrin Keepnews" 2008). The second common type was the variety concert, featuring a series of acts, often with some kind of programmatic intent. Benefit concerts, on the whole, were of this second type.

    The state of affairs for jazz concerts in the 1950s had roots going back nearly to the turn of the century. Concerts, of one type or another, featuring jazz or jazz-derived musical styles are as old as the music itself, in at least some sense. In the 1910s and 1920s—as in later years—concert halls were certainly a less common venue for jazz performance than were night clubs, taverns, and ballrooms; nevertheless jazz occasionally found a concert stage. Carnegie Hall—which was by all measures the most prestigious concert hall in the city throughout the twentieth century—actually hosted jazz-oriented music as early as 1912. The Clef Club orchestra, under James Reese Europe's direction, most commonly played for dances at public and private venues, but at least two of their massed gala concerts were held in Carnegie Hall, in 1912 and 1913. Descriptions of the Clef Club's conglomerated events suggest an aura of spectacle and festivity: multiple pianos, hundreds of musicians playing mandolins, banjos, violin, viola, cello, bass, harp-guitars, a smattering of winds, including at least one "saxophone," and a combination of "legit," reading musicians and those who played by ear all appearing on one stage (Howland 2009, 21). Europe's concerts, which Howland describes as featuring "a decidedly non-classical, variety-oriented spectacle," may have been less formal events than later jazz concerts, but even so they could have inspired presenters in the following decade—W. C. Handy, for instance, and Paul Whiteman.

    The opportunity to work on the concert stage was clearly a matter of prestige in the 1910s and 1920s, and it remained so through the 1940s and 1950s (as it continues to do for musicians working in popular styles today, to some extent). Trumpeter Rex Stewart's description of the hierarchies of black musical employment in New York in the 1920s bears this out, with the "first tier... still occupied by the Clef Club musicians," and musicians whose primary employment was in nationally touring vaudeville companies immediately behind them (Howland 2009, 30). The precise ranking was shifting, as Stewart suggests, with vaudeville and variety per se rapidly declining in prestige and significance, being replaced by big bands (often with dancers), which retained some aspects of the variety show but in a much updated style and form.

Even if Whiteman and Handy, both of whom presented jazz-derived work in concert settings in the 1920s, were intent to make "a lady out of jazz"—to present it with the utmost seriousness and demonstrate its highbrow potential—nevertheless they relied on the variety show to provide genre norms. As Howland shows, both Whiteman's concert at Aeolian Hall in 1924, featuring the premier of George Gershwin's *Rhapsody in Blue*, and Handy's concert at Carnegie Hall in 1928, including the first performance of James P. Johnson's *Yamekraw: A Negro Rhapsody*, built on the format of the variety show. The common format for such a show involves two halves, each divided into a series of acts roughly ten to fifteen minutes in length, following a typical sequence: "dumb" or wordless acts, comedy, drama, songs, and so on organized in such a way as to accommodate normal audience behavior (late arrivals, bathroom breaks, and such), build interest, and retain audiences after the intermission (Howland 2009, 85). Handy's program—like other, later programs that incorporate jazz on the concert stage in a "variety" format—was more serious than Whiteman's, importantly less inclined to incorporate elements of hokum and tomfoolery derived from the minstrel stage but had its share of comic and up-tempo bits in the right places (the "character songs" that ended the first half, the Cake Walk that began the second half, and a grand "Jazz Finale," for instance; 89).[5]

Later, prominent jazz concerts in Carnegie Hall—Benny Goodman's in 1938 and Duke Ellington's in 1943—may be seen as retaining echoes of this variety show format, even as they largely dispensed with nonjazz content, as could concerts such as John Hammond's extravaganza *From Spirituals to Swing*, also from 1938. Goodman's concert seems the closest to the Whiteman format, in the sense that it followed a similar kind of rhythm, opening with a short introduction and historical featurette ("20 Years of Jazz"), moving on through (among others) a staged "jam session" and ending with a grand finale, "Sing, Sing, Sing (With a Swing)," with Gene Krupa's wild drumming providing a kind of novelty. The precise contents and order of the variety show's acts may not have been followed—there is not much of a gesture toward comedy here, for instance—but in the combination of vocalists and acts without words, and in the rhythm of movement between short pieces and longer pieces, between lighter and heavier, and between segments with a narrative arc and those without, Goodman still seems to have built on the jazz concert model that had itself built on the variety show.

From Spirituals to Swing offered a very different kind of variety, and yet it continued to relate to the jazz concert model established in previous events if not directly to the variety show model itself. For the concert, Hammond expanded on the historical narrative that both Whiteman and Goodman had incorporated into concerts. His concert differed from the others by drawing the history of jazz back not only to ragtime and New Orleans jazz but to boogie-woogie, blues, spirituals, and ultimately to Africa, heard through Hugh Tracey's recordings of "African Tribal Music" from coastal West Africa. There was no longer a real relationship to the older variety entertainment, in terms of the number or order of events, and in a sense the program suggests that the jazz concert—or the concert presentation incorporating jazz and other African American music—had become a schematic format in itself. The most compelling principle at work in crafting an evening's entertainment now appears to have been managing energy. The first half of the program starts at the most exotic, with West Africa represented on recording, followed immediately by the most familiar, the Count Basie orchestra, playing one brief number. The audience was then brought from that high of excitement into a more contemplative section of spirituals, which then built in intensity with "Holy Roller Hymns," sung by Sister Rosetta Tharpe. A small group drawn from Basie's orchestra once again drew the mood back with "Soft Swing," setting a point of departure for a gathering intensity with Sonny Terry on harmonica, a series of blues singers (including Joe Turner, Jimmy Rushing, and Helen Humes), and a finale featuring Meade "Lux" Lewis, Albert Ammons, and Pete Johnson in "A Cutting Session." Thus the curtain came down for intermission at a high point, which was picked up in the second half, featuring only two acts, Sidney Bechet and his New Orleans Feet Warmers demonstrating "Early New Orleans Jazz," and the return of the full Basie orchestra as well as smaller combos drawn from it to end with swing.

Duke Ellington's 1943 concert at Carnegie Hall, which featured the premiere of *Black, Brown and Beige*, brought together aspects of various earlier jazz concerts, including the series of acts (now all played by his band in some format or another) and the historical narrative (now basically confined to the piece *Black, Brown and Beige* itself). There were fewer acts than on a typical variety show (six in all), but the continued division of the show's program into numbered acts clearly points to the variety show rather than the symphonic concert. That said, the ordering of the acts themselves can be seen as drawing on the American orchestral concert. By the mid-1940s the genre norms for a symphony concert had become well entrenched.[6] Concerts were generally in two parts, with an intermission, and each half commonly included two or occasionally three works. The first half often began with a shorter, lighter piece—Mozart's and Haydn's works were typically programmed here—and concluded with the longest, most grandiose piece of the evening; Brahms and late Beethoven were common first-half ending choices. Note the similarity in this regard between the symphonic program and a variety show: as George Gottlieb, a booker for a New York theater in the teens said, the number immediately before intermission was a "big act," which had to have "something really worthwhile to...crown the first half of the bill" (quoted in Howland 2009, 85). In the 1945 concert Ellington opened with lighter fare—nodding, perhaps, to the symphonic program, but also to the importance of comedy in the variety show, with his homages to Bert Williams and Bill "Bojangles" Robinson—and closes the first half with his big, symphonic work, the multimovement "tone parallel," *Black, Brown and Beige*. The second half of a symphonic concert at this point usually started with a concerto or other work for vocal or instrumental soloist with orchestra and then concluded with a big, often showy work. It is no accident, then, that the second half of Ellington's program in 1943 included a series of pieces featuring one or another instrument, referred to in the program notes as "Concertos," and a final act of three songs, two of which were among the band's biggest hits, "Don't Get Around Much Any More" and "Mood Indigo."

Ellington's concert in the symphonic mode was not the direction in which most jazz concerts would go in the following years, although there was a slow but regular production of jazz and jazz-derived pieces in the "third stream" that were programmed in otherwise nonjazz symphony concerts. Perhaps as a symbol of jazz coming into its own, and in tandem with the ongoing opportunity to program longer but formalized collections of music on LPs in the 1950s, jazz concerts took on a form more clearly their own over the course of the 1940s and 1950s. Though they often retained the practice of incorporating elements that made them clearly special in comparison with night club and dance hall settings, concert formats usually drew on the forms of small-group swing and modern jazz combo performance: tunes used as vehicles for extended solo improvisation. Part of the problem with concert programming before the mid-1940s must have come from anxiety about the need to maintain an audience's interest over multiple hours of music without dancing (either in a floorshow or social dancing). The extended "programmatic" concerts and the grouping of short pieces into "acts" both address this need. Neither element was common in jazz concert programs by the mid-1950s. Instead, most concerts had programs that look more like the playlists of the new LP format. As the two formats—the modern jazz concert and the LP—emerged at basically the same time, it is hard to say precisely what the relationship between them is, but it is plausible to think that they, along with changes in social mores around jazz audience behavior and clear changes in the music itself, were all part of a complex, shifting cultural ecology that was responsible for similarities between the two formats.

Jazz, along with the jazz concert, was surely coming into its own in the period between 1944 and 1960. It was developing a level of cultural capital in America that would eventually lead to its being named a national treasure by the U.S. House of Representatives, among other things (Gabbard 1995). The number of jazz concerts increased rapidly, with virtually every kind of jazz being showcased in concert halls, in major cities, and, importantly, on college campuses. Concert dates were single-night events as part of a mixed touring schedule for an orchestra like Duke Ellington's or Stan Kenton's; they were special one- or two-night events for groups that existed only for the purpose of the concert, as with Thelonious Monk's 1959 Town Hall concert; and they were tour packages, as in Norman Granz's Jazz at the Philharmonic (JATP) series. Programs for all of these sorts of events tended simply to showcase a series of pieces, selected to create a dynamic sense of energy and repose. In this regard, they may have had a distant relation to the variety show, but if so, only the softest of echoes.

Two interconnected aspects of the new approaches to presenting modern jazz in general at the time seem to be responsible for this shift. First, the "head-solo-solo-solo...head" format, was infinitely flexible and infinitely expandable, allowing as many or few solos and as many or few choruses per solo of whatever piece was being played as a bandleader and soloist wanted. It gave bands a way to explore pieces of music in some depth and at some length without having to search for extended forms, along the lines of what Ellington did with *Black, Brown and Beige* in 1943 (and with various pieces both before and after). This meant that they no longer had to think in terms of "acts," which might have been necessary, to give coherence to an hour-long string of three-minute-long pieces. Second, audiences and musicians were both becoming accustomed to the experience of jazz as a "music for listening," in addition to jazz as dance music. This meant that some of the extra trappings and special pleading that were typical of jazz concerts in the 1910s, 1920s, and 1930s were unnecessary.

That this change did not only apply to "modern" jazz concerts at the time is clear in the programs for Granz's JATP concerts. Beginning in 1944, Granz endeavored to present major figures from swing along with younger modern jazz musicians in varied concert programs. He started with concerts at the Los Angeles Philharmonic, which gave the series its "at the Philharmonic" moniker, and quickly developed the JATP brand into one of the premier jazz concert institutions in the world. Groups working under the JATP heading included a wide variety of musicians—Ella Fitzgerald, Oscar Peterson, Benny Carter, Lester Young, Roy Eldridge, Illinois Jacquet, Charlie Parker, Dizzy Gillespie, Stan Getz, Zoot Sims, and Ray Brown, for instance—and could be heard in the top concert halls of the United States and Europe. There are no scholarly studies of Granz's work or the JATP series, but it does not seem to be an exaggeration to say that the series holds a key place in the history of jazz concerts as a whole.

Granz's vision for the JATP series may not have been fully formed when he organized the initial event—a concert featuring Nat "King" Cole, Ella Fitzgerald, and Lester Young—but it seems quickly to have taken shape. Granz was a consummate businessman (in 1953 he said, "If I didn't make at least $100,000 a year take-home pay, I'd quit"), and the concerts clearly reflected this (Severo 2001, D7). The groups were advertised lavishly in newspapers and trade journals, highlighting the star power of their unusual lineups. Beyond this, however, Granz had a fundamental social and artistic goal for the concerts: to present jazz in such a way that it would be heard by contemporary audiences as a music with the seriousness, depth, and quality to match the major classical stars of the day. As he said, "I insisted that my musicians were treated with the same respect as Leonard Bernstein or Heifetz because they were just as good" (ibid.). Moreover, his obituary in the *New York Times* reports: "In all his Jazz at the Philharmonic presentations Mr. Granz emphasized that he wanted no dancing or unruly behavior when the music was played. He wanted people to listen, just as they might listen to Bach or Brahms" (ibid.). In spite of what might now be thought of as a fetishization of the Western classical canon and misguided or condescending attitudes toward jazz audiences and the ebullient, interactive nature of jazz performance styles, the concerts were enormously successful for more than a decade, earning Granz the admiration of many musicians (ibid.).

This normalization of jazz concerts may have made them less remarkable, but it did not make them less popular or less valuable to musicians or promoters. Indeed, they were clearly enormously popular, with the major festivals (just starting in the early 1950s) becoming fixtures of American cultural life. Nor, I think, did it make the musicians less prone to see concerts as an opportunity to make a significant artistic statement, or at least to treat them with a measure of formality they may not always have given club shows or dances. Such a position is borne out in the later chapters of this book, which look closely at the individual performances from Monk's sets at the Morningside Community Center benefit.

ORGANIZING A CONCERT: THE SOCIOECONOMICS OF JAZZ CONCERTS

The concert on which this book focuses was not organized for strictly musical reasons, as were those discussed above, but rather as a way to raise money and awareness for a cause. The convention of holding benefit concerts for one thing or another has a long history, being established in Europe, for instance, as early as the eighteenth century, as Dennis Arnold's and Brian Boydell's studies of such events in Dublin have shown, but in jazz it was not common until the Civil Rights era (Arnold 1968; Boydell 1992).[7] Citing concert organizers such as Nat Hentoff and musicians including Clark Terry and Bernice Johnson Reagon, Ingrid Monson, dates the massive growth in benefit concerts for the Civil Rights movement to the early 1960s (Monson 2007, 154). In the wake of such concerts as the Congress on Racial Equality's 1960 event featuring Monk, Jimmy Giuffre, Bill Henderson, and Clark Terry, and Max Roach's initial public performance of the *Freedom Now Suite* in 1961, also as a benefit for the Congress on Racial Equality, Monson says, "Although benefit concerts generated considerable amounts of money for civil rights organizations, their purpose and popularity cannot be fully explained by the economic dimension alone.... They also created social spaces in which musicians and audiences could feel as though they were *doing something* to aid the Southern struggle" (Monson 2007, 155–57, emphasis in the original).

The concert benefiting the Morningside Community Center is somewhat distinct from the history of the 1960s as Monson describes it, inasmuch as the center was not a radical organization in the way CORE and SNCC were—nor even an explicitly political center-left institution like the NAACP. Nevertheless, it should reasonably be seen as a part of the larger picture. In fact, events such as this one, which were organized for more local, but still socially committed, organizations, may even reasonably be seen to have set the stage for the flourishing of benefit concerts in the 1960s. The Morningside Community Center was at least implicitly engaged not only in outreach and development but also in the Civil Rights Movement. Established in 1938 by Presbyterian minister James Robinson, the center provided broad-based social services in its upper Manhattan neighborhood. Its charge, in keeping with Robinson's interests as both a pastor at the Church of the Master and the valedictorian for his class at Lincoln University, was to create access to education and health care, especially mental health services, for the local African American community (Sarkella and Mazzeo 2006, 40). Robinson and the center were highly visible in the period immediately surrounding this concert, appearing in *Ebony* and *Jet*, for their educational programs, "interracial summer camp" (which was the immediate beneficiary of the Carnegie Hall concert), and work-study trips to West Africa. Duke Ellington played a benefit concert for the center in 1959, and Robert F. Kennedy visited the center in 1963 (Compston 2002, 126; Vail 1999, 153).

Perhaps the clearest way in which this concert anticipates events such as the SNCC concert of 1960 is in its presentation of an all-star, "billboard," multi-act lineup. As noted, the only CD release to come from the Morningside Community Center benefit features Thelonious Monk and John Coltrane, but they were not alone on the bill and were not even the headlining act of the evening. Only Sonny Rollins, who was billed as a new act ("introducing..."), had lower billing than Monk and Coltrane. Even though this may seem surprising in retrospect, it made sense in 1957. The other acts were notable not so much for having been active longer than Monk; Billie Holiday had been performing since 1929, but Dizzy Gillespie's career had begun along with Monk's in the late 1930s, Ray Charles had been recording only since the late 1940s, and Austin Cromer shared billing with Dizzy Gillespie starting that year, for instance. What they shared, in contradistinction to Monk, Coltrane, Chet Baker, Zoot Sims, and Rollins, was that they could reasonably be expected to draw a broad audience, from core jazz fans to more casual concert attendees. Ray Charles, for instance, had been working the R&B circuit for more than a decade by the time of the benefit, releasing a series of top-ten singles throughout the early and mid-1950s that were collected on an eponymous LP with Atlantic in 1957. He may not yet have become the household name he would become with albums such as *Modern Sounds in Country and Western* and *Genius + Soul = Jazz*, but he was definitely a star in Harlem already. Monk, it should be said, was also well on his way to being a household name by then, but not in a way that would make him a huge audience draw for a benefit concert. In 1959, when *The Many Loves of Dobie Gillis* premiered, Monk's name was recognizable enough to be a talisman of hip for the beatnik outsider Maynard G. Krebs, and a few years later, in 1964, his portrait would grace the cover of *Time* magazine. Still, in 1957 he had just gotten his cabaret card back, and in any case, in all the instances cited here he represented the obscure taste, not the mainstream.

Monson suggests that this kind of concert programming—the creation of lineups featuring jazz stalwarts alongside pop acts (often jazz-leaning pop acts)—presented a series of aggravations to the jazz musicians in the events. Audiences may well have wanted to hear the pop stars—the Ray Charleses and Billie Holidays, and in later concerts the Frank Sinatras and Sammy Davis, Jrs. on the programs—but by the mid-1960s jazz musicians who were participating, generally for no pay, were acutely aware of differences in status that these events highlighted (Monson 2007, 165–68). This may not, however, have been as needling in 1957 as it was by 1967, if only because it was still common for jazz musicians to appear on mixed bills in the 1950s. The pages of *Variety* list regular nights at auditoriums such as Harlem's Apollo featuring Monk or Miles Davis, to name just two, along with R&B acts, comedians, dancers, and so forth—everything but contortionists and plate jugglers. In a way, it seems as if these lineups—particularly when they show up in theaters such as the Apollo, which had originally presented burlesque and transitioned to variety entertainment in the 1930s—represent an echo of the historical relationship of jazz with American theatrical traditions. I am even more inclined to see them as evidence of the less strict divisions in the past than today between jazz and other African-American music traditions—especially R&B—as well as more general pop.

Regardless of how musicians felt about billboard lineups like the one for the Morningside Community Center concert, it seems clear that audiences loved them. It is difficult to know precisely—or even in a general sense—who was at the Morningside Community Center benefit, but it seems plausible that it was a broader audience than would have seen Monk and Coltrane together in the months before at the Five Spot in Greenwich Village. Ira Gitler remarks in his contribution to the reissue's liner notes that not only was he not there but "I am still wondering...why I've no memory of the event, nor do friends of mine, like Dan Morgenstern, who have been in and around jazz for a long time" (Gitler 2005, x). I take this to mean that the concert was aimed at an audience other than the jazz insiders represented by Gitler, Morgenstern, and their friends. Monk's Town Hall concert of only a year later, for instance, clearly was on their collective radar, and it was a very different sort of event. In comparison with the Town Hall concert, which featured one band and an important musical experiment (Monk's work scored for a jazz chamber orchestra), or his regular appearances at the Five Spot (gradually becoming one of the premier jazz clubs, largely because of Monk), the concert at Carnegie Hall may have seemed pedestrian to the jazzerati of the time.

It is maddeningly difficult, however, to catch a glimpse of who the audience for this concert and others like it was, even if it is possible to say things about who it was not. The price of admission can tell us something. At $2, $3, $3.50, and $3.95, ticket prices were moderate, akin to something like $20–$40 in 2012 dollars. By comparison, a movie ticket at the time was around 60 cents (perhaps $0.75 in Manhattan). The venue might also tell us something: as a grand concert hall in a well-to-do part of Manhattan, the concert was likely attended by people of some cultural status. This really is not much, in the end. It does not, reliably, tell us anything about the racial and gendered makeup of the audience. All of the music on the bill certainly had substantial followings among both black and white New Yorkers, not to mention Hispanic and Asian Americans, and among both men and women.

Firsthand reports of the evening are also little help. *Billboard* announced the concert in their November 25 issue, giving the lineup and noting the profits were to benefit the Morningside center, but it did not review the event. The *Saturday Review*, which regularly covered the jazz beat at the time, also had a notice but gave even less information. The *New York Times* review says little about who was in attendance, though it does give some insight into what was commonplace and what unusual about this event. Ray Charles's set was the highlight for John S. Wilson, largely because of the novelty of seeing him in such a setting. "The event of particular interest in a program that included Billie Holiday, tenor saxophonist Sonny Rollins, the Thelonious Monk Quartet, the Zoot Sims Quartet with Chet Baker, trumpet, and, of course, Mr. Gillespie's band," he said, "was the New York concert debut of Ray Charles, a pianist and blues singer" (Wilson 1957). Monk, he said, "who is rarely heard in concert, made several of his oddly oriented, quixotic compositions glow with an eerie pianistic light," and the Gillespie band, "which turns up frequently at such affairs, was more flexible and sure-footed than it has often been in the past" (ibid.). Whitney Balliett, writing in the *New Yorker*, was less excited by the whole event, which he described as "a rundown circus" (1957, 208). He seems to have been only to the early show and was particularly unimpressed with Gillespie's band and the Zoot

Sims quartet, but he also found Ray Charles's set uninspired. About Monk he was more positive, saying, "Monk...appeared with a quartet...and worked his way through five fascinating if somewhat calculated numbers, which had such fearless titles as 'Crepuscule with Nellie,' 'Nutty,' and 'Epistrophy'" (209). He described Coltrane as "a hard-toned, uninhibited performer" and said he "took several solos, during most of which he relied on a series of complex, dancing runs that seemed, nonetheless, more automatic than inspired" (ibid.). Balliett saved his strongest praise for Billie Holiday's set, which he called "a memorable twenty minutes" (210). The general tenor of the review, which also covered the "Jazz for Moderns" concert a few days before, featuring Miles Davis's Quintet, Gerry Mulligan's Quartet, and others, was one of dissatisfaction with jazz concerts altogether. His complaints run the gamut: they start late, the emcee is "that pale descendant of the old circus barker, the disc jokey," the staging and lighting is abysmal, and sound reinforcement is routinely inappropriate (208). At best, however, one can say only that an average reader of the *New Yorker* (largely white and at least aspirationally well-to-do, to judge by the magazine's never-ending cavalcade of advertisements for hi-fi systems, luxury clothes, and international travel programs) may have shared Balliett's familiarity—and ennui—with concerts such as this one.

CONCLUSION: WHY CONCERTS?

Concerts moved from being a marginal but by no means unheard-of context for jazz in the early twentieth century to being one of its regular settings by the end of the 1950s. However, even as they became more common, they remained special in an important sense. Audiences and musicians alike continued to see the concert setting as something that conferred prestige on the music being performed. Concerts in general may have involved some kind of trade-off for musicians, as the setting involves a loss of some of the intimacy and interaction that smaller club performances facilitated. To the extent that this was so, however, only some musicians felt it as a real loss. Charles Mingus's hostile spoken introduction recorded in the studio for the performance of "Original Faubus Fables," on *Charles Mingus Presents Charles Mingus* in 1960, suggests the downside to club dates: potentially inattentive audiences, a perceived lack of respect for jazz as an art, and real distractions to playing well.

Beyond this, however, concerts may have represented the best employment jazz musicians had available to them at that point. A cursory review of Duke Ellington's contracts, housed in the Ellington collection at the Smithsonian Institution, for instance, shows a stark disparity between concert dates and dance hall shows. Every contract has a slightly different set of terms, but in general when the band played a dance they could expect to have committed to four grueling hours (generally 8:00 p.m. to 12:00 midnight or 10:00 p.m. to 2:00 a.m.) of relatively short, danceable numbers for somewhere around $1,000. By contrast, an average concert performance brought in closer to $2,000 for less than two hours of work, typically in two sets in which they could stretch out and play longer arrangements that might have been more musically interesting to the musicians. Concerts, then, offered a high degree of musical satisfaction for something like four times the hourly wage. At a time when Ellington—to judge from his correspondence, at least—was still struggling to bring in enough from performing to end his tours in the black, concerts must have been seen as the best option. For other musicians, with less star power, the distinction could have been even more significant.

Obviously, benefit concerts specifically would not have had the same financial value to jazz musicians, since they often donated their time. Still, compared with other gigs, it is not hard to see why benefit concerts would have appealed to performers. They had most of the same qualities of any other concert—that is, they allowed musicians flexibility in programming and put them in front of an attentive audience without the distraction of cash registers, clinking glasses, conversation, and so on. Beyond this, at least in the 1950s they gave jazz musicians the opportunity to play for broad audiences, as seems to be the case with the Morningside Community Center benefit that Monk and Coltrane's recording comes from. These audiences may have had less familiarity with the intricacies of modern jazz than did club audiences, but they were clearly still open to its musical codes. Moreover, they represented a much larger market than the gradually diminishing jazz fan base. Even more importantly, however, as Monson documents, benefits gave jazz musicians an opportunity to visibly demonstrate their commitment to a cause in the best possible terms. Their music clearly had value in this political economy, and their contribution truly mattered. Monson focuses on benefits specifically for the civil rights movement, which proliferated after 1961; but the prevalence of benefits for various causes in the 1950s shows, in a sense, the range of commitments jazz musicians had.

This chapter and the previous one were primarily conceived to bring some historical context to a discussion of Thelonious Monk and John Coltrane's performance at the Morningside Community Center benefit concert at Carnegie Hall. As discussed above, one of the key things concerts—whether benefits or not—offered musicians was a chance to present versions of what they were doing elsewhere in a more formal setting than normal. This may have led to less spontaneous performances, but it also often led to more polished ones. That trade-off may well have been disappointing to the music's fans, but for the musicians it may not have been. Recording sessions were similarly opportunities to play more formally, since by then musicians had come to think of their recordings as the part of their music that would be known to posterity. This often produced a different kind of playing, but not a less valued kind. As the following chapters will show, on the two sets they played that November evening, Monk and his quartet took the opportunity to program polished, considered versions of tunes they were playing night after night at the Five Spot. The results may not have been electrifying in the way their nightly gigs were, but from a vantage point in the early 2010s, we can say they have a depth and power that make them compelling evidence of one of the most important collaborations in the history of modern jazz.

CHAPTER 3
Playing Ballads
"Monk's Mood" and "Crepuscule with Nellie"

THE QUARTET'S FIRST set of the Carnegie Hall concert was around the length of one side of an album at the time, roughly thirty minutes, but it had an unusual set list, alternating between slow, introspective pieces and quick vehicles for virtuoso display.[1] The set is unusual not only for incorporating more than one ballad but also for starting with one. The two slow pieces are somewhat different from one another— "Monk's Mood" is a journey through Monk's poignant sense of dissonance, and "Crepuscle with Nellie" is a set piece for his beloved wife—but they share a key element of their arrangement. There are no solos in either performance, in the standard sense, and no one improvises on either piece. Rather, as on other recordings of the songs, Monk plays through each piece alone once and is then joined by the band, which continues to play the head, at times indulging in a free rubato. The creative interest in these pieces, beyond coming from the formal structures of the compositions themselves, arises from the ways in which Monk and the rest of the band collaborate in interpreting, or "realizing," them. Although they appeared in the concert and on the CD release in alternation with the first set's up-tempo pieces, I have chosen to look at "Monk's Mood" and "Crepuscule with Nellie" together in this chapter because of the significant similarities between the two performances, and in order to illuminate the differences between them. Moreover, I do so to bring out the significance of Monk and Coltrane's voices as balladists, in contrast to the more common attention they have received for other kinds of playing.

In these two tunes, perhaps more than anywhere else, Monk and his group make a case for Nat Hentoff's judgment from around this time that "[Monk's] works are *compositions* in the sense that relatively few jazz 'originals' are" (1960, 137). In most cases jazz tunes are successful to the extent that they serve as vehicles for improvisation, but "Monk's Mood" and "Crepuscule with Nellie" have to be viewed in a different light, simply because they were not, at least for Monk, really understood this way. The two songs might more reasonably be viewed as miniatures with, not surprisingly, a striking level of inventiveness in details of both melodic and harmonic construction. That said, there is a very real difference between pieces like these and compositions in the Western classical tradition, as is clear from this performance. Although the band does not use the songs as vehicles for soloing, neither do they play through them "as written." Instead Monk has his band interpret the songs' basic parameters—melody, harmony, rhythm—within a narrower range than in most jazz performances, but still with space for each musician to bring something, to make them new in the act of performance. The exercise of art and craft here is in the group's attention to detail, rather than in larger improvisational gestures.[2]

These two ballads offer an interesting set of theoretical questions, inasmuch as they represent some of Monk's most challenging harmonic writing. An analysis of the two pieces has to come to terms with how they create effective, clearly audible experiences of melodic direction without necessarily using standard harmonic procedures. Monk's peculiar harmonic choices are, therefore, a significant object of analysis in this chapter, but they are in some ways driven by and secondary to melody and rhythm, rather than vice versa. Most importantly, "Monk's Mood" and "Crepuscle with Nellie" are windows onto Monk's particular genius for combining the conventional and unconventional—or of using the unconventional to signify and illuminate musical conventions.

"MONK'S MOOD"

"Monk's Mood," at nearly eight minutes, without the standard timekeeping device of the regular rhythmic groove or the form-defining articulations of the movement from solo to solo common to most jazz performances, is a challenging statement. Originally titled "Feeling That Way Now," Monk wrote the piece that would become "Monk's Mood" in February 1946 on commission for Gil Fuller to arrange for Dizzy Gillespie's post–Billie Eckstein modern jazz big band (Kelley 2009, 113).[3] Fuller was a prodigious arranger, having worked with quite a number of major swing bands, and in the early 1940s he was responsible for finding ways to use the orchestrational language of swing in the service of bop for Gillespie's group. The piece suggests at times, through a constantly shifting set of approaches to voicing, harmonization, and counter melodies in the bass and interior voices (typical of Monk's pianistic style), that Monk "heard" the piece even in its earliest compositional stages as a work that could be performed by big band, as well as by solo piano or small modern jazz quartet. There is no extant recording of the Gillespie band's version of "Monk's Mood," but it appears Monk made Fuller's job somewhat easier, as an early score of the piece, in the Mary Lou Williams papers, shows Monk conceiving of it from the start not only in "lead sheet" form—a melody with schematic chord changes—but fleshed out with bass lines, chord voicings, and an "orchestral" piano arrangement laid out on a grand staff (ibid.).

It may come as no surprise that Monk programmed "Monk's Mood" on the Carnegie Hall concert, inasmuch as it was a piece he played regularly in the late 1950s, and that he had already recorded with Coltrane. Beyond this, there may have been an even more compelling reason not just to include it but to play it first on that night's program. As noted in Chapter 1, "Monk's Mood" seems to have held a special place for Coltrane, because it was the composition that first drew him to work with Monk and was the first piece that Monk taught him (Kelley 2009, 218). Although it is hard to speculate on the reasons for any particular decision about a given concert program—aside from how the music fits together— the special interest Coltrane took in the piece, as well as Monk's satisfaction with how Coltrane played it, helps explain its inclusion as part of a somewhat odd set list.

The piece is based on two melodies, an arching opening melody that covers mm. 1–4 of the A section, and a second melody that is introduced in m. 5 and taken up and in one form or another to provide almost all the rest of the melodic material for both the end of the A section and the bridge.[4] The first melody is composed of two parts: an opening statement of four eighth notes, a quarter note, and a final long note—the long note is five beats but might be thought of as a whole note in the second measure that is preceded by a one-beat anticipation—and then its conclusion, a quarter-note triplet group and dotted-quarter-eighth pair that resolves to a whole note in the fourth measure. Melodically the first part moves through an upward-directed arpeggio of an Fmin7 chord in eighth notes—C–E♭–A♭, with a B♭ upper neighbor reaching up past the A♭ and then resolving down, followed by a leap down to an E♮ quarter note on beat 3 (which Monk harmonizes with a B♭7 chord), and a large step up of a third to the last note on beat 4 of the first measure (which Monk harmonizes with a ringing CMaj9 chord, voiced with an open fifth in the bass). The second part picks up from the G that concludes the previous motive, stepping down to F, which Monk ornaments with a complete upper neighbor, and then it continues down through E, leaps down to G for the penultimate eighth note, and resolves to C for the ending whole note, as the seventh of a D♭Maj7 chord.

Monk presents the second, more clearly motivic, melody initially in the third measure and then transforms it rhythmically and harmonically over the course of the rest of the A section and the bridge. The initial form of the motive is a quarter note, two eighths, and a final two quarter notes, moving D–C♯–E–F–E. Harmonically this takes place over a stepwise movement from B♭7 down to A7, with D as the third of the first chord and E as the fifth of the second. The F works as a suspension, which is approached by step from below. This motive is repeated in the next measure, starting on F, with the rhythm unaltered, but with an alteration in the intervals to allow it to end on G♭ rather than G. It is then repeated starting on G, with further alterations to the intervallic structure (G–F♯–G–B–D–G), the last two quarter notes transformed into a dotted-quarter-eighth pair and the final eighth note extended with a whole note in m. 8. Measures 7 and 8 are further altered in the repeat of the A section (and in the final A section), so that the rhythm is a quarter followed by constant eighths, with the final eighth note of m. 7 tied to a whole note in m. 8 of the second A section, and not tied but rather followed by a rearticulated whole note in the last A section. Versions of this motive, characterized by the opening quarter-eighth-eighth and/or a down-up melodic contour, are found in mm. 1–5 of the bridge, with the final measures of the bridge winding up in nonmotivic material.

Harmonically the piece displays a characteristically "Monkish" ambiguity. It is perhaps best thought of as projecting a sense of C tonality (with some major/minor modal mixture, though perhaps more strongly suggesting C minor), yet it does so without ever including a ii–V–I (or even a simple V–I) progression ending on CMaj7 or Cmin7. The melodic line is easier to hear in relation to C than are the changes. Major points of arrival are all drawn from the C major diatonic scale, with the exception of the E-flats in mm. 5–6 of the bridge. Moreover, the A section can be seen as projecting a movement from G, in m. 2, to C, at the end of the second and last A, through its primary structural notes (that is, those notes that are the focal point of elaborating devices, such as suspensions or neighbor tones, or notes that are simply points of stasis or arrival in the individual melodic segments). The fact that the first A and the bridge both end on G supports the idea of a kind of structural melody in two parts. The first part begins on G as scale degree 5 of C, moves downward toward C, returns to G at the end of the first A, and completes the movement to C at the end of the second A. The second part then moves back to G, which it arrives at only by the end of the bridge, and finally completes a large-scale descent from G as scale degree 5 to C as scale degree 1 over the course of the final A. Monk's alterations to the melody in mm. 7–8 of the A section strongly support hearing the piece in this way. The first A section ends on G, and the melody is reconfigured to allow an ending on C in the second A section, which is arrived at by leap from a low G. This altered melody is then further altered in the final A section so that the C is withheld until the downbeat of m. 8, rather than being anticipated in m. 7. Moreover, in order to withhold the C until m. 8, Monk introduces a D on the second half of beat 4 of m. 7, thereby completing a descending C major scale from G to C. Though this is by no means a classic *Urlinie*, Schenkerian scholars will recognize elements of tonality as Schenker described them in this reading of the melody.[5]

If the "Monk's Mood" melody is relatively straightforward and projects a sense of tonality while incorporating some chromatic surprises, its chord changes are less so. The A section opens with a ii–V progression in E♭ (Fmin7–B♭7♯11), which resolves not to E♭ but to C major, which Monk usually played with an open voicing emphasizing a perfect fifth in the bass. The implication of this move—creating a sense of nonresolution—is not really developed. Instead, Monk moves to another ii–V progression, this time in C major (Dmin7♭5–G13), but does not clearly resolve it to C. The chord at the beginning of m. 4 is generally represented in lead sheets as a D♭Maj7, which might be thought of as a substitution of some kind. I would argue that it makes more sense to understand this not as a "substitution" in the sense in which the term is generally used in jazz theory—the tritone substitution, particularly—whereby two closely related chords can be used interchangeably, but rather to hear the D♭ in the bass as a half-step displacement of the more obvious resolution of the progression. A similar move comes at the end of the second and final A sections, where Monk moves from A♭7, which can be heard as a tritone substitution for D, down to G7, and then ends on D♭Maj7. The joke, as it were, of this whole A section, and in some sense of the whole piece, is that the only CMaj7 chord is arrived at from a ii–V progression that aims somewhere else, and multiple ii–V progressions that aim at C do not reach it.

Monk's first recording of this piece, from the Blue Note session on November 21, 1947, sheds some light on this. He may already at that point have thought of the chord in m. 4 of the first A section, and both mm. 4 and 8 of the second and last A sections, as incorporating a D♭ as part of a moving bass line, but he does not sit on it the way he did in various recordings of the piece from the late 1950s. Rather it sounds as if D♭ is intended at that point as a dissonant flat ninth, or more simply as a nonharmonic dissonance in the context of a CMaj7 chord. Likewise, in the 1957 studio recording Monk made with Coltrane that was released on *Thelonious Himself*, Monk treats the D♭ in the bass in m. 4 of each A section like a chromatic suspension that he resolves to C just before moving on to the following harmony. On the other hand, in the same recording the final harmony of the second and final A sections is very clearly a D♭Maj7. voiced in such a way as to highlight the open interval between root and fifth in the bass.[6] The implication from these few recordings, at least, is that Monk initially thought of the progressions at these moments as fairly conventional tonal gestures (ii–V–I, with or without a tritone substitution) and over time developed them into more distinctive, "Monkish" ones by shifting the chord of resolution by a half step. A recording of the piece in its early arrangement for the Gillespie band might have shed some interesting light on this issue, were one available.

Monk and the quartet extend "Monk's Mood" in the Carnegie Hall performance, playing two and a half ornately ornamented choruses without solo improvisations. Monk's initial chorus functions, as his initial choruses often do, in an introductory way, showcasing the tune in a relatively simple context. Coltrane then enters for an extended cadenza starting over the D♭Maj7 harmony that ended the first chorus, stepping down to a B7 while Abdul-Malik holds a bowed low B, and Monk plays arpeggios over the range of the piano. Toward the end of the cadenza, Monk uses a descending whole-tone flourish to shift down to B♭7, landing on Fmin7, the first chord of the A section, at which point Coltrane enters with the primary melody. Throughout the rest of the first two A sections of the second chorus, the band continues to take the melody out of tempo, with Abdul-Malik bowing long notes, and both Coltrane and Monk playing scalar, arpeggiated, and occasionally less regular patterns through the full range of their instruments, to extend nearly every note longer than an eighth note. At the bridge Wilson enters, playing a double-time shuffle groove, slightly behind the beat, with brushes, and Abdul-Malik switches to a plucked bass line, not in double time, emphasizing the downbeats of each measure. The final A section brings a return to the nonmetric feel and the texture of the first two A sections. Finally the band repeats the bridge and last A sections with the same arrangement as in the second chorus. Altogether the introduction of out-of-time, substantially ornamented playing stretches out the sections, so that whereas Monk's first whole chorus took just under two minutes, the band's chorus-and-a-half fills nearly six minutes. This amounts to an unusual, and frankly challenging, way to open a set in the late 1950s.

The arrangement of "Monk's Mood" that the band played on this concert, with its alternation between metric and nonmetric sections and extended cadenzalike passagework, echoes the arrangement Monk recorded with Coltrane for Riverside just months before the Morningside Heights Community Center benefit, but it shows a dramatic expansion of the idea. The amount of passagework and the length of the extensions are both substantially increased. Moreover, although Coltrane played most of the passagework on the Riverside recording, here both he and Monk play in counterpoint. This is an excellent place to see how Monk and Coltrane were affecting each other as musicians during the period. Not only is it possible in this recording, among others, to see Coltrane working out the so-called sheets of sound style that became his signature thereafter, but it is also possible to hear Monk's playing as "sound-sheety" as well.[7]

Monk's passagework, of course, has other precedents—in the piano playing of his predecessors in New York, particularly Art Tatum for instance, but others as well. Monk's own work is riddled with these kinds of virtuoso flourishes, so much that certain whole tone scale passages and arpeggios up and down the keyboard can be reasonably thought of as emblematic, if not stereotypical of his playing, as much as dissonant clusters that resolve to a single held note, stride left hand interjections, or particular chord voicings. That said, I would be hesitant to think of this as evidence simply that Coltrane was influenced in the development of his "sheets of sound" by Monk's pianism. He does seem to have been influenced in this way, to at least some extent, but Monk also seems to be affected by Coltrane here. More interesting, though, is the recording Monk made just over a year later with a larger ensemble at Town Hall in

February 1959, without Coltrane. In this instance Monk could easily have played extensive passagework, even in spite of the somewhat different arrangement, but he did not. What is the best way to think about the relationship between Monk and Coltrane's playing styles here? It sounds as though the younger musician, developing a radically new approach to his instrument—an approach based at least in part on material drawn idiomatically from harp and piano techniques—heard something in Monk's music that inspired him, and in turn Monk supported him with playing that was at once compatible with Coltrane's conception but at the same time based in his own personal style.

"CREPUSCULE WITH NELLIE"

The other ballad Monk programmed on the first set of the Carnegie Hall concert was "Crepuscule with Nellie." Unlike "Monk's Mood," which was one of Monk's older compositions and which he recorded only sporadically, and seems even to have played live relatively seldom after 1957, "Crepuscule with Nellie" was a new piece, likely unknown to his audience, and one that would come to be central to his repertoire in the following years. Monk does not appear to have had a dogmatic position on interpreting "Monk's Mood," but by contrast he treated "Crepuscule with Nellie" as a more or less fixed composition, changing the arrangement in some ways, but not using it as a vehicle for extended improvisation. Indeed, even though Monk had played a short solo on the Blue Note recording of "Monk's Mood" and gave Charlie Rouse a solo on it for the Town Hall concert, he never played improvised solos on "Crepuscule with Nellie" or had his sidemen do so on it. A close analysis of this performance can uncover aspects of the composition, as well as aspects of the band's work together on the evening, though obviously it does not shed light on their approach to soloing.

Monk often drew on and paid tribute to his friends and loved ones in the titles of his compositions—in ballads, but also in medium and up-tempo songs. It is not always clear that the compositions themselves were, in every instance, written with the tributee in mind, particularly given the shifting quality of many of his song titles; "Ruby, My Dear," for instance, was originally titled "Manhattan Moods," though the opening motive of the melody does perfectly fit the words in the title. That said, the relationship between the work "Crepuscule with Nellie" and Monk's wife is altogether clear, not only in title but in intention. Monk began writing the piece for Nellie in early May 1957, when she was hospitalized and eventually underwent surgery for a thyroid condition (Kelley 2009,

221). According to Robin Kelley, Monk, "Driven to mania...was desperate to finish the song because he feared he might lose his precious wife" (221). The piece was finished just in time for a recording date on June 25, 1957, and after numerous takes it was recorded to Monk's satisfaction with Coleman Hawkins, Ray Copeland, John Coltrane, and Gigi Gryce, ultimately appearing first on *Monk's Music*.

"Crepuscule with Nellie," true to its impressionistic Latinate title, is a miniature that bears some comparison with nineteenth-century piano character pieces. Debussy's *Preludes* might be the most obvious comparison; Debussy and Ravel's impressionism, particularly their use of seventh chord planing, was notoriously appealing to modern jazz musicians, and the title "Crepuscule with Nellie" is, perhaps, reminiscent of Debussy's "Des pas sur la neige," or "Le vent dans la pleine." But Chopin's *Preludes* are, if less obvious, perhaps an equally apt comparison. Although Debussy comes up in jazz discussions regularly and Chopin does not generally, we know that Monk was familiar with Chopin's work and thought highly of it. Kelley reports a story told by Monk's niece Benetta Smith, who remembers seeing a book of Chopin pieces on Monk's piano in 1959 or 1960, and moreover remembered Monk playing "a very difficult piece" (an *adagio*, no less) from it (Kelley 2009 viii). Moreover, Vladimir Horowitz's recordings of Chopin were in Monk's personal collection. I would hesitate to venture too direct a link between "Crepuscule with Nellie" and any specific classical work, but aspects of "Crepuscule with Nellie" are similar to mid-to-late-nineteenth-century character pieces. Without belaboring the comparison, even if "Monk's Mood" is more conventionally lyrical, "Crepuscule with Nellie" is more clearly pianistic, or at least instrumental in its conception. Its melodic angularity, extensive chromaticism, and shifts in range all imply a pianistic background. Beyond this, the harmonic complexity of "Crepuscule with Nellie" seems as much related to nineteenth-century classical practices as to American popular song. Finally, the fleshing out of the form, which is nominally a thirty-two-bar AABA song form but eschews regular two-bar phrasing and appends an extensive, motivically significant, harmonically remarkable coda to it, moves out of the formal rhetoric of the pop song in a way that many jazz compositions do not.

Unlike "Monk's Mood," which has a melody that draws heavily on a C diatonic set and projects a sense of C as tonic but undercuts any simple tonality with its harmonies, "Crepuscule with Nellie" has a slippery, tonally ambiguous melody that Monk supports with a harmonic structure that is complex, nevertheless fairly clearly projecting a sense of A♭ major tonality. The melody of "Crepuscule with Nellie" starts with a strongly swung, dotted-eighth-sixteenth melody in parallel sixths that connotes a 1920s-era blues, of the sort W. C. Handy or Clarence Williams might have written. The principle melodic line, which starts on E♭ and moves up to B♭, serves as a brief opening phrase. The point of the rise to B♭ (and an interjected C–D lick at the end of m. 2) is not to create some kind of line in that register but rather to start with an expansive, opening-up gesture, as rising lines often do. This rising line is then followed by a phrase that stands in opposition to it, spatially. This phrase, which fills the rest of the A section, involves a long, ornamented, chromatic descent from F through middle C. Its metric organization is irregular, being grouped in units of six beats, five beats, seven beats, and four beats. The final measure of the first A section returns chromatically back to the E♭ on which the first opening melody began.

The bridge begins on C and moves, with some chromaticism (a B♮ lower neighbor, a D♮ upper neighbor, and an F♯ passing tone) but largely through the A♭ major diatonic set, up to an arrival on A♭ (but importantly not A♭ as the root of a chord) in m. 5, and it is then immediately left, again by a scalar motion. The rest of the bridge—three measures—involves another ornamented, chromatic line, moving from C down to B♭ and back up to the E♭ that starts the final A section. The last A section is a nearly exact repetition of the second A section, moving from E♭ up to B♭, and from F down to C, but it is then followed by a five-and-a-half-measure coda. The coda's opening gesture is a reinterpretation of the final motive of the A section, a three-eighth-note pickup that surrounds the point of arrival with two whole steps above and one half-step below, landing on the arrival note on the downbeat of the following bar, all transposed up one step from last measure of the A section. The first full measure of the coda ends with a fanfarelike gesture in a higher register that repeats a similar motive in the second measure of the A section. Monk then uses rising block chords, in parallel motion, through a B major triad to C. The ending C triad then supports a return of the opening motive, shifted up two octaves.

Although the piece ends on a C dominant seventh harmony, there is no reason to think of it in either C, with a bluesy flat seventh, or F major, ending on V. Rather, the chord structure that Monk devised for this melody is perhaps best heard as an extended game of gesturing toward A♭ major but undercutting resolution to the tonic A♭ in a number of ways. The opening chord progression, which underscores the bluesy melody in parallel sixths, starts in the middle of a process, so to speak, with an implied B♭ dominant seventh chord in bar one moving to an E♭ dominant seventh in bar 2. This could resolve to A♭ major, and the prominence of the low E♭ in the bass in the first A section along with the bass riff that strongly implies a dominant harmony, with its first three notes, E♭–B♭–D♭, and its final G, support that implication. The suggestion of a resolution on A♭ is immediately undercut, however, and instead the initial B♭ dominant seventh to E♭ dominant seventh move has to be reinterpreted when, in the second half of m. 3 the next melodic bit begins with an A♭ dominant seventh, not an A♭Maj7, and A♭ becomes the jumping-off point for more rotations in a cycle-of-fifths progression, rather than a point of resolution. The second phrase moves through the cycle of fifths from A♭ to D♭ and G♭, all in dominant harmonies, each half a bar long. The cycle is interrupted in mm. 5 and 6, which leap by a tritone to a Cm7–F7 ii–V progression. Measure 6 follows with a series of fifth progressions, descending by half step, B7–E7–B♭m7–E♭7, which finally, in m. 7, resolves to an A♭Maj7 harmony.

The tonic of the piece, underscored by an open fifth in the bass, and harmonized with the third of the chord in the melody, arrives one measure before the end of the form, making the A section sound not so much like an eight-measure, regular song form unit but rather like a seven-measure, irregular unit, with a one-measure tail afterward, which repeats the final melodic gesture while slipping away from the melodic resolution that went with it. Here the C–B♭ pair that was initially the third and ninth of A♭ major become flat fifth (or sharp eleventh) and third of a G♭ dominant seventh harmony. G♭ stands in no particular tonal relation to A♭ in this case; it is both arrived at and left by movements that do not imply harmonic progression. Given the voicing of the G♭ chord, and the whole-tone-scale flourish that Monk plays after landing on it, it is reasonable to think of the G♭ instead as part of a whole-tone movement between A♭, G♭, and B♭ (which follows it on the repeat of the A section).

The bridge begins with a move back to A♭, now as part of a rising sequence that spans two measures, reaching a B♭min7 chord that prepares the way for the piece's biggest A♭ major gesture, a two-measure V chord over an E♭ pedal. Again, the big tonal gesture comes at the wrong moment, and even though its harmonic implications are ultimately realized, with a move to A♭ major in m. 6 of the bridge, the following two measures again undercut the stability of that tonic chord, moving back to the B♭ dominant harmony that starts the final A section.

The most important harmonic gesture of the final A section, which is otherwise identical to the first and second A sections, comes in the first measure of the coda. Having moved away from A♭, and reinterpreted the C as the flat fifth of G♭, Monk then repeats the melodic gesture

(F–E♭–B♮–C), returning to an A♭Maj7 chord. This is not an independent harmonic movement—the A♭ is not prepared in any way—so much as a way of revealing that in a sense the G♭ in each of the previous iterations was an incomplete neighbor that is finally, in what feels like the end of the piece, completed. The material that follows, then, is a wink, one last move away from the tonal center of the piece, suggesting an open-ended, rather than completed or closed, sense to the piece as a whole.

The single most notable thing about Monk's performances of "Crepuscule with Nellie"—with Coltrane, and with other musicians—is the extent to which they are all similar. Even more than with "Monk's Mood," which actually shows some substantial differences in conception (allowing improvisation or not, taking the whole piece more or less in time or taking sections with so much rubato as to produce a free, nonmetric feel to time, and so on), Monk and his collaborators stayed within fairly tight limits in general, at least for recorded performances of "Crepuscule with Nellie." All the recorded performances are roughly four and a half minutes, with small deviations coming as much from the length of the final note and the presence of applause before or after the piece in live recordings as from differences in tempo, rubato, or pauses at structural junctures. In general, each performance entails two statements of the melody, first played by Monk, either alone or with just the rhythm section, and then by the full band. The most notable nonnormative recording in this sense is a live recording originally released as *Thelonious Monk in Italy*, on Riverside in 1961, which is half as long because the band plays through the form only once. Deviations from the standard orchestration for the piece can be heard in two cases, but both follow the general percept of growth from a thin texture using fewer instruments to more instruments and a thicker texture. In the *Town Hall* concert performance, Monk plays only the first two A sections solo and is joined by Charlie Rouse for the bridge and last A section of the first chorus; the full band then enters for the second chorus. Given the expanded ensemble Monk had to work with in this concert, it is reasonable to hear this as an expansion of the basic principle. In the single-chorus live version from Italy, Monk plays just the first two A sections solo, and the band joins him for the bridge and final A section. This might be seen as the same basic principle, in abridged form, to fit the shorter duration of the performance as a whole.

Given the extensive similarity of various performances, the differences come mostly in how the performers interpret very small-scale aspects of the piece, of which the smallest—accent and rubato—are possibly the most interesting in terms of giving the piece its character. The Carnegie Hall concert is only the second recording of the piece, but it shows a profound growth and refinement from the first recording, the one released on *Monk's Music*. Monk recorded "Crepuscule with Nellie" five times, plus a partial take between the third and fourth full takes, for *Monk's Music*, and three of the full takes are available for comparison. It seems clear from the materials available that Monk and the band, which included Coltrane, along with Coleman Hawkins, Gigi Gryce, Ray Copeland, Wilbur Ware, and Art Blakey, struggled to achieve a performance that was polished in the way Monk wanted. In the series of takes there is a general trend toward streamlining, or better put, cutting away elements that the band was not executing well. Notably, for instance, Blakey plays a drum part that should build rhythmic intensity over the course of the second half of the bridge, beginning in m. 5 of the bridge with a quarter note figure that shifts to eighth notes along with the melody and then shifts to triplet eighths in the following measure and sounds as if it is intended to hit sixteenth notes in the last measures of the section and end with a cymbal crash on the last melody note of the section, immediately before the E♭ anacrusis that signals the return to the A section. This might have been a compelling gesture, but Blakey's interpretation of the groove and the rest of the band's do not come together, and what might have been sixteenth notes on the snare drum are out of time to the extent that they become a pattern bearing no simple fractional relationship to the melody or bass line. This gesture is much curtailed in subsequent takes, and in the "keeper," the sixth take, it is replaced with a much more straightforward triplet pattern in m. 3 of the bridge.

The horns also had problems with ensemble in the earlier takes, most obviously in Gigi Gryce's painfully loud top line in the C–C–D response figure on beat 4 of the second measure of the A sections. This is ultimately solved in the keeper by holding back the full entrance of the horns until the bridge of the second chorus, so that they play the A section in full only once, the last time through.[8] The final clear excision of an aspect of the piece that creates a simpler, more streamlined final version is a whole-tone run that Monk plays during the G♭7♭5 in m. 8 of the A sections. In the first take Monk plays the flourish in the first A section of both choruses, in the fifth take he plays it only in the first A section of the second chorus, and in the keeper he does not play it at all. It is not clear that the flourish was a problem in earlier takes, but its absence in the keeper does notably streamline the performance.

Even though Monk and his band eventually produced a satisfactory take of "Crepuscule with Nellie" on the June 26, 1957, recording date, the

Carnegie Hall live version represents a much more refined, subtle performance of the piece as a whole. This is true in terms of ensemble issues, for instance. Abdul-Malik and Wilson's accompaniment is emblematic in this respect. Ware's playing on the *Monk's Music* version was unobtrusive; Abdul-Malik's in the Carnegie Hall concert is a genuine support. His articulation, for instance, of the rising bass line in m. 2 of the A section is solid and confident, defining the triplet rhythm precisely.[5] His tone and rhythm in mm. 6 and 7 of the A section likewise project the ii–V motions strongly, underscoring how important this moment is to the piece as a whole. Shadow Wilson, similarly, plays a combination of time and interjections with an authority that Blakey never quite managed in the *Monk's Music* sessions. This is part of the arrangement in the A sections, where he plays along with the triplet bass line in m. 2 and with the melody figures in mm. 4 and 6, as well as playing a response of quarter notes during the held notes in mm. 7 and 8. Even though the response is not complex, it produces a feeling of anticipation during the held notes that pushes forward into the next rhythmic figure. Coltrane likewise plays the melody with confidence that he and the other horn players did not appear to have on *Monk's Music*. Possibly the most difficult moment, getting from the C–C–D interjection at the end of m. 2 back to the main melody on F in m. 3, which is partly difficult because of the rhythmic precision needed and partly because of the registral shift, is accomplished as well here as anywhere in Monk's catalog, or better. Monk gave himself some leeway with this figure when playing it solo, by inserting often quite long moments of rubato, drawing out the second half of the fourth beat of m. 2 (in this performance even adding an arpeggiated figure before coming back to time in the first beat of the following measure), but he generally had ensemble choruses take that measure in time. Charlie Rouse solved the trick by playing the eighth note D staccato, shortening it by half or more. Coltrane, here, sounds as if he hits the first sixteenth note of the figure incrementally late, but he catches up and holds the final note out to its full length, still coming in smoothly on the first note of the following measure.

Monk's own touch in this performance is similarly smoother and more expressive than in the recording for *Monk's Music*. Such a difference is notoriously difficult to show in a transcription yet is of great effective significance. A spectrogram or even waveform analysis might provide a way of visualizing the differences, but it would also incorporate extraneous information. In any case, the difference is readily audible. In the *Monk's Music* version Monk interprets the rhythms such that he hesitates ever so slightly before each of the long notes, and hits them harder than the surrounding notes. This projects the key points of arrival clearly, but it also creates a sense of disjointedness to the piece. Disjointed rhythms are often pointed to as an idiosyncratic aspect of Monk's style, but I think in this case they are better heard as a technique to signal form to his band, and they actually get in the way of a tender interpretation of the ballad. With a band playing the piece confidently as on the Carnegie Hall recording, it is possible to hear Monk play more flowingly, with a more even articulation, and more even dynamics, calling attention to changes in volume, accent, and texture as ways of shaping the interpretation.

MONK AND COLTRANE AS BALLADISTS

The inclusion of "Monk's Mood" and "Crepuscule with Nellie" on this recording highlights aspects of Monk and Coltrane's playing together that are not always at the forefront of descriptions of the two musicians, and that show an expressive grace and subtlety that are compelling. Although the two and their rhythm section do not solo on either of these pieces, they all play with a level of attention to interpretive detail that is notable. Monk may be most commonly thought of for pointillism. As trumpeter and producer Don Sickler said, "With Monk there's some things, I think, where if you took out the bass and drums it could confuse a lot of people as to where the time is some of the time. A lot of the time it would be very relative, because he actually knows where it is, it's just he places his stuff in a unique, very personal way."[10] Here, though, as in other recordings, he plays with a lush sense of completeness that makes these ballads genuinely expressive. And even though Coltrane may be thought of as having been most influential in the quest for prodigious technique, mastering the art of speed and complexity in thinking through melodies that expand the harmonic language of jazz tonality, here his biggest contribution is a rich tenor voice that states the melody directly. This is, of course, also an important part of his playing at least until 1963, during which year he recorded *The Gentle Side of John Coltrane* and *John Coltrane and Johnny Hartman*.

It is not that others have not noticed these sides of Monk's and Coltrane's playing, but rather that they have not received the attention they deserve. As noted before, this recording is an exceptionally good place to hear this band's work with ballads because of the unusual inclusion of these two on the first set.

CHAPTER 4
UP-TEMPO TUNES, CONVENTION, AND INNOVATION
"Evidence" and "Nutty"

MONK PAIRED EACH of the ballads on the first set of the concert at Carnegie Hall with an up-tempo piece, following "Monk's Mood" with "Evidence," and "Crepuscule with Nellie" with "Nutty." As noted in Chapter 3, it was somewhat unusual to program two ballads, both without improvisation, in a single set, but the two faster pieces provided a balance, giving Coltrane and Monk room to stretch out in solos, and giving Wilson and Abdul-Malik more extensive supporting roles. The two quick pieces show different sides of Monk's compositional output, in terms of style and procedure. "Evidence," one of his most fragmented melodies, was composed on the changes from "Just You, Just Me," a Tin Pan Alley pop song from Monk's youth, that had become one of his favorites at the time.[1] "Nutty," on the other hand—a more playful piece—was entirely from Monk's hand, but using a highly repetitive, stock harmonic progression.

These two works and their performances gave Monk, his band, and their audience a new set of challenges and experiences in playing and listening from the ballads that each one follows. The most obvious differences, of course, are in tempo and form (up-tempo tunes versus ballads, works without improvisation versus performances oriented around solos with brief statements of the heads at the beginning and end), but they also differ in terms of the sensibility of the tunes and relative familiarity to audiences in 1957. The pairing of ballads and up-tempo tunes is felicitous, at the very least, suggesting that Monk was thinking more than incidentally about how his tunes interacted in making a set list. "Monk's Mood," which was a truly challenging opening to the set—probably for the musicians as well as for the audience because it required control and attentiveness if it was to remain interesting—gives way to the righteously indignant "Evidence." Here there is an alternation between interiority—"Monk's Mood"—and exteriority—"Evidence"—or between the subjective and the objective. Yet both share a sense of gravity and seriousness; both are "heavy" pieces, emotionally. "Crepuscule with Nellie" and "Nutty," by contrast, involve an alternation of affect, from tender to playful, but both in some sense are lighthearted. Even "Crepuscule," in spite of the strained context of its composition, has a buoyancy that is very different from many of Monk's other slow pieces.

It is hard to find Monk speaking directly to the kinds of affective associations I ascribe to these pieces. He seems to have been fascinated in the first instance and for the most part with the more abstract logic of musical relationships in their own right, but it is not hard to believe he would have appreciated the connections. His approach to titling suggests he thought of the pieces as songs—even if he wasn't himself a lyricist. Many of his works' titles (in either their original or their later versions) scan well as the first line of a song ("Ruby, My Dear," for instance, or "That's the Way I Feel Now"), and when choosing standards Monk seems to have been drawn at least in part to lyrical content as well as music ("Everything Happens to Me," for instance, or "Just a Gigolo"). In thinking about how to move from song to song, Monk could certainly have considered such meanings. Moreover, these meanings in Monk's work are largely signified not only in titles but in musical content, and thus the technical aspects of crafting a program (moving among tempos, harmonic types, melodic characters, and so on) would, even if incidentally, tend to produce this kind of juxtaposition.

Another important difference between the two ballads on the first set and these two up-tempo pieces, beyond their strictly formal and affective context, was their relative familiarity to audiences. "Monk's Mood" was not a new piece in 1957, but it has an entirely *sui generis* harmonic and melodic structure, which means that for those who had not followed Monk's work carefully it would have been quite unfamiliar territory. The fact that he had just recorded it for *Thelonious Himself* should mean some people in the audience would have recognized it, but they still might not have fully integrated a sense of its harmonic logic. "Evidence" would probably have been more familiar ground, since Monk had been playing it regularly for many years by then and had recorded it, and what's more he based it on an older set of changes from a pop song. In theory, at least, the piece could have been doubly familiar to audiences. Fans—or even regular listeners—of the time would likely have had a feel for the kinds of harmonic rhythm it incorporates and thus would have had something stable and familiar to hear even as the surface of the head melody—and much of the solo material—may have been shocking. "Crepuscule with Nellie," the newest of the pieces and in a sense the hardest to intuitively understand, came as the climactic third piece, followed by "Nutty," which was fairly new but which has a harmonic structure that is immediately recognizable and easy to grasp. Even audiences who had never heard the prior recording on the album *Work* and who had not seen Monk play it live in the preceding months would have grasped its schematic regularity at once.

In both pieces Coltrane takes solos that show him working through the possibilities for dissonance treatment suggested by Monk's idiosyncratic way of voicing chords, and playing solos that build from clipped motivic statements to cascading displays, reaching climaxes of volume and intensity that make him a "hot" foil to Monk's "cool" approach. In contrast, Monk solos in the idiosyncratic way for which he was known at that point on both songs. He alternates between minimalist statements, built up in an unrelenting musical logic and formulaic, but still, somehow, witty *passaggio* flourishes—arpeggios and scale patterns that show him to be a deft technician at the keyboard when the moment calls for it. Beyond this, these pieces nicely illustrate how Monk worked with rhythm sections—and played as an accompanist, himself—as well as with soloists.

"EVIDENCE"

"Evidence" was a tune Monk programmed often, first recording it on one of the sessions that made up his *Genius of Modern Music* releases on Blue Note, in July 1948 (with Shadow Wilson on drums, incidentally). It is not clear when he wrote it, but Robin Kelley has identified Monk playing something like the head of "Evidence" as an accompaniment figure for Dizzy Gillespie's solo on "Groovin' High" in a 1946 recording (Kelley 2009, 114). In any case, throughout the late 1950s and 1960s Monk played the song regularly and recorded it a number of times.

The piece is a study in dissonance, and in Monk's attention to the forms of Tin Pan Alley song. The original song, written by Jesse Greer and Raymond Klages, follows the harmonic conventions of the American pop tune of its day, firmly establishing E♭ tonality and using progressions by fourths and fifths to mark major structural elements of the form. The A section established the key of E♭ major with a progression that starts on the tonic, with an E♭Maj7 chord, and moves to the dominant, with a B♭7 chord in the final measure. This chord, preceded by a subdominant Fmin7 in m. 7, sets up the cyclical return to the tonic in the repeat of the A section. The bridge, like many similar songs, pivots through a dominant chord on E♭ now interpreted as V/IV to establish an arc moving from a large-scale IV to a large-scale V over eight measures, setting up the return to E♭ as I at the beginning of the final return of the A section. The original melody is similarly a smart, engaging rendering of conventions of the genre. It grows out of a single two-note motive of a rising major second, first heard as the initial melodic gesture of the A section (Fig. 4.1). This motive is repeated immediately, but at a lower pitch level, marking the rhythmic parallel of the lyrics "Just you" and "Just me." After this the A section continues a downward trend, with the next motive beginning yet another step below, and then concluding with a sweeping gesture up to the high tonic, E♭. The bridge also begins with the primary motive, starting on the high E♭ and reaching the highest note of the piece, an F. It then cascades downward to set up the return of the A section.

One of Monk's most pointillistic compositions, "Evidence" has a sparse, almost melodyless head, in striking contrast to "Just You, Just Me." The melody of the head is a series of rhythmically surprising jabs. Its surface motion is a play of regularity and irregularity, with only a small amount of normatively motivic or melodic material to hang on to. The opening five measures of the A section are particularly difficult to

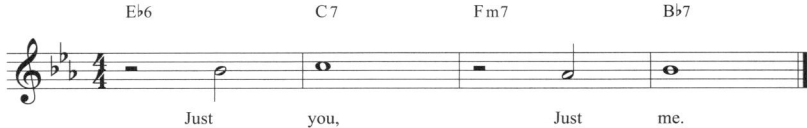

FIGURE 4.1. "Just You, Just Me," Head, mm. 1–4

hear in terms of any kind of schematic pattern, with the piece resolving into a unified harmonic, rhythmic and motivic pattern only at the end of the A section and in the bridge. The overarching drama of the tune, then, becomes the cyclical alternation between initial irregularity and its resolution into pattern, in total creating a kind of meta-regularity.

The first note of the melody, a D, is the major seventh over the opening E♭Maj7 chord. It leaps away to an F that can be reasonably heard as the seventh of a G half-diminished chord, displaced from the second half of m. 1 into m. 2. The following melody notes, G♭, E♭, and F♭, are all either sevenths or flatted fifths of the chords on which they fall, and the melody note in m. 5, D♭, would be the seventh of the original chord in that measure, an E♭7 chord, except that Monk harmonizes it with a tritone substitution A dominant seventh, which makes the D♭ a major third. To say that in the first five measures Monk consistently emphasizes harmonic dissonances in relation to the chord structure of the source material, "Just You, Just Me," is true, but not the whole story. It is at least as important to note that first, some of the dissonances (for example, the downbeat of m. 2 and the second half of beat 1 in m. 5) are dissonant only with regard to imagined notes; and second, the dissonances Monk chooses to emphasize are notable particularly for the fact that they go unresolved, giving what is a fairly coherent source harmonic progression the impression of disjuncture. This impression is further supported by the rhythmic irregularity of these five measures. The underlying meter is a standard jazz 4/4, with swung eighth notes, and, importantly, harmonic changes at the same pace as "Just You, Just Me," one or two per bar. However, the melody hits imply a sequence of primarily three-beat groupings, with occasional one- and two-beat groupings, coming to a clear four-beat group only for m. 8.

Measures 6–8 of the A section resolve this sense of disjuncture with a pair of motives that partially resolve the sense of irregularity of the beginning of the section. Monk establishes both tonal and rhythmic normativity in m. 6 by playing an ornamented descending melody over a fifth progression in the bass. The chords move, from A♭min7 to D♭Maj7, on beats 1 and 3, with the step in the melody (G♭–F) resolving the seventh of the A♭ chord to the third of the D♭ (ornamented by a quick drop to the fifth of the A♭ chord). The final measures of the A section elaborate the original chords of "Just You, Just Me," suggesting a move to the tonic chord, E♭, in m. 7, followed by an alternation between B♭7 and F7 in m. 8 to set up a progression through the circle of fifths beginning on B♭ in the bridge. The melody from m. 7 into m. 8 is among the piece's most memorable one, and iconic, moving from

E♭ through a G–B♭ pair to an A♭–C♭ pair, emphasizing the V chord of the tonic key with a stark dissonance. The final, hanging A♭–C♭ pair and rising motive leaves the head feeling open and dynamic.

The bridge presents a different kind of regularity from the end of the A section, but regularity nonetheless. The melody notes are parceled out, one to a measure, and thus never make the kind of motivic sense that the final measures of the A section do; but unlike the beginning of the A section, they all land on the same part of the bar—the "and" of beat 1—and constitute a very clear melodic trajectory, rising from A♭ to E by half steps (except for the final move from D to E). This rising pattern begins as a way of schematically moving through a circle of fifths progression, but it is retained through mm. 5, 6, and 7, even as the harmonies break from the rotation through fifths, in order to set up an F7–B♭7 progression in mm. 7 and 8.

The performance of "Evidence" on this recording particularly highlights the way Shadow Wilson's drum work integrates with the band. Monk had a preference for bassists and drummers who primarily kept solid time and provided unobtrusive, hard-swinging support, and Wilson was one of his favorites (Kelley 2009, 230). Throughout the solos Wilson does just that, marking the formal structure and adding little fills in relation to the soloists' playing, but in the head he has the chance to do more. Wilson hits all of the notes of the melody, but between them he fills out the space with a combination of playing a rhythmically interesting ride cymbal pattern and adding fills as a sort of countermelody on the snare, toms, and bass drum (Fig. 4.2). While Wilson keeps time moving regularly, he adds a significant layer of complexity, keeping the head even more rhythmically unpredictable. His playing here gives the head a level of tension that he is able to nicely relieve by playing a relaxed, in-the-pocket pattern as soon as Coltrane's solo starts.

Coltrane plays a three-chorus solo in this performance—relatively short, by the standards of his later career, but in keeping with the kind of solo length Monk's sidemen generally played on recordings at this point. Over the course of the three choruses, Coltrane generally uses standard figures—scalar patterns, arpeggios, and skip-step combinations—that outline the harmonies of the piece (largely hewing to the original harmonies of "Just You, Just Me," in fact). By highlighting primary chord tones as much as chord extensions, Coltrane seems to be moving from a Parker-esque bebop language to the development of what would become his "sheets of sound" language in his recordings as a leader from just a few years later. This may also be heard as echoing Monk's own preference for clearly projecting the precomposed structures of his—and

FIGURE 4.2. "Evidence," Shadow Wilson's Playing on the Head

others'—pieces first and only thereafter showcasing inventive harmonic alternatives.

The thing that makes Coltrane's solo interesting, and more than a calisthenic etude or pattern study, is how he uses rhythm and tessitura to build and shape the solo into one large statement, rather than three self-contained choruses. Coltrane works with and against the chorus structure in doing this, at times highlighting the head's form in his choice of points for movement and stasis and at times undercutting it. In the first chorus, he starts with a phrase structure that hews to the head's form. The first A section starts with material in eighth notes that accents a high D♭, the opening melody note of the head, and then moves both down in the tenor's range and gradually faster, hitting a low point in m. 6, and blowing to a small conclusion at the end of m. 8 (Fig. 4.3). He marks the beginning the second A section with a brief pause, followed by a clear arpeggio of the tonic chord reaching up to a high E♭, the root of the chord and tonic pitch of the piece. He then accents the notes D and D♭, over the course of mm. 2 through 4, descending from each of them, and creating a reminder of the high D♭ at the beginning of the first A section. Next he moves through the end of the second A section with a series of sixteenth-note patterns. Coltrane marks the B section with a precipitous drop back to eighth-note patterns, speeding up to triplets by m. 5 and sixteenth notes

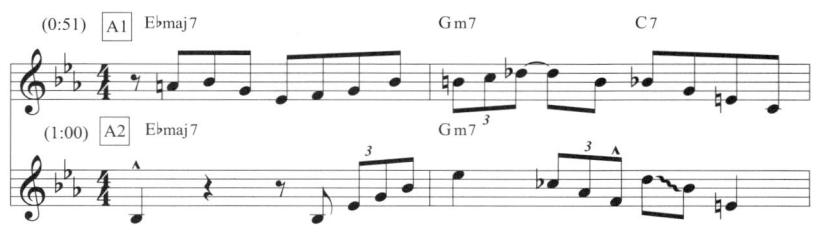

FIGURE 4.3. "Evidence," John Coltrane's Solo, First Chorus, mm. 1–4 of A1 and A2

in mm. 7 and 8. Having relatively clearly established the form over the first three sections of his first solo chorus, Coltrane then deemphasizes regular two-, four-, and eight-measure phrasing in the final A section, continuing the sixteenth-note phrase from the end of the bridge through to the end of the chorus and into the downbeat of the second chorus.

In his second chorus, Coltrane follows a pattern similar to the one he established in the first chorus, yet shifting the beginnings and endings of phrases so as to specifically obscure the section breaks. He uses an arpeggio up the tonic chord in m. 1, reaching E♭ and then descending, in turn, from E♭ and D♭, to establish a motivic connection with his playing on the A sections of the first chorus. He ends the principle phrase of the first A section in m. 7 and then in m. 8 begins a phrase that will occupy the majority of the second A section, thus deemphasizing the regular eight-measure cycle, as well as the harmonic significance of the return to the tonic chord at m. 1 of the second A section. In the second A, Coltrane uses an A♭Maj7 arpeggio in m. 3 to set up a strongly accented high D♭, echoing similar gestures at the beginning of each previous A. He ends the first phrase of the second A section in m. 5, largely rests through m. 6, and then plays a concluding phrase in mm. 7 and 8, drawing attention to the end of the first half of the chorus. He begins the bridge with another iteration of the high D♭, now as the third of a B♭min7 chord, drawing it into a part of the chorus in which he had not played it previously. This sets off a phrase that ends on the downbeat of m. 7. Rather than mark mm. 7 and 8 with a phrase that signals ending, he uses the F7–B♭7 cycle that points so strongly to the beginning of the final A section to begin a phrase that crosses over the section break, pausing in m. 2 and then immediately resuming with a phrase that takes a quick breath in m. 7 and flows across the line marking the end of the chorus immediately into the first A of the third chorus.

Coltrane's third chorus is the least sectionalized of the three, driving through nearly the entire thirty-two bars with sixteenth-note passages. He does mark the beginning of the first A section once again with a line that reaches up to the high E♭, D, and D♭, ornamenting each with a descending arpeggio, creating a sort of sonic reminder of the form as it moves by, without necessarily organizing his phrasing in relation to it. Coltrane aligns his phrasing schematically with the background form only at the end of the final A section. He shifts from the ongoing sixteenth-note pacing in m. 5 of the final A section to play a section in eighth notes, which eventually brings the solo to a close with a gentle drop from G to E♭ in m. 1 of the following chorus (Fig. 4.4). This last gesture signals closure, in part through coming to rest on the tonic pitch, in part by

FIGURE 4.4. "Evidence," John Coltrane's Solo, Third Chorus, A3

holding the last note out for three beats, and in part by inverting the closing gesture of the head. Where the head's last motive, the rising three note passage, E♭–G/B♭–A♭/C♭, created a sense of openness by moving away from the tonic and lingering at the top of a rising gesture, here Coltrane creates a sense of closure.

In what was his common practice at the time, and indeed throughout his career, Monk based essentially all of his comping during Coltrane's choruses on material drawn from the head. For the first chorus this amounted to more or less straightforwardly playing the head as an accompaniment to Coltrane's improvisation. In the first A, Monk plays the head nearly verbatim, with only small shifts in rhythm; in the second A he does the same but does not play the melody in mm. 7 and 8. In the bridge Monk once again plays the melody nearly verbatim, except for the last two measures. It is only in the final A section of this chorus that Monk moves away from playing the head as accompaniment, playing a countermelody to Coltrane's growing sixteenth-note lines up to m. 5. In the second chorus Monk works with two figures: he uses a succession of two-chord figures in the first A section, and he switches to a rising three-note motive, sometimes shortened to two notes by the elision of the initial anacrusis, throughout the second A sections. This three-note motive is itself derived from the material in mm. 7–8 of the A section, the only truly motivic element in the head. In the bridge he returns to the one-chord-per-measure figure from the head, which leads to a continued use of figures from the head for the final A section. Monk lays out the whole of the first A section of Coltrane's third chorus, and when he comes back in in m. 2 of the second A, he moves from the chordal punctuations that defined the head material into the three-note motive he had established in the second A section of chorus 2. The effect is to tie all three choruses together into a single musical thought, in dialogue with the formal logic Coltrane establishes concurrently, and helping make the end of the third chorus a satisfying end to Coltrane's solo.

Monk's solo shows quite clearly his own mode of deriving new material from the pieces he played. Coltrane's final note stretches into the opening measure of Monk's first chorus, and rather than blow over Coltrane's final statement Monk rests for the start of his solo, using the first four bars of the first A section as a buffer zone before he begins his own idea. He then fills the second half of the first A section and the entire second A section with a nearly verbatim statement of the head. He follows this opening with a B section that starts with a five-note melody that sounds like a reference to the opening melody of his composition "Well, You Needn't." This figure quickly morphs into the rising chromatic line from the head in a top line alternating with a static E♭, which functions as a tonic pedal, working against the harmonic implications of the section's changes. He moves away from head-based material altogether for the final A and the first A of the second chorus (Fig. 4.5). In m. 3 of the second A section of the second chorus, Monk introduces a tritone figure that is again reminiscent in rhythm and contour of "Well, You Needn't," and very close to the piece "Raise Four," which he follows by a quick descending flourish in fifths and fourths that is the most recognizable "Monkism" of the entire solo. This leads to a return to the material from the head for the B section and final A of his solo. His closing gesture alters the last figure of the head, the three-note rising motive, giving it a swing inflection and changing it, as Coltrane had, from an open I–V move to implying a closed, cadential V–I. He also plays this at the highest register he has used thus far in the piece, with principle melodic notes, an A♭ moving down to G, in the portion of the piano that does not have dampers, giving it a much brighter timbre than the preceding material.

Monk obscures the transition from solo to final head by replacing the first hit of the head, Ds played in octaves, with a rootless E♭Maj7 chord, voiced so that the same G he has just played at the end of his second solo

FIGURE 4.5. "Evidence," Thelonious Monk's Solo, Second Chorus

FIGURE 4.5. (Cont'd)

chorus is prominent in the texture. Coltrane seems surprised by what turns out to be the return of the head, coming in with his opening notes each a beat late. It seems plausible that Coltrane might have expected Monk to play a third solo chorus, or that he simply missed the entrance. In any case, Monk then makes something out of the off-kilter timing of Coltrane's entrance, consistently playing the melody notes late for the rest of the final head. The effect is a kind of heterophony, where Coltrane holds down an unornamented version of the melody, while Monk ornaments it exclusively through rhythmic displacement, one of his most common techniques.

"NUTTY"

Unlike "Evidence," which Monk had recorded and played often, "Nutty" was nearly a new piece when the band played it at Carnegie Hall. Monk had written it three years earlier, in the studio on September 22, 1954, to fill up space on a trio date with Art Blakey and Percy Heath, ultimately released on the Prestige album *Work* (Kelley 2009, 179). The piece certainly has the feel of something organized on the spot, a little four-measure melody hummed out and harmonized in the most straightforward way, repeated with only the slightest modifications to signal its function within the schematic thirty-two-bar AABA song form. Monk recorded the piece relatively seldom—in comparison with "I Mean You," "Blue Monk," or "Round Midnight," for example—and only once between its original recording and the Carnegie Hall concert; but that one recording is noteworthy because it was on one of Coltrane's first dates with the group, in the summer of 1957. That recording was among those held up by contractual disputes between Riverside (for whom Monk was recording) and Prestige (with whom Coltrane was under contract) and thus audiences at the Carnegie Hall concert would not have heard it. Monk's groups appear to have played "Nutty" with fair regularity at the time; not only is it on the studio recording and the Carnegie Hall concert, but it is also on *Misterioso*, one of the two live recordings Monk made with Johnny Griffin, Roy Hanes, and Ahmed Abdul-Malik in 1958.

Regardless of whether audiences would have heard "Nutty" before, it made a good choice for the last full piece of the first set. Like the quick final movement of most classical symphonic or chamber works, "Nutty" makes a welcome closer. The tune is recognizable and easy to follow in a way that many Monk pieces are not. Moreover, its upbeat, bouncy—in a word, "nutty"—qualities, coming around twenty-five minutes into the set, would have been appreciated by an audience that had, by that point, been given some fairly heavy fare. To emphasize this, the band takes the piece at a significantly quicker tempo on the Carnegie Hall evening than they generally had up to this point, pushing by as much as 10 bpm faster than other recordings. It is hard to say how this compares with the range of tempi that Monk would have set for "Nutty," since it is reasonable to assume that the majority of his performances of the piece were not recorded, but it brings to mind Ben Riley's assertion, as mentioned above, that Monk had the ability to play "in between all of the tempos."[2] In fact, in the Carnegie Hall recording, the band seems at least somewhat taken aback by the tempo Monk set, making m. 6, which is set off by a drum fill by Wilson and set of quarter-note triplets in the melody, fairly messy. After that brief instability, time seems to settle in, and the band plays tightly for the rest of the performance.

For a soloist working motivically on transformations of materials from the head, "Nutty" supplies a relatively small but rich set of ideas. The opening leap of a fifth, from B♭ to F (transposed to E♭–B♭ in the bridge), which is filled in with a chromatic passing tone, B♭–E–F in the A sections and E♭–A–B♭ in the bridge, in m. 5 of each section, provides one striking motive to work with. The leap can be filled in, repeated, transposed, expanded, or contracted, and its short-long rhythmic profile can be altered. These possibilities are suggested, in fact, in mm. 4–5 of each A section and the bridge, as well as mm. 7–8 of the final A section, which repeats the quarter note to held-note rhythm, the rising melodic shape, and the *marcato* articulation, but beginning on beat 3 instead of beat 1 and contracted to a whole step instead of a fifth. Measures 2 and 7 of each section provide the only other motive in the piece, an answer to the opening leap that first moves up from E♭ to G by step (from A♭ to C in the bridge) and then moves away by step, to end with a descending skip from A to F (D to B♭ in the bridge). This motive, which remains partially open by virtue of ending on scale degree 5 (F in the A section, B♭ in the bridge) and by ending with a skip rather than a step, is transformed to provide more of a sense of closure in m. 6 of the bridge and the last A section by continuing up the scale, entirely by step, from scale degree 4 to the octave tonic. Though the melody is highly repetitive and clearly outlines a series of eight- and four-measure sections, it provides some potentially interesting ideas for phrase structure, inasmuch as it does not break down into clear two-measure groupings, instead being divided, to the extent that it is clearly divided, into three asymmetrical subphrases.

For a soloist working largely with the head's chord changes, "Nutty" offers immensely regular, frankly commonplace ground. Each section is divided into two four-measure phrases, which are themselves nearly identical. The first four bars move from the tonic, B♭, through a chromatic, passing B diminished chord, to a ii–V progression in the tonic key, Cmin7–F7, in m. 2, with a deceptive resolution to a minor 7 chord on D in m. 3—scale degree 3 in the key of B♭. The Dmin7 starts a ii–V sequence, moving through G7 in m. 3 to Cmin7 and F7 in m. 4, which prepares for a return to B♭, as I, in m. 5. The second half of the A section begins with the I–vii/ii–ii–V progression from mm. 1 and 2, but instead of a deceptive resolution Monk then resolves the F7 chord to a B♭Maj7 in m. 7. There follows a ii–V in B♭ as a turnaround in m. 8 or an immediate pivot with a ii–V in E♭, the key of the bridge, in m. 8 of the second A section. Because the melody of the bridge is identical to the A section, with the exception of its transposition to the key of B♭, its harmonic scheme is also the same, save for its transposition and its turnaround in m. 8 being in the tonic key. The challenge with a piece of this sort, harmonically both extremely repetitive and commonplace, is to find ways of playing that sound new enough to be interesting, while still remaining comprehensible.

Coltrane takes two solo choruses in this performance—somewhat shorter than those he took in the studio with Monk earlier in the year. The two performances are similar in outline—in both cases Coltrane treats the form fairly similarly, and in both cases Monk comps in quite a similar way—but the Carnegie Hall performance is more polished. It is tight, clear, and nicely interactive, and it deals interestingly with what is, after all, a fairly simple head, while the studio performance (quite possibly the first time Coltrane actually played the piece) is none of these. Much as a few months playing the same material night in and night out with Monk can be heard in Johnny Griffin's playing on live recordings made from the Five Spot the following year, in "Nutty" the difference between Coltrane working out the possibilities made available by the piece and Coltrane confidently crafting a musical statement is clear.

For the most part, Coltrane treats the standard ii–V based changes as an opportunity to play long, boplike strings of sixteenth notes, largely outlining the chords and common substitutions, as he did in the studio recording from July. What makes this seem more confident and clear in the Carnegie Hall performance is, first, that with only two instead of three choruses he has less time to fill, and thus less opportunity to sound repetitive and generic; and second, that he punctuates the passage work with references to the head that are sensible and give the solo an overarching form.

Coltrane sets up the first chorus with a descending passage starting on the turnaround in m. 8 of the head. This passage descends from the final note of the head, a high D, which is the third of the preceding B♭ chord and a pungent ninth against the Cmin7 chord that begins the turnaround. The line lands on a D an octave lower, which Coltrane holds through nearly an entire measure. Here he references the long note from the head, while actually avoiding both melody notes of the head and playing the third of the chord in their place. He then plays a version of the m. 2 motive, approached by an eighth note F on the second half of beat 4 of m. 1 and with the E-flats played as a single quarter note. He ends the motive in m. 3, which gives Monk, who has been playing a reduced version of the melody as a comping pattern, the opportunity to play the hits from the head in beats 3 and 4 of m. 3 as a response figure. As Monk responds, Coltrane begins a long sixteenth-note passage. He plays passage work with no clear relationship to the melody for the rest of the first A section, ending on the tonic pitch B♭ in m. 7, signaling the measure's role as the major cadential point of the section even more clearly than the head melody does. He takes a breath and then plays a long B♭ in m. 8 as an anticipation of the return of the tonic chord in m. 1 of the second A section.

Coltrane begins the second A section with a passage of sixteenth notes that descends through two octaves of a B♭ major scale with a chromatic G♭ between scale degrees 6 and 5, and then ascends by arpeggios, clearly referencing the chords, but with no obvious connection to the melody. The clearest implication that he continues to play with the head melody in mind is that he breaks the passage work with a descending leap from an eighth note D to a held F on the downbeat of m. 3, a slightly delayed echo of the A–F descent on beat 4 of m. 2 in the head. Coltrane then fills

FIGURE 4.6. "Nutty," John Coltrane's Solo, First Chorus

FIGURE 4.6. (Cont'd)

the rest of the second A section with sixteenth-note passages, largely composed of standard four-note scalar and arpeggiated patterns and following the changes clearly.

Coltrane prepares for the modulation to IV with the use of a descending B♭ Mixolydian scale in the last measure of the second A section and confirms the tonicization of E♭ major with a prominent E♭–B♭ leap in m. 1 of the bridge. He then plays the motive from m. 2 of the head, rhythmically transformed as was done in m. 2 of the first A section of the chorus. The effect is, in a sense, not just a reminder of the head but rather an architectonic gesture. It signals both the importance of the bridge, as the halfway point in the chorus, and the overall form of the solo as a series of passages set up by the melody of the head and ultimately returning to it. The rest of the bridge is taken up, then, with sixteenth-note passage work, during which Coltrane notes the tonicized IV chord in m. 7 with a E♭–B♭ leap in eighth notes. Having signaled the moment of formal articulation this way, Coltrane then continues on with a long sixteenth-note passage that crosses over the break from the bridge to the third A section, effectively making the second half of the chorus a single phrase group. Significantly, rather than referencing the head in m. 2, as he did in the first A and the bridge, and rather than largely not referencing it at all, as in the second A section, Coltrane continues the passage work through m. 5 and then plays a rhythmically altered version of the head melody in m. 6, now expanded with an ascending arpeggio at the end of the measure so as to set up a D–B♭ descending leap at the end of m. 6 as a gesture of closure that anticipates the harmonic resolution to the tonic in m. 7.

Coltrane begins his second chorus with a long sequence of sixteenth-note passages, all played with bass and drum accompaniment while Monk lays out. He carries this through until m. 2 of the final A section, where he returns to the head motive. Monk comes back in at this juncture, as well, playing the hits from m. 3 as a response, and supporting the end of Coltrane's solo. Coltrane finishes the chorus with a series of sixteenth-note patterns that end in m. 1 of the following chorus. The effect is to expand on the formal logic of the first chorus, essentially widening the distance between references to the head, but continuing the basic structure of cyclical journey away from precomposed material and eventual return. In fact, Coltrane's solo on the studio date from July of that year showed a similar approach, being composed of regular references to the head (mostly to the ascending leap of m. 1, rather than the more melodic motive in m. 2), alternating with sixteenth-note passages; yet the earlier recording seems less clear in its formal conception. In part this is a result of Coltrane's use of the two-note leap as the main reference to the head in the earlier solo. The link between the melody of m. 2, which contains stepwise motion and a leap of a third, and Coltrane's passage work, which is largely composed of scalar and arpeggiated patterns in thirds, is easier to hear. Moreover, the sixteen, sixteen, thirty-two-measure patterning created by Coltrane's references to the head in the Carnegie Hall solo is easy to hear and satisfying, whereas in the earlier recording over three choruses Coltrane does not give listeners such a schematic periodicity to hold on to. Finally, Monk's decision to return to comping during the final A section of Coltrane's second chorus reinforces the formal logic of departure and return that Coltrane creates in his solo. In the earlier recording Monk laid out for the duration of Coltrane's second and third choruses, giving him space to explore, but no support for crafting a clear statement.

As in his solo on "Evidence"—and as was his common practice—Monk derives much of the material for his two-chorus solo on "Nutty" from the head. In this instance, however, rather than creating formal logic primarily through a kind of ABA pattern of head-related material, new material, and return to head-related material, as he had in "Evidence," Monk works significantly with two distinct arrangements of the head material, the alternation of which imparts a sense of form to the piece. The first A section of Monk's first chorus serves, as elsewhere in his work, as a transition (Fig. 4.7). Coltrane has played over the section break, ending his line on the tonic chord that resolves the turnaround at the end of the preceding A section; recognizing this, Monk continues to use comping patterns through the end of m. 4 of the section. This comping material works as an introduction for the first phrase of the solo, inasmuch as it leans heavily on parallel sixth movement, which comes to be motivic. In mm. 5–7 of the section Monk then plays the material from the head in the first of the two arrangements he uses in this solo, an arrangement dominated by a homophonic handling of the melody, primarily in parallel sixths and seconds. Monk rests in mm. 7 and 8, clearly marking the end of the section and giving Shadow Wilson space to be heard as he plays a fill that signals the section break.

Monk introduces the second arrangement of the head material in the second A section of his first chorus (Fig. 4.8). In this arrangement he uses the tonic B♭ that starts the melody as a midregister pedal, decorated by a trill to the A half a step below. He then plays the rest of the melody staccato, which retains a clarity that might have otherwise been lost due to the ongoing half-step trill underneath the moving notes. In a move that opens up the range of the solo and provides a contrasting surface movement to the

FIGURE 4.7. "Nutty," John Coltrane's Solo, Transition into Monk's Solo, A1

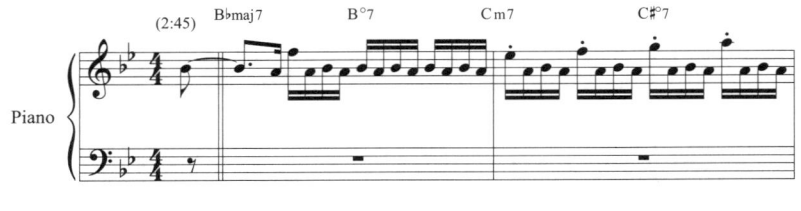

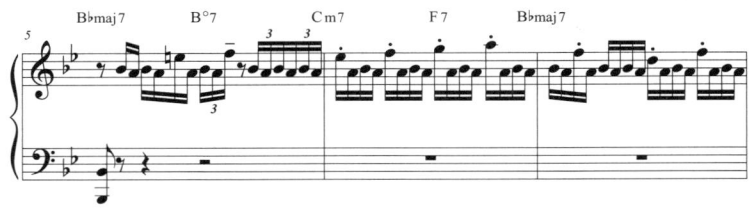
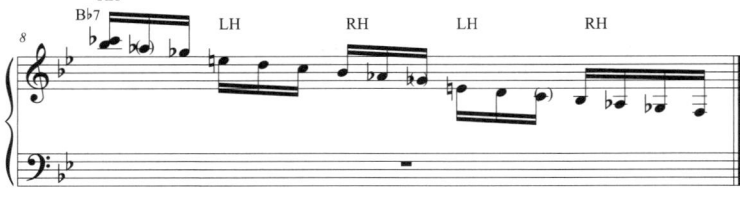

FIGURE 4.8. "Nutty," Thelonious Monk's Solo, First Chorus, A2

static trills in mm. 1–3 and 5–7, Monk punctuates the head material in this section with big whole-tone descending runs starting on F in m. 4 and on a B♭/C dyad in m. 8, as suggested by the harmonies.

Having now played almost exclusively, and quite clearly, head material for half a chorus, Monk extrapolates from the head for the bridge. His playing in this section is much more open, relying extensively on single-note lines and rests. This emphasizes the AABA structure of the head—which is a result of harmonic, rather than melodic, change in the precomposed material. To reiterate the effect, Monk returns to the arrangements he introduced in the first and second A sections for the final A section of the first chorus. In something like a synthesis, he plays the second arrangement, the one characterized by the A–B♭ pedal trill and a staccato melody, in mm. 1–4, and the first arrangement, the one characterized by homophony and a reliance on parallel sixth movement, in mm. 5–6. Rather than finish the chorus with a sweeping whole-tone run, Monk plays the rising two-note figure from m. 7 in a higher register and as though it were a horn hit in a big band piece.

The horn hit, which Monk plays three times, serves to tie the end of the first chorus to the beginning of the second, blurring the section break. Monk then leaves behind the material from the head, which dominated his first chorus, dividing the first A section into two subphrases but softening the strong break at m. 5 in the head. In mm. 1–3 he plays the final iteration of the two-note hit from the previous chorus in its original register; then he plays a series of figures that echo it, dissipating its energy through a gradual descent through the piano's low register. In m. 4 Monk introduces a line that sounds somewhat reminiscent of the melody from the sixth and seventh measures of "Take the A Train" and that initiates a series of single-note lines in mm. 6–8. These lines end with a B♭–F flourish that foreshadows his playing at the beginning of the second A section.

Monk starts to point to the head material again in the second A section, with a strong B♭–F–E♭ gesture that clearly derives from the first three notes of the precomposed melody. This gesture has the sound of a phrase begun but abortively turned away from, as though Monk is preparing for a big return to familiar material but wants a transitional section. After the E♭, instead of continuing the head melody, then, Monk returns to single-note lines reminiscent of the material from the previous section. He points these lines to a big landing on B♭ in m. 5, which also suggests the melody of the head but, once again, does not complete the gesture. Finally, in mm. 7–8, Monk plays an A–B♭ trill, now displaced from where he initially played it, but still bringing to mind the head and its earlier use in Monk's first solo chorus.

Monk delivers the return to the head in the bridge, as he so strongly suggested in the preceding A section, now played in a homophonic texture as at the beginning of his solo. He plays it through, largely without other material, deriving variation primarily from note choice in his harmonization, not just in the bridge but through most of the final A section as well. Only in m. 6 does he deviate from the head melody, becoming stuck, so to speak, on a set of chordal hits that support an E♮–F melody, similar to the hornlike hits he played at the end of the bridge in his first chorus. These hits function as a closing gesture, and he plays them right up to the downbeat of the next chorus, when Coltrane returns and the band plays the head out.

With this, the group concluded the main portion of their first set of the evening. They had only to play their theme song, "Epistrophy," which, to anyone even passingly familiar with Monk by that time, would have been a clear signal of the end of the set. As an opening set it was strong, creative, and coherent. It moved through grand, prickly, tender, and lighthearted sentiments, and it had an ebb and flow that would have kept an audience engaged; and although it showed the various talents of everyone in the band, it particularly highlighted Monk's vision. I would note here the way this set speaks to considerations raised in the introduction regarding composition and improvisation as modes of creativity. The distinction between aspects of these pieces on this performance that were fixed ahead of time and those decided in the moment does not map neatly onto a dichotomy between formal structure and its elaboration, nor onto a distinction between works and their interpretation. Rather we hear a blending of these at every level, from the moment-to-moment, to the individual pieces, to the management of the complete set as an aesthetic experience.

CHAPTER 5

Scripting the Sound of Surprise
"Bye-Ya" and "Sweet and Lovely"

MONK PROGRAMMED A more common, and in a sense more easily digestible, second set than the first for this concert. His group worked through three longer pieces, rather than the first set's four relatively short ones, using a more standard fast-slow-fast sequence for the pieces and closing with a rendition of "Epistrophy." Although there is a certain overall unity of approach to the entire evening—a single, basic, overarching sound and musical concept—the band also clearly treated each song as a distinct musical statement. As was Monk's usual approach, rather than thinking of a piece simply as a specific set of harmonic prompts for improvisation, they treated the songs holistically, approaching them melodically, harmonically, rhythmically, and motivically as complex entities, with musical challenges but also historical contexts and meanings to themselves and their audiences. The second set included two originals and a standard, in addition to "Epistrophy." They were all songs in fairly regular rotation in Monk's repertoire and would likely have been well known to at least a portion of the audience at Carnegie Hall that evening. This chapter looks at the first two pieces, which, as thirty-two-bar song forms, share some formal properties but also throw into relief the contrasts Monk and his band were able to achieve within a performance.

"BYE-YA"

The second set opens with "Bye-Ya" (a corruption of "Vaya," Spanish for "Go") Monk's only work with references to Latin jazz. The song is not, strictly speaking, a Latin piece, but like Dizzy Gillespie's "A Night in Tunisia" or Horace Silver's "Nica's Dream" it uses Latin rhythms in the A section of the head, switching to swing at the end of the A section and throughout the bridge. In this way, Latin and jazz rhythms "call" and "respond" to one another, so to speak, dramatizing the form of the head. Writing about this performance of "Bye-Ya," Robin Kelley notes that it showcases Monk's "ability to evoke Caribbean rhythms" (2009, 238). This is true, but there is more to it. The most compelling element of the performance is not just the use of a Latin groove but Monk's, and his band's, ability to shift between swing and Latin rhythmic concepts from measure to measure. Beyond rhythms, Monk hints at the Latin music of the 1940s, in the syncopated melody, built on arpeggios, and its alternation with a punctuating response in the bass—as though the head were a condensed version of a mambo chart, where the primary melody might be played on alto saxes and trumpet and the response might come from the trombones and bari sax. Wilson's drumming is, as elsewhere, an important addition to the head. Because the melody only hints at Latin rhythms in the A section, it is Wilson's work on the toms that most clearly signals a mambo groove. When he switches to a ride cymbal pattern for the swing sections, the effect is unmistakable.

Kelley notes a connection between "Bye-Ya" and "Bemsha Swing," which Monk co-wrote with drummer Denzil Best, as pieces evoking the Caribbean in Monk's repertoire, yet leaves the potential implications of these two pieces largely unexplored (2009, 23, 160–61). The two tunes are in fact quite different, one evoking Afro-Cuban and Puerto Rican musical forms and the other the Calypso typical of black communities in the Anglophone Caribbean.[1] Both styles were to become important Afrocentric references in midcentury, as well as statements of personal identity, in such pieces as Sonny Rollins's "St. Thomas," and of course both styles allowed variety and upbeat, danceable (or at least dance-invoking) sounds in recordings that might otherwise be too grave, but they are by no means the same. If nothing else, there was a whole genre that had developed in the United States linking jazz and Afro-Cuban traditions by the mid-1940s, but no equivalent for Anglo-Caribbean music.

The Latin feel in "Bye-Ya" had at least two significant connections to Monk's world. First, Latin rhythms were fairly common in modern jazz—certainly in hard bop—as a way of providing variety. Through their association with Afro-Caribbean culture, they were also a way of signaling racial solidarity, Afrocentrism, and diasporic connections for many musicians (Monson 2007, 133–37). When Monk first began working on "Bye-Ya," sometime in 1945 or 1946, these political undercurrents were emerging as a part of the reception of jazz, and in certain cases in its production as well. "Black, Brown and Beige," for instance—Duke Ellington's "Tone Parallel to the History of the Negro in America"—which explicitly linked the black experiences of North America with those of the Caribbean, was premiered in 1943. The piece was not "militant," in the way that expressions of Afrocentrism would become in the 1960s, but its expression of racial pride was clear nonetheless. Dizzy Gillespie's work in earnest on Afro-Cuban/Jazz fusion also dates from the mid-1940s, when he hired conguero Chano Pozo to work in his big band. In his memoir, *To Be or Not...to Bop*, Gillespie makes extensive connections between Afro-Cuban music and Africa, using the drum as a symbol of African authenticity and resistance. As he says, during the era of slavery, "In the United States they wouldn't let us use our primary means of expression, which was the drum because we could talk with the drum, and they figured you could foment revolution with the drums. So what the hell are they gonna let you talk for? So you can talk to somebody two miles over there and say, 'Let's get these muthafuckas [sic]. Get ready'" (Gillespie and Fraser 1979, 318). Bringing Pozo into the band was, for Gillespie, a way of broadening both their musical palettes and their depth of connection to diasporic cultures.

Second, as all of Monk's biographers point out, the Latin "tinge" in Monk's music, especially "Bye-Ya," must have had some overarching resonance with his childhood in the "San Juan Hill" neighborhood. The neighborhood was notable for its large, well-established West Indian community, and Monk would have heard Afro-Caribbean music from house parties and on the street, growing up there (though as I argue elsewhere, he would also likely have heard popular music of the day and, importantly, light opera in the neighborhood, since the tastes of black Caribbean people at the time were hardly limited to autochthonous musical styles; Solis 2008, 20). Given this background, it may be surprising that Monk did not write more pieces using Latin sounds.[2]

It seems likely that all of these issues were present in "Bye-Ya" for Monk, though the song's upbeat groove provides the most obvious, and probably the most compelling reason for programming it to open the band's second set on this concert. One further element of Monk's biography and history with the song may have added significance to the song that night. More important, perhaps, than Monk's general musical background, and more immediate, it would seem, than the political implications of Latin music for black musicians in the 1940s was the fact that Monk composed "Bye-Ya" (originally as "Playhouse") for Dizzy Gillespie's reconstituted big band in the mid-1940s, around the same time he provided the band with "Monk's Mood" (Kelley 2009, 113). Gillespie's band had been an important conduit for Modern Jazz/Afro-Caribbean fusions—so-called Cubop, for instance—by then, and it seems plausible that Monk had this in mind when writing "Bye-Ya." It is notable that Dizzy Gillespie was one of the other featured performers on the concert that night. Monk was subtle and clever in many ways, and he might well have taken some pleasure in the connection. That said, Monk played the piece fairly regularly in the late 1950s, recording it first in 1952 in a trio setting and again in 1958, with Johnny Griffin on tenor, and it would be a mistake to read too much into his selection of the piece for this particular concert.

As in so many other performances, Monk began "Bye-Ya" with a solo statement of the A section. The eight-measure introduction serves to set up the basic dynamic of alternation between the implication of swing and Latin grooves, as well as the head's two-voiced texture. The texture is implicit in the rhythms and tessitura of the motives, but Monk also highlights it through subtle attention to articulation. The first gesture of the piece is the descending fifth that establishes the bass line, from an A♭ pickup to a D♭ on the downbeat of the first full measure. Monk plays these two notes dryly, with separation between them (though not staccato, and not heavily accented). This is followed, starting on the *and* of beat 2, with a rising arpeggio through the upper extensions of a D♭7 chord ending on G (the eleventh of the chord), in eighth notes. Since one of the biggest differences separating swing and Latin feels is in the distinction between even and uneven eighth notes, the interpretation of the rhythm here is of paramount importance. Monk plays this arpeggio with a clear swing feel—more strongly uneven, in fact, than he might in other contexts, since the unevenness of eighth notes in his swing is not usually terribly pronounced, even at moderate tempos. Measure 2 completes the subphrase, with the G on beat 4 of m. 1 stepping down to an F in the melody, harmonized with a block chord voicing and reiterated on the *and* of 2 (a rhythm that implies the *clave* pattern that is a hallmark of Latin feels). The next two measures repeat the first two, and Monk plays them in the same way. The fifth and six measures have the same basic structure, in a new harmonic context (an alternation between G♭7 and A♭, rather than D♭7 and A♭6), and with the ending rhythmically condensed to two off-beat hits, on the *and* of 4 of the first measure and the *and* of 1 of the second. Monk plays the bass line somewhat differently, starting with three eighth notes beginning on the *and* of 3, and harmonizing them with a dissonant second, rather than playing a single note. These are the first straight eighths of the performance, and Monk hammers them loudly. He then plays the answering arpeggio (F♭–A♭–C–E♭) in conspicuously even eighth notes, signaling the potential for a Latin feel when the rest of the band enters. Monk ends the introduction with the final two measures in a groove that suggests the swing rhythmic feel that characterizes the ends of the A sections throughout the head. There are only two eighth notes in the last two measures (m. 7, beat 3), which Monk plays unevenly, but this is enough, along with his phrasing of off-beat hits preceding it, to indicate a swing feel.

The whole band does not come in immediately on the first A section in this performance, because in m. 1 and throughout the head Monk plays the bass line motive solo, but the whole band does enter on m. 2 and plays consistently thereafter. The head is a standard thirty-two-bar AABA form, but it has some distinctive segmentations. The A section, as suggested above, breaks down into four two-measure units, aaa'b, with a climax in m. 6, and a contrasting figure that provides a conclusion in mm. 7 and 8. The bridge, which works through alterations to a single motive, involves a process of intensification through diminution, with the first statement of the motive taking up four measures, the next taking two, and the final ones one measure each.

Harmonically "Bye-Ya" is clever, as Monk's pieces often are. The piece is nominally in D♭, inasmuch as it begins and ends with D♭ harmonies, and its opening gesture in the left hand of the piano can best be heard as a $\hat{5}$-$\hat{1}$ movement, implying V–I in D♭. Here, however, the straightforward implication of standard harmonic and melodic procedures clearly indicating D♭ tonality comes to an end. The A section has relatively little in the way of coherent melodic trajectory, with the arpeggiated motives making clear local logic (the move from G to F, for instance, across the bar from m. 1 to m. 2 sounds like a compelling one), but not pointing toward any larger melodic direction. The strongest melodic trajectory in the section is in the final two measures, where the descent from G♭ through F to E♭ sounds convincingly conclusive as a line that aims not at the tonic but at the ninth of the D♭ chord that ends the section (and the piece, ultimately). The bridge is, by contrast, highly melodically directed, and clarifies the centrality (if not in strict terms the "tonality") of D♭. Here a series of neighbor tones moves chromatically downward, with the higher of the two neighbors the point of rest. Thus, the F♯ in mm. 1 and 2 of the bridge steps down to the F in m. 4, whose neighbor E♭ takes up all of m. 3. The melodic form of the first two measures is then taken up in mm. 5 and 6, this time focusing on E♮, and then foreshortened versions of the neighbor pair focus on E♭ in m. 7 and D in m. 8. This descent clearly points to D♭ as its next step (and, given pacing, its resting point or even goal), but the resolution of the line is displaced, happening, if one can hear it doing so, two octaves below, in the left hand of m. 1 of the return of the A section.

Harmonically the piece is similarly focused on D♭, without, particularly in the A section, using standard tonal gestures. The opening bars of the A section involve an alternation between D♭ and A♭ chords, but the D♭ is harmonized as a dominant chord, and the A♭ with the somewhat ambiguous sixth. The piece moves through a G♭7–A♭ sequence and finally concludes with a settling-in gesture that leads to D♭6/9 movement in mm. 7 and 8. This final harmonic movement is surely best heard as a combination of parallel motion in the bass (E♭–D♮–D♭) with descent in the melody (G♭–F–E♭), but since the second chord is either a Dmin9 or a Bmin7, it does not, ultimately, function as a tritone substitution for the V chord, A♭7. The bridge is clearer harmonically than the A section just as it is melodically, and it more obviously gestures toward D♭ major. The opening move to A♮ is unusual, but it sets up a large-scale root movement that ends on the D♭ opening the A section, a classic bridge procedure. After two measures of A7, the piece moves to two measures of A♭, followed by a series of chromatically descending ii–V progressions, Bmin7–E7 in mm. 5 and 6, B♭min7–E♭7 in m. 7 and Amin7–D7 in m. 8. This is, perhaps, the only true jazz commonplace in the whole thirty-two bars, and its ultimate progress is undercut by the fact that it resolves not to a D♭ Major 7 chord but to the D♭ Dominant 7 that opens the final A.

Coltrane launches into his solo immediately from the last note of the head, inverting the closing F–E♭ interval for his opening gesture (Fig. 5.1). The use of a gesture with such a clearly audible motivic relationship to the head suggests the thinking Coltrane intends for the solo at large, as something that may not so much state the melodies of the head directly as use them loosely. Thus they become the basis for the only solo on the evening's concert that actually works within the "sheet of sound" concept he would

FIGURE 5.1. "Bye-Ya," John Coltrane's Solo, First Chorus, A1, mm. 1–4

go on to develop more extensively in the following years. With a somewhat longer solo than he took in the pieces of the previous set (four choruses, rather than two on "Nutty" and three on "Evidence"), Coltrane shows less of an inclination to build a schematic, structural form on this piece. Instead the solo breaks down into a set of largely discrete sections. If there is an overarching formal concept at play here, it is one of gradually extending section lengths over the course of the solo. Coltrane clearly marks the ends of the first and second choruses and internally subdivides each of those choruses, generally by eight-measure sections as well as subdividing within each eight-measure section, but he plays through choruses 3 and 4 without the same level of regular segmentation.

The first section, which starts at the beginning of the solo, is characterized by the repetition of the E♭–D–E♭–F melody. Following this, however, there is almost no development of distinctive melodic material. Instead, Coltrane plays a combination of arpeggios and scalar patterns, treating each chord, to some degree, as a unit, as in mm. 2 and 5 of the first A section of his first chorus; mm. 1, 5, 6, 7, and 8 of the second A of that chorus; or mm. 1–6 of the bridge. Where he clearly suggests meaningful voice-leading gestures, they are commonly in places in which half-step motion readily connects one chord to another, as, for instance, in the move from the A6 chord in m. 2 of the bridge to the A♭6 chord in m. 3. In the first chorus of his solo, Coltrane ends the second measure with an A♮. After a breath, he picks up on the second half of beat 1 in the third chorus with a figure that begins on A♭. This moment also allows Coltrane to connect the chords, if only for a moment and perhaps only incidentally, to an idiomatic aspect of the tenor sax, since the roots of these two chords, concert A and A♭, are the lowest two notes of the instrument.

In a sense the third and fourth choruses of Coltrane's solo can be heard as a contrast with the first two; in the first two he worked with a range of figures, and even more importantly he showed no particular gravitation toward recurring focal pitches. Though perhaps somewhat favoring root tones as boundary pitches for his melodic gestures (as with the low A♭ in m. 2, the high D♭ in m. 3, and the midrange A♭ in m. 4 of the first chorus, for instance), he generally worked with the entire range of the instrument, varying his points of arrival. In the third and fourth choruses, by contrast, Coltrane used a more limited set of gestures, honing in more resolutely on a small number of focal pitches. This is immediately clear in the first six measures of the third chorus, where he plays an extended series of ascending and descending arpeggios with a top pitch of B♭ and a bottom pitch that alternates between C♭ and C♮, to project the alternation between D♭7 and A♭6 harmony (Fig. 5.2).

Unlike most of the rest of the concert, Monk comps throughout Coltrane's solo. In a dialogue of sorts, Monk seems to be alternating between keeping the melody of the head in our—and Coltrane's—ears and dropping dissonant punctuations into the texture. Coltrane, meanwhile, takes one of his least complex solos in the concert. It is as though with Monk's more active presence behind him Coltrane was happy to leave some space in his playing. When he leaves off, bringing his solo to an end more than to a clear conclusion, Monk takes up in a similar vein. His solo is almost entirely devoid of virtuoso fills, opting instead for a wry, disjointed collage. In a style he had honed for years, Monk fills his solo with brief snippets quoted from his other compositions, and a deconstruction of the head of "Bye-Ya" itself.

FIGURE 5.2. "Bye-Ya," John Coltrane's Solo, Third Chorus, A1, mm. 1–6

Monk's three-chorus solo moves along at the elevated pace that Coltrane, Abdul-Malik, and Wilson established by the end of the saxophonist's solo (Fig. 5.3). Perhaps following Coltrane's example, Monk does not give this solo the kind of extensive overall formal patterning that he did in other cases; nevertheless he uses a number of formal gestures that suggest moment-to-moment, if not large-scale, planning. Broadly, Monk works with three kinds of material in this solo—material from the head, quotes from other pieces, and new material (some of it common to his language elsewhere and some of it particular to this performance)—and by managing the alternations among these three types he is able to highlight the formal drama of each chorus and give some shape to the three-chorus solo.

In the first chorus Monk clearly marks the eight-measure section breaks, starting new material at the beginning of each section. The first A section involves the statement of a motive starting with a descending leap from F to A♭, and then rising from A♭ to B♭ and B♮. He then repeats the second half of the motive, adding a concluding D♭, and again this time harmonized and ending on E♭. A third, somewhat altered statement marks the end of the motive, and in m. 7 Monk moves on to a figure that starts with a reiteration of the F from the beginning of the solo, but now centering on a descending Fmin7 arpeggio. In the second A section Monk works with comping-derived chordal hits, and markedly more silence. To suggest a tie to the material from the first A section, Monk continues to work with the high F as an important note. This section ends with an arpeggiated figure that points toward and ends with the B section. Only in the bridge does Monk reference the melodic material from the head. As in that evening's performance of "Nutty," Monk uses references to material from the head in alternation with new material here as a way of focusing attention on both the form of the piece itself—there is no way to miss the fact that they have reached the bridge, since Monk plays the melody of the head just as the bridge starts—and as a way of giving formal structure to his solo overall. Having played material closely connected to the head melody at the beginning of the bridge, Monk moves away from it, beginning in m. 4, where he plays a heavy, descending line from A♭ to G♭ in the lower register that sounds like a reference to the opening motive of his composition "Off Minor." Monk brings back the smallest suggestion of the melody of the first two A sections in the final section of the chorus by focusing, again, on the high F that started his solo. Here, rather than play it as part of the type of moving lines he created in the first two A sections, Monk uses the F as the high note in tritone-heavy comping-style hits for the first half of the section. He ends the section with a descending figure starting on an E♭ a seventh

FIGURE 5.3. "Bye-Ya," Thelonious Monk's Solo

FIGURE 5.3. (Cont'd)

FIGURE 5.3. (Cont'd)

FIGURE 5.3. (Cont'd)

above the F that serves as a focal point for the entire chorus, aiming at and ending on a figure focused on B♮ that has its final note on the downbeat of the second chorus.

In the second chorus, Monk solos in a way that elides section breaks much more than in the first chorus. The overall form, in a sense, remains similar, inasmuch as the A sections are composed primarily of material that derives harmonically, but not thematically, from the head; he contrasts this with the bridge, where he largely plays material from the head. In the first A section Monk begins with an eighth-note motive focusing on an alternation among B♭, B♮, and C in the melody, moving chromatically between the flat seventh of a D♭ chord and the third of A♭. This motive in the middle register of the piano gives way to sweeping, multi-octave descending runs. The second of these runs ends in the final measure of the section, but in order to elide the section break Monk picks up the descending run as the opening gesture of the second A section. Rather than continue with the descending melodic runs throughout the second A section, which would create the sense that there was one large idea governing the two sections together, Monk moves on to a new eighth-note melody reminiscent of his playing in the third A section of the previous chorus for the rest of this A section. Monk thereby gives the impression that the continuation of the descending motive into the first measure of the second A section was intended principally to elide the section break. Perhaps responding to this, Shadow Wilson, who consistently marked the eight-measure sections up to this point (including the first A section of the second chorus) by playing fills in the final measure of each, does not play a fill in the final measure of either the second A section or the bridge.

Once again, in this chorus Monk marks the bridge by playing material clearly derived from the head. In fact, he foreshadows this move by playing a rhythmically compressed version of the final motive of the A section in m. 8 of the second A section in this chorus. In this bridge he begins by playing the head essentially untransformed and gradually transforms it. By m. 5 he introduces a very clear three-layer texture, including melody on top, a stepwise descending line (A–A♭–G–G♭) in the middle, and punctuating bass notes. At the same time he foreshortens the rhythms so that the melody ends early. Then, to elide the transition to the final A section, Monk plays material derived from this new arrangement of the bridge as the opening measure of the A section. The rest of the A section is then taken up with new material, the motivic transformation of a triplet gesture that is, in a way, a free inversion of the motive from the first A section of this chorus, with its goal notes moving down from C through B♮ and B♭, with B♭ now serving as the third of a G♭7 chord (delayed into m. 6) and finally as the sixth of the D♭6 chord in m. 8. Wilson marks the end of the chorus strongly with a fill, anticipating Monk's attention to the larger-scale formal unit.

Monk starts the final chorus of his solo with a two-part texture, a chordal call followed by a midregister melodic response, and then moves to ethereal-sounding chordal hits in the highest register of the solo. These chords continue on into the second A section, and Wilson, taking a cue from Monk's playing in the previous chorus, does not strongly mark the transition to the second A. Only in m. 4 does Monk move away from this comping-like chordal material, and when he does he moves to a descending run like those he has already interspersed in the second half of various A sections previous to this one. The final measure of the second A section is strangely disconnected from the rest of the first two A sections. Here Monk plays a motive that sounds like a reference to the last measure of the A section of "Well, You Needn't." There is no particular relationship between the two pieces, but it is an effective motive for imparting momentum into the downbeat of the next section. In contrast to the first two choruses, Monk does not clearly reference the melody from the head in the bridge of this chorus. Instead he plays a series of short gestures that work with the ii–V progressions that characterize the section. The last A section is the most interesting moment of Monk's third chorus, inasmuch as it is the first in which he introduces truly new, clearly motivic content. Monk starts squarely on the downbeat of the section's first measure, playing a motive that features a prominent repeated B♮. After playing this motive again an octave below in m. 3, Monk introduces a final gesture made of rising, tightly voiced chords in a low register, reaching a point of conclusion in the second half of m. 6. He follows up with open-voiced chords in a high register. Middle register hits in m. 8 lead to an authoritative first note of the head, on which Coltrane reenters and Shadow Wilson returns to the Latin feel and prominent use of tom-toms. The band then plays the head out to end the piece.

"SWEET AND LOVELY"

At the end of "Bye-Ya" the band jumps immediately into the only standard of the evening, "Sweet and Lovely." Taken at a stately tempo, it stands as a lyrical point of repose in the set. From the standpoint of sheer length, at more than nine minutes, but also in terms of complexity of arrangement, "Sweet and Lovely" amounts to the heart of the second set, and of the CD release as well. As a thirty-two-bar AABA pop song, "Sweet and Lovely" shares a basic formal outline with "Bye-Ya," but in most other ways the two performances are a radical contrast. Obviously, the tempos are not the same, but other, less obvious divergences are equally important. The contrast in the extent of arrangement is most immediately (and arguably most importantly) striking. "Bye-Ya" virtually does not have an arrangement—in stock bebop style, the band plays the head and a series of solo choruses and ends with the head, with a bare minimum of pre-arranged elements. "Sweet and Lovely," by contrast, shows Monk the Hard Bopper arranging large-scale formal elements more substantially.

Like virtually all of his choices of standards, "Sweet and Lovely" was a hit pop song from Monk's early teens (DeVeaux 1999, 170–71). Its original recording, which reached number one on the pop charts, was released in 1931, when Monk was fourteen years old. The song charted with remarkable consistency in various recorded versions in that year and also in a revival version more than a decade later. The initial recording was directly connected to its composition. Rather than coming from a musical, as did many standards adopted by jazz musicians, "Sweet and Lovely" was written as a stand-alone piece for Gus Arnheim's band, with vocalist Donald Novis interpreting the lyrics. Composer credit is given to Arnheim, Jules Lemare (one of a number of pseudonyms used by Charles N. Daniels), and Harry Tobias, but it seems likely that Arnheim had relatively little to do with its actual composition. He actually wrote very little, being principally known as a bandleader, but Daniels was a prolific songwriter, and owner of a song publishing company until 1931 (Jasen 2003, 17; Burlingame 2008). Tobias was the lyricist, "Sweet and Lovely" being one of his many hits (Vosburgh 1995, 16). The song was immediately released in four more versions, including two directly connected to the Arnheim recording: one by Russ Columbo, who had begun as a member of Arnheim's string section, and one by Bing Crosby, who had sung with Arnheim's band until 1930 (Jasen 2003, 17). Monk most likely knew one or more of these versions, but by 1952 when he first recorded it he and his listeners would have been more likely to have had the last charting version, Bing Crosby's revival from 1944, in their ears. Crosby's recording stemmed from the 1944 release of the film musical *Two Girls and a Sailor*, which featured the song in an arrangement played by Harry James and his Music Makers.

Monk's interest in the song surely derives from the pop versions from the 1930s and 1940s. If nothing else, there were relatively few jazz versions of the song between its publication in 1931 and Monk's first recording of it, in a trio arrangement on Prestige Records in 1952. Tenor saxophonists Flip Phillips, Dexter Gordon, and Wardell Gray each recorded a version of the piece in the mid-1940s and early 1950s, and Howard McGhee and Milt Jackson recorded it in 1948 (released on Savoy 12026). Otherwise, however, the vast majority of jazz recordings of "Sweet and Lovely" come from after Monk's 1952 version. After the 1952 trio version, Monk recorded the song again with Gerry Mulligan in 1957, with Charlie Rouse in 1962, and solo in 1964; he played it live countless times, a number of which were recorded.

One can only speculate about why Monk liked "Sweet and Lovely," and why he programmed it on any one concert or another, but the song may have been linked in some significant way to "Bye-Ya" for him. His first recording of it, with Art Blakey and Gary Mapp, was the last of four songs cut in Beltone studios on October 15, 1952, immediately following "Bye-Ya." It is unfortunate not to have more evidence about the context for pairing these songs in two instances. I imagine the first recording session needed an up-tempo piece and a ballad, and the two were somewhat fortuitously chosen; Monk's choice to repeat the pairing on the Carnegie Hall concert may simply have represented his sense that the two songs worked well back to back.

THE HEAD

It is hard to gauge why Monk chose to play "Sweet and Lovely" often, along with a handful of other favorite Tin Pan Alley ballads, such as "Just a Gigolo," "Everything Happens to Me," and "I Surrender Dear." Scott DeVeaux notes that Monk's choices commonly speak to his undocumented early career, mostly as an acknowledgment of the impact the "endless string of jam-session favorites" had on his developing aesthetic (DeVeaux 1999, 171, 175). This seems generally true, particularly for songs such as "Nice Work (If You Can Get It)" or "Liza," though many of the songs Monk chose to play also had lyrics that one can imagine him finding poignant or telling. "Sweet and Lovely," in contrast, does not really fit either of these categories of song: to judge by the surviving recordings, at least, it became a standby of jazz repertoire in the later 1950s and especially the 1960s rather than being common jam session material in the 1930s and 1940s; and the lyrics are the least interesting kind of Tin Pan Alley love song. The song does not quite use the "moon, June, spoon" rhyme, but its description of the object of affection as "sweeter than the roses in May," with eyes bluer than the sky, is the zenith of blandly generic lyricism. Instead, two formal elements of the song—the chord progression in the first four bars of the A section, and the melodic and harmonic implications of the last two measures of the bridge—fit Monk's language and approach to interpreting pop songs neatly, and they may have been precisely what kept Monk coming back to the song.

The head follows a standard thirty-two-bar AABA form originally in C major (although Monk routinely played it transposed up a minor third, in E♭, as he did on this concert).[3] The A section, which is repeated verbatim every time it appears, has two four-measure phrases, which function as an antecedent-consequent pair. Each is further divided into two two-measure subphrases, which also have antecedent-consequent qualities, or perhaps better put have contrasting motivic qualities that give them beginning and ending characters. A four-measure section begins with a cantabile figure that encompasses a small rise (a step in the first section and a third in the second), followed by a fall of a fifth. This opening lyrical gesture is then concluded by a contrasting passage in eighth notes that lands on a long note corresponding to the end of the phrase and the end of a line of poetry in the lyrics. Monk shifts the phrasing on these sections so that the note concluding the first four-bar phrase is anticipated, coming on the *and* of the fourth beat of m. 3, and the note that concludes the second four-bar phrase is preceded by a syncopated gesture, thus coming right on the downbeat of m. 8 of the section. Melodically the entire section entails a drop of an octave, from the E♭ an octave above middle C to E♭ immediately above middle C, or from a high tonic to the tonic an octave below. The antecedent-consequent quality of the two phrases is signaled by ending the first phrase on scale degree 5, B♭. At its simplest the first four measures constitute an extended prolongation of a ii–V in A♭, the fourth of the main key. Monk uses this as an opportunity to map a strong chromatic descent in an inner voice onto a progression that uses the circle of fifths and tritone substitutions to even more strongly tonicize A♭. The second four-measure section then moves, somewhat unconventionally, from A♭ through D to a E♭Maj7 chord on the downbeat of m. 7 and a ii–V in E♭ (Fm7–B♭7) on the second half of m. 7, which brings a full cadence on I in m. 8.

The bridge uses quite different phrasing from the A section, setting up a clear impression of the kind of departure and return that is the hallmark of the AABA song form. It has three short, two-measure phrases, the last of which is extended to four bars. It is possible to hear the melodic motion of the B section phrases as a transformation of material from the A section, since its shape (one measure of eighth notes followed by a long note) is similar to the subphrases in mm. 3–4 and 7–8 of the A section. The most striking motivic element to the bridge, however, is not this incidental similarity but rather an entirely new three-note rising figure that is heard initially in the second measure. This motive is not repeated in m. 4 but is repeated in m. 6, and then a sequence of repetitions of the motive becomes the basis for the extension of the third phrase into mm. 7 and 8. This motivic quality underscores the most interesting formal aspect of the lyrics, which is a quick internal rhyme in the final line. The first three lines of the bridge's lyrics have an aba rhyme scheme (When she nestles in my arms so tenderly / There's a thrill that words cannot express / In my heart a song of love is taunting me), and the fourth line then is nothing more than two further iterations of the rhyme (Melody, haunting me). The extensional quality of the melody in mm. 7 and 8 of the bridge highlights this and points to the fact that even though each of the previous lines in the lyrics is a complete phrase, the final line of the stanza is itself an extension of the immediately preceding line and not syntactically independent.

The final two measures are perhaps the most obviously "Monkish" of the piece, and I suspect this was what caught his ear. The first instance of the three-note rising motive, in m. 2 of the bridge, has a half-step/whole-step sequence, as it does in m. 6. Its reuse in mm. 7 and 8, however, involves transformation to an intervallic structure of two whole steps. This melody (two sets of rising whole steps separated by a half step, A–B–C♯ followed by B♭–C–D), harmonized by two dominant-seventh chords a half step away from one another (A7 followed by B♭7), clearly implies at least the possibility of voicing the chords with a flatted fifth, and playing with whole-tone scales in each measure. Unsurprisingly, given his penchant for mapping whole-tone scales onto dominant-seventh chords, Monk does indeed play whole-tone figures in these two bars, not only of this performance but in numerous recordings as well. That this is part of Monk's interpretation of the piece—his way of making it his own—is clearly suggested by the fact that none of the other notable recordings of the piece before Monk's exploits this possibility. For instance, in recordings from near that time Wardell Gray turns the dominant-seventh chords (particularly the second one, the B♭7) into a moment to highlight a bluesy quality in his playing, and Dexter Gordon extends what he did in the rest of the piece, elaborating the tones of the chords with significant chromaticism.

THE PERFORMANCE

"Sweet and Lovely" is on the one hand the most extensively arranged piece on the concert, and on the other the most disjointed. The arrangement is not unlike the sort commonly used by Horace Silver or Art Blakey—a "Jazz Messengers" kind of approach. It opens with Monk playing a portion of the A section of the head alone, with a grand, updated, "Monk-ish" stride accompaniment. The rest of the band then comes in for a full chorus of the head, with Coltrane playing a slow, descending countermelody and Monk chomping away at the main melody, presenting it in alternation with dissonant asides. There are then two choruses of what I call interstitial or transitional playing, somewhere between additional head choruses and solos. Monk plays the lead on the first of these choruses, roughly a minute and a half of music, with Coltrane playing the countermelody throughout the A sections. Coltrane then restates the melody, both himself and Monk ornamenting it extensively for an entire chorus. Throughout these first three choruses the band hints at double time, particularly in the last two measures of each A section. Heading into the fourth chorus, which marks the moment at which Coltrane takes a more standard approach to soloing, the band shifts into both a significantly faster tempo and a consistent double time, which they continue for the remainder of the solo. The band then returns to the original tempo and rhythmic feel for a final statement of the head, ending with a brief tag and cadence for piano and tenor.

The disjointed quality comes in even at the very beginning of the performance. Monk's introduction is what critics often called "angular," which in this instance is to say dissonant and rhythmically dogged, if not exactly square. The simplicity of the A section's rhythms (two notes in each of the first two bars, followed by eight quarter notes in the third bar) lends itself to the interpretation Monk gives it, hammering every beat in the left hand, while giving the melody notes just enough detachment one from the next to push against any expectation of cantabile phrasing that the piece's history as a vehicle for crooners might have suggested. His interpretation of the eighth notes in m. 3 is nearly even, rather than swung, adding to the impression of angularity, and it might have made the song seem deliberately old-fashioned to an audience used to hearing hard-swinging bop interpretations of standards. The sense of angularity is not necessarily disjointed itself, but it certainly produces the opposite of the pulsating, forward momentum generated by the feel of the immediately preceding "Bye-Ya." Whatever sense of movement Monk created in the first few measures of this introduction, he then undercuts in the fourth measure, at least for an audience familiar with the song. Rather than continue into the fourth measure of the tune, a point of rest that is central in producing the song's balanced, regular phrasing, Monk jumps to m. 7, to play the last two measures of the head. The introduction, then, is an odd five measures, disrupting the melodic and formal expectations of anyone who knows the song and creating an off-kilter tension at the outset.

TRANSITIONAL CHORUSES

The two choruses that follow the head showcase Monk's characteristic approach to solo interpretation of standards—particularly Tin Pan Alley ballads—here expanded to a quartet setting. Each of the two choruses interprets and expands on the piece's main melody, phrasing consistently in terms of the song and always returning to the original composed material at key formal moments. Monk takes the lead part in the first of the two choruses, and Coltrane takes the lead in the second; in each chorus the rest of the band—Wilson and Abdul-Malik—strongly supports the impression that these are intermediate choruses, somewhere between head and solo.

Monk's playing on the first of these two choruses sets the format, in a way that he had no doubt done any number of times before when playing this in clubs. He anticipates the main motive that he goes on to use in the first four measures, a rhythmic motive that consists of three eighth notes and a syncopated quarter note followed by an eighth-note rest, in the final bar of the previous chorus. What sounds initially like transitional figuration used over a harmonic turnaround comes to stand in place of the opening melody. Monk plays it twice in the turnaround bar, starting it on beats 1 and 3, producing a sense of regular periodicity. He then transforms the motive in the immediately following measures, reconfiguring the pitches to fit the new harmonic framework, but perhaps more interestingly he also uses a metric shift to undercut the predictability established in the motive's first appearance and to echo the rhythm of the head melody. In mm. 1–3 of this chorus Monk plays the motive starting on beats 1 and 4, beat 2 of bar 4, and finally beat 1 of bar 5. This phrasing creates an additive three-plus-two-plus-three beat structure in the first two measures, which is pleasantly asymmetrical and echoes the rhythm of the first three pitches of the melody (E♭–F–B♭) though without marking the reiteration of F on the downbeat of the second bar. Monk then leaves behind this briefly explored motive for the second half of the first A section, instead playing a longer melodic phrase in quarter and eighth notes that touches on, without strongly highlighting, the pitches of the head melody in mm. 5 and 6 (C–E♭–A♭). The clearest evocation of the shape of the head melody at this moment is Monk's rapid flourish up to the highest note of the section (a B♭ three octaves above middle C) on beat 4 of the fifth measure. Having suggested, but never really stated, the head melody for the first six bars of this solo, Monk then plays the concluding, cadential figure of the head in mm. 7 and 8.

The pattern Monk established in the first A section characterizes his approach to the rest of the chorus: he suggests, but does not actually play, the main melody most of the time, producing a kind of tension as his actual playing creates a ghostly presence of the head. This tension is relieved every time mm. 7 and 8 of the A section come around and he plays the cadential melody. In the second A section, Monk inserts a motive in the first four measures that highlights the static quality of the harmony by juxtaposing melodic notes (E♭, F, F♯, G, and D) against a reiterated B♭.

FIGURE 5.4. "Sweet and Lovely," Thelonious Monk's Solo, First Chorus, A1 (Notated in Double Time)

This incorporates the first three notes and the final note of the head melody in these four bars, but it deflects their implications by separating the trajectories: the E♭–F movement becomes part of a rising line, and the B♭ is moved to a lower voice-leading part. In m. 5 Monk avoids a clear use of the head melody, but in the sixth bar he hits the E♭ and A♭ of the main melody on beats 1 and 2, setting up a return to the eighth notes in m. 7. Monk largely plays new material for the bridge, though still retaining the phrasing of the head, with a series of three two-measure units followed by two similar one-measure ideas. This increases the drama of the AABA song form, creating an even stronger expectation of a conclusion with the head melody at the end of the third A section. Monk satisfies this expectation with materials that recall both of the first two A sections of the chorus. He starts by hitting the E♭ that is the opening pitch of the main melody, now in repeated eighth notes. Rather than use it as the upper voice of a two-voiced arrangement, akin to the second A section, he sets in motion a rising line that moves to E♮ instead of F, in what sounds like the opening of the motive from m. 3 of the head, and then on to an F♯, a ninth over the E♮ in the bass. Passage work in m. 4 brings Monk to a substantially ornamented version of the C–E♭–A♭ melody in mm. 5 and 6, and finally a satisfying return to the main melody in mm. 7 and 8.

With a subtle gesture from Wilson marking the end of the section, Coltrane then starts a similarly organized chorus. In the first A section he plays the head melody nearly as written. Adding an anacrusis figure to lead into the first measure, he arpeggiates the notes of the E♭ chord that the previous chorus ended on, rather than implying a harmonic turnaround; he adds two flourishes of passagework, rising to a C, the ninth of the B♭ chord in m. 4 and arpeggiating up from the A♭ in m. 6; and he substantially ornaments the notes of the second half of m. 7, subdividing the four eighth notes into sixteenths and triplet sixteenths. Despite these small changes, however, the song's melody is entirely present in Coltrane's interpretation, as much as it might be in any head chorus of a ballad. In the second A section, Coltrane moves further from the head melody in mm. 1–4 (Fig. 5.5). Here, unlike Monk, who largely derived new material from a complicated revision of the song melody, Coltrane appears to be playing figures derived from a rendering of the harmonies without reference to the head. He returns, however, to an interpretation of the head melody in mm. 5–8, this time elaborating the long A♭ in m. 6 and the final E♭ in m. 8, rather than the eighth notes in m. 7.

In the bridge, Coltrane largely eschews the pitches of the head melody, much as Monk did in his chorus. He does however, again as Monk did,

FIGURE 5.5. "Sweet and Lovely," John Coltrane's Solo, A2 (Notated in Double Time)

retain the basic phrasing of the head as a guide to his improvisation. At the end of every two-measure unit Coltrane breathes, putting a short space between his musical ideas. Moreover, not only does Coltrane subdivide the form in the same way as the head, but he also improvises melodies with shapes that subtly echo the phrases in the head. The fundamental shape of the head melodies is a quick, large rise (a sixth, E♭–C♭, in m. 1, for example), followed by a slower, more gradual descent and finally another rise (this last rise being the characteristic three-note motive discussed above). Coltrane subdivides time into more than the predominant eighth notes of the head, which allows him to rise and fall further than the head melody and to fill in the open space between the boundary notes. Still, all of his phrases amount to the same overall shape: a steep rise and more gradual descent (now spilling over from the first and into the second measure of each phrase), and then another rise. Coltrane clarifies the relationship to the head melody that is implied in each of the first two of these phrases in m. 5, where he begins the phrase with exactly the open G♭–E♭ (or, enharmonically, F♯–D) interval of the head melody. The only place his phrasing does not quite fit the scheme of the head is in mm. 7 and 8. Here, where the head has two rising motives, each one constituting a subphrase, Coltrane initiates a rising gesture that he could have played twice (once per measure), but instead he allows the figure to flow over into m. 8, treating it as a single phrase. In the final A section, Coltrane returns to the head melody, playing it even more straightforwardly than Monk did. As in the first two times, he adds ornamental passagework and uses the same reconfiguration of the eighth-note melody in m. 7 that he did in the second A section, ending with a descending scale degree 2 to scale degree 1, rather than 7 to 1. Nevertheless the head is recognizably present throughout.

In both Monk's and Coltrane's choruses, the rhythm section plays in a way that supports hearing these choruses as extensions of the head, as does Coltrane when he is not soloing. This is where Abdul-Malik's bass playing becomes most clearly form-defining in the entire evening. In the first chorus Abdul-Malik played what sounds like a pre-arranged, maximally direct line, highlighting the differences among the first four measures of the A section, the fifth and sixth, and the seventh and eighth, and differentiating as well these subsections and the bridge at large (Fig. 5.6). He did this partly through note choice and partly through rhythm, playing a chromatic descending line in half notes for mm. 1–4, rather than either playing a static figure or implying a set of substitute chords. Then, with the change in harmonic structure in m. 5, Abdul-Malik plays his most rhythmically active accompaniment figure. And finally, in mm. 7 and 8,

FIGURE 5.6. "Sweet and Lovely," Ahmed Abdul-Malik's Playing, Head, A1

the most tonally directed moment in the head, he plays E♭–G–F–B♭, projecting a I–iv–ii–V progression in rhythmically energetic quarter notes. Wilson supports essentially the same sound in the head, particularly in the first A section, where he plays a figure in quarter notes in mm. 1–6 and then shifts into a bouncy four-beat jazz shuffle rhythm in double time for mm. 7 and 8. In the bridge, both Abdul-Malik and Wilson move to playing more regular timekeeping patterns, but returning to this more complicated set of patterns for the final A sections. In the two transitional choruses, both Abdul-Malik and Wilson expand on the pattern they set in the first chorus, but still projecting the head's subdivision into a number of component parts in similar ways, rather than treating the choruses as longer units to be reconceptualized and redivided by a soloist in dialogue with his accompanists. Coltrane adds to this impression by playing precisely the accompaniment figure he did in the first chorus (a chromatic descent in mm. 1–4 that doubles Abdul-Malik's bass line).

COLTRANE'S SOLO

Altogether the first three choruses could have been a nearly complete performance of "Sweet and Lovely." Monk often treated Tin Pan Alley ballads this way, particularly when he played solo or in a trio setting. The band could have ended with one slightly less ornamented version of the head, perhaps with Monk playing the melody and Coltrane once again playing an accompaniment, or they could even simply have ended after the third chorus; at almost five minutes it would not have been a peculiarly short performance. On the other hand, it would have left Coltrane without the opportunity to play an extended solo, and would have been somewhat short in comparison with the previous piece. Instead, after a pronounced pause, each of the musicians seeming to take a big breath, the band jumps into a double-time groove that is also at a significantly faster underlying tempo.

Wilson has prepared the audience for the move to double time, by playing double-time patterns regularly throughout the preceding three choruses, and Coltrane played rapid figuration in his transitional chorus, but the gap between the last regular time chorus and the first in double time, along with the tempo change, separates the sections more than they might have if there was only a shift to double time. In fact, Wilson and Abdul-Malik's time-defining gestures become one way of hearing the creation of large-scale form over the course of the entire performance. Wilson is the first to gesture toward double time, doing so at the end of the first A section of the ensemble head chorus. The other musicians hold him back at this point, notably Abdul-Malik, whose walking bass line is definitively in "single" time. At various points, but importantly as the band reaches the end of the various A sections throughout the piece, Wilson plays double-time patterns, gradually ratcheting up the energy and expectation of a leap to a full-band double-time section. Even as Coltrane also suggests a double-time feel in the beginning of his solo, Abdul-Malik's steady bass holds the group back from a full-fledged shift in feel. All of the tension generated by the repeated gestures toward double time may be responsible, in fact, for the faster underlying tempo once the full band makes the shift—a way of underlining the explosive power of their interpretation of the double-time feel. Here the players generate overarching form through repetition and difference in the moment of performance, again in a manner not easily explained with recourse to the language of composition and improvisation. All of them, but particularly Wilson and Abdul-Malik, engage in creative gestures that are perhaps the clearest example of "comprovisational" practice in the whole piece.

Coltrane's three-chorus solo follows a common pattern in his playing, and in hard bop improvisation in general, largely playing new (if formulaic) passagework that relates primarily to the harmonies, and that seldom suggests the original melody in pitch content, overall contour, or even phrasing. To the extent there is a sense of overall form in Coltrane's solo—and that is only a minimal extent—it comes from the alternation between even phrasing in two- and four-measure units that reflect the original phrase lengths of the head, and irregular phrasing in odd measure units that obscure the original phrase (and even section) lengths of the head. Looked at in this way, the solo does not so much have a single formal drama as it is a series of three iterations of the same basic formal drama carried out in slightly different ways. In each chorus Coltrane begins the first A section with material that in one way or another is regular—notably involving four-measure phrasing—and then moves to greater irregularity. He returns to a sense of regularity and relationship to the head's phrasing, generally in the bridge, and always in mm. 7 and 8 of the bridge, and then returns to irregularity in the final A section, obscuring the chorus break after each of the first two choruses. Only at the end of the third chorus—the end of the solo—does Coltrane play material that creates a sense of closure.

In his first chorus, after a break in m. 8 of the previous chorus where he sets the new tempo and implies the shift to double time, Coltrane begins with a four-measure statement of the head melody. This is the only clear reference to the original melody in the entire solo, and it neatly bridges the solo section to the transitional choruses that precede it. In the second half of the first A section, Coltrane plays passagework largely in sixteenth notes (eighths in relation to the double time being played by Abdul-Malik and Wilson). This material does not clearly differentiate between mm. 5–6 and 7–8, as the head did, but a breath at the end of m. 8 allows Coltrane to still make the section a succession of two regular, even phrases. For the second A section, Coltrane largely departs from this formal division, instead playing a flurry of figures in sixteenths from mm. 1–7 without strong internal division into subphrases (Fig. 5.7). A second phrase carries Coltrane over the section break into the bridge, even while Wilson plays an extended fill to articulate the formal division. Coltrane carries the second phrase of A2 over into m. 2 of the bridge, and after a breath he continues with material in much the same vein until m. 6. Only in mm. 7 and 8 does Coltrane phrase in a way that echoes the head, and here the relationship is distant. Rather than play a set of repeating figures in mm. 6, 7, and 8, Coltrane plays a rising figure in m. 6, followed by a descent in m. 7 and another rising figure in m. 8. The relationship to the head is only in the use of clearly delineated one-measure phrases at this moment. After this fairly limited reference to the head, Coltrane then plays a third A section that bears virtually no relation to the head, instead playing constant figuration with breaths that give an asymmetrical patterning—breaking at the end of m. 5, in m. 7, and then playing across the chorus break and breathing in m. 1 of the following A section.

In the second chorus, Coltrane follows a similar pattern. Although his playing in the first A section does not reference the melody of the head, he does subdivide the section clearly into two four-measure units, as does the song's melody, playing distinct material in each of

FIGURE 5.7. "Sweet and Lovely," John Coltrane's Solo, First Double-Time Chorus, A2

the two half-section phrases, and breathing at the end of mm. 4 and 8. The second A section bears some relation to the song melody, primarily through phrasing (Fig. 5.8). In particular, the first three measures all have notes suggesting the head melody. In the bridge of this chorus, Coltrane moves away from the head once again, playing one long phrase in mm. 1–6, with irregular subphrasing that does not suggest the song melody. He returns again to the head phrasing in mm. 7 and 8, playing a single, one-measure phrase in each. It could be argued that the single-measure phrasing at this moment is as much a response to the chords (half-step-related dominant chords); yet Coltrane could have phrased across the measure line, using, for example, suspension or anticipation to blur the boundary between the chords but manifestly did not, here or in the other choruses of his solo. Shadow Wilson suggests a strong

FIGURE 5.8. "Sweet and Lovely," John Coltrane's Solo, Second Double-Time Chorus, A2 and Bridge

climax at the beginning of the last A section of this chorus, playing much more actively on the snare and toms throughout mm. 1–4 than he had elsewhere. Coltrane builds on this moving back into passagework, playing with short subphrases, and no significant points of rest until after the end of the chorus.

The final chorus of this solo largely recapitulates elements Coltrane has already played. The first A section has a clear pause at the end of m. 4, helping return the audience to the form of the song, but the section's second phrase, which starts in m. 5, crosses over the section break. The second A section, which Coltrane starts with the continuation of this phrase, has irregular phrase lengths, and very little reference to the song itself. The only moment in the section that articulates the underlying form of the head is a rise to an altissimo arpeggiation of the tonic chord in m. 8, giving a sense of arrival and rest (albeit slight) to the end

FIGURE 5.9. "Sweet and Lovely," John Coltrane's Solo, mm. 5–8 of Bridges, Double-Time Choruses

of the section. He pushes on strongly into the B section, this time transitioning to altogether regular phrasing—a four-measure phrase, followed by a two-measure phrase, and finally ending with two one-measure phrases—echoing the structure of the head. By this point the figure in m. 7 and 8 has the effect of a return to recognizable material, highlighting this spot's formal significance (Fig. 5.8). The last A section is one long phrase, a kind of drive to the end, which Coltrane signals with a stock arpeggiated melody that brings a sense of closure on the downbeat of the next chorus.

The most disjointed moment of the entire performance is the transition from the fast double time of Coltrane's solo back to the slow regular time of the closing head chorus. Solo endings are always somewhat fraught, and the transition between double time and regular feel can be disruptive, but when both happen along with a shift in the underlying tempo, there is the possibility that the whole performance could fall apart. In this case Coltrane helps by musically signaling the end of his solo in the last A section. He most likely also made a physical gesture, and the group could have decided the number of choruses for his solo in advance, quite possibly both. The overarching rhetoric of Coltrane's solo is a steady movement that gains intensity as it goes along by virtue of being sustained. Such a slow ratcheting up of energy, common in jazz solos, is not usually or obviously directed toward any specific end point—Coltrane could have played another chorus or two, or even more, before playing a final A section that implied closure—which means that the band has to sustain its energy along with the soloist up to the moment of the new chorus. Importantly, there is no point of transition. In this performance, it takes only a few beats for Monk, the rhythm section, and Coltrane to coalesce around the new tempo and feel for the final chorus, but those few moments are some of the most memorable in the concert. They are worth hearing because in a sense musical events like this are the stuff of jazz. They are the "surprises" in Whitney Balliet's classic description of jazz as "the sound of surprise" (1959).

Together "Bye-Ya" and "Sweet and Lovely" offered audiences two of Monk's three characteristic kinds of music: original composition in the Tin Pan Alley song tradition, and a standard drawn from that tradition. They made for a lighter set of pieces than those Monk chose for the first set, with more freedom, and more fire. For a midnight set, they would have been invigorating and exciting, showing a range of the band's abilities that had not yet been explored in the early set.

CHAPTER 6

Abiding Favorites
"Blue Monk" and
"Epistrophy"

THE MONK QUARTET's performance at Carnegie Hall that evening in November ended with a six-and-a-half minute performance of a blues staple from Monk's repertoire, "Blue Monk," and finally a version of his theme song, "Epistrophy" (which they had also played to end the first set). The two songs make a particularly fitting conclusion to a Monk concert—or to Monk's part of a star-packed concert such as this one. Together they are, along with "Round Midnight," among those he played the most, and they are two pieces it is reasonable to think he felt a particular, personal affection for. "Blue Monk" is one of his ur-blues, a piece that is at once distinctly in the traditions of blues he would have known from his youth, and at the same time clearly individualized, recognizably his own. It is so much so that he named it after himself, putting it in the category of explicitly self-identified pieces, along with "Monk's Dream" and "Monk's Mood." "Epistrophy" was undoubtedly the piece he played most often, inasmuch as he was in the habit of ending his sets with it and often included it on recordings to mark end points. Though not named in a way that calls out Monk's identity, the piece itself is suffused with Monk's characteristic economy of materials and overwhelming love of motivically unified melodies and hard-swinging grooves.

"BLUE MONK"

The last full piece from the second set on the Carnegie Hall concert recording is "Blue Monk." The band plays a version of the song that compares interestingly with earlier recordings of it by Monk in other settings and with other blues performances by Coltrane. Monk recorded "Blue Monk" more than ten times for major label sessions, and he was recorded playing it in concert at least that many times over the course of his career. He first included it on the trio sessions with Art Blakey and Percy Heath that were released on the album *Work* in 1954. According to Peter Keepnews, Monk may have composed it in the studio for that session, in response to Bob Weinstock's complaint that Monk "never played the blues" (Keepnews 2000, 23). He next included it on the May 1957 sessions with Art Blakey and the Jazz Messengers, where Monk first recorded with Johnny Griffin. Shortly after the Carnegie Hall concert, Monk hired Griffin as his regular tenor player and included "Blue Monk" on both of the live recordings they made in 1958. Set lists for Monk's regular performing are hard to come by, but he must have played "Blue Monk" with enormous regularity, since many of the informal recordings of live sets that are available also include the song.

Weinstock's complaint about Monk's limited use of blues seems odd, in retrospect. In fact, from today's vantage point Monk can be thought of as one of the midcentury jazz masters most engaged with the blues, and with a particularly "bluesy" sense of the blues form. And yet "Blue Monk" was only the third blues—of his or anyone else's—that Monk ever recorded (having recorded "Misterioso" and "Straight, No Chaser" for Blue Note in 1948 and 1951, respectively). The old saw that modern jazz somehow straightforwardly cut its ties with blues is largely discredited, but it does seem true, as David Ake argues more subtly, that "most New York–based bebop musicians consciously avoided traditional blues chord changes and stylistic devices" (2001, 49). Monk probably played blueslike pieces in his early experience touring with an evangelist, though it is unlikely that he played blues songs themselves, since gospel and blues were held by sanctified audiences in much of the midtwentieth century to be incompatible genres. He also may have played blues forms as house pianist at Minton's, although the eighteen songs captured on bootleg recordings from that period do not include a single blues. In a sense Monk appears to have come to a full embrace of the blues, like the New Jersey–born pianist Count Basie, largely as a mature musician (Ake 2001, 50).

Although Ake excepts Charlie Parker from the argument that "early bop players largely sought to distinguish themselves from the perceived backwardness of their Southern relatives," which the blues represented, I suggest that Monk is actually the clearest counterexample (2002, 49). Monk's blues songs tend to use the most straightforward, simplest blues progressions and have melodies that most clearly relate to those of the generations of blues performers (both "city" and "rural," to the extent that those terms are meaningful) who came to national attention in his youth. Moreover, his recordings of blues pieces give the impression that as much as his blues songs are individuated—"Blue Monk" is clearly different from "Straight, No Chaser" or "Bolivar Ba-Lues-Are"—they are all also iterations of a single basic form, in a way that his take on standards, or his composition of new pieces in standard song forms, is not (Solis 2008, 57–59).[1] This strikes me as a particularly "down home" attitude toward the blues, in comparison even with Parker's, whose blues tunes—"Blues for Alice," "Au Privave," "Billie's Bounce," and so on—typically include substitute changes that add complexity to the 4 x 4 x 4 measure blues form and have melodies that often do not point to the kind of riff-based or altered pentatonic forms common in blues as such.[2]

"Blue Monk" is more melodically distinctive than most of Monk's other, riff-based blues compositions. The piece is a blues in three clear sections, each four measures long, related in an aa'b pattern reminiscent of so-called "classic" blues.[3] Each section involves some transformation of a chromatic call-and-response melody introduced in the first four measures. The initial presentation of this melody has a classic arch shape, leading in parallel thirds from B♭ and D, the root and third of the tonic chord, up by chromatic steps to D and F, in the first measure. This melodic kernel is repeated, transposed up a fourth to imply the IV chord in the second measure. The third measure, the response, then descends back to the B♭–D interval, having introduced a low E♮, which stands outside the main register of melodic movement. The primary arch is complete at this point, and Monk adds a tail to this in m. 4, stepping down chromatically to A♭ and C, which provides a harmonic push to the IV7 chord in m. 5. The second four measures repeat this set of phrases, but with alterations to account for a new harmonic context. The first two measures both take place over a IV7, so rather than separate the two rising chromatic melodies in thirds by a whole step, the first starts on E♭ and G, and the second starts on the same pitches on which the first ended, G and B♭, so that the whole figure outlines the E♭7 chord, E♭–G–B♭–D♭. The following measures repeat the figure from mm. 2–3 but stop on the B♭–D interval. The final four measures, which are anticipated with an anacrusis figure in triplets at the end of m. 8, do not follow the same two-plus-two measure breakdown as the first two sections. Instead this section focuses for one measure on a static D–F pair in the main melodic voice, with a return to the lower register that differs from one version to another but focuses on an F and sometimes E♭, the root and seventh of the V7 chord that is common in this bar of the blues form in more rootsy blues traditions. Following this interjection, the melody picks up again in the main register with two iterations of the figure from mm. 2 and 3, the first starting on beat 1 of m. 10, and the second transformed by a metric shift to start on beat 2 of m. 11. This shift means that the second time the figure appears it turns the backbeat accent pattern around, creating a rhythmic clash at precisely the moment the chords cadence on the tonic. The melodic interrelation of the song's three sections is somewhat "down home," and its chord progression is even more so. Unlike with other modern jazz blues compositions—at least, unlike those from the 1940s and many from the 1950s—Monk uses a limited set of changes here (one per bar, at most), and no ii–V substitutions. The changes are more reminiscent of Bessie Smith's or Mississippi John Hurt's recordings from the 1920s than those of Monk's modern jazz contemporaries.

The performance on this concert is significantly different from Monk's previous recordings. First and foremost, although Monk often took "Blue Monk" at an excruciatingly slow tempo—so slow that it can be unnerving to listen to at times—here he counts it off at a refreshingly upbeat mid-tempo. The speed of this performance is good evidence of two things: first, of the fact that Monk had a flexible approach to tempo; and second, that the band grew comfortable with the material and with one another over months of regular gigging and Monk now trusted them, musically. As with this concert's performance of "Nutty," discussed above, here is a record of Monk playing a piece demonstrably faster than he often did. His reasons for taking "Blue Monk" at such a tempo on this night and not on previous recording sessions are more interesting, ultimately, than the simple fact that he does so. Robin Kelley describes the sessions that produced Monk's album with the Jazz Messengers, which included "Blue Monk" as notoriously beset with problems, and notes that the first day's takes of the piece were unusable, because the sidemen (saxophonist Johnny Griffin and trumpeter Bill Hardman) were uncomfortable with the tune. Monk's particularly slow tempo on the recording of "Blue Monk" from the second day was "a test of wills between himself and Blakey, whom he sometimes accused of pushing the tempo" (2009, 221). The previous recording, also with Art Blakey, was very slow, and if it is true that he wrote it in the studio that day, it would necessarily have been new to the band. None of these problems hinder the quartet at Carnegie Hall, which gives Monk the freedom to set any tempo he chooses.

The group plays through two statements of the head, as was common for Monk's blues performances at the time, but they play a somewhat unusual variant. Monk initiates this by playing the melody solo one time, as an introduction with a series of shifts to what is otherwise a regular, if syncopated, melody. The effect of the shifts is to even out the flow of short, moving notes and long, held notes. Monk plays the first two bars not as series of eighth notes and anticipated half notes, but rather as eight straight quarter notes. He then plays m. 3 in eighth notes as usual, but rather than holding the B♭–D interval as a syncopated quarter note he pushes through in consistent eighths until the A♭–C pair at the end of the tail, which he holds through the end of the fourth bar. Monk plays the second section as written, in contrast to the first section, although he cuts the last note short in order to play four eighth notes as a pickup to the third section, rather than three triplet eighths. Finally, he alters the last melodic subphrase of the introduction, syncopating the opening B♭–D interval of the melody in m. 11, giving it additional rhythmic bounce as he prepares for the head chorus.

The full band's statements of the head do not use Monk's rhythmic alterations from the introduction. Rather, they play a standard version of the tune both times until the end of the eighth bar of the chorus. In a somewhat unusual move, however, Coltrane plays the lower of the parallel parts throughout the first eight bars (that is, he starts the melody in m. 1 on B♭, rather than D). In its effect this is not a crucial difference, but it is noteworthy inasmuch as it was, at least judging by the recorded evidence, quite uncommon. Musically, highlighting the lower of the parallel lines this way strengthens the force of Monk's root movement in the harmonic scheme, since it means that in mm. 1 and 5 the first melody note in the saxophone is the root of the measure's chord, rather than its third. In the last four bars of each chorus, Monk and Coltrane disrupt the expected melodic flow by riffing on the figure from the end of m. 8 and m. 9, trading it back and forth (Fig. 6.9). Since this figure so strongly implies the V chord (which creates a sense of expectation for resolution in the listener), the effect is to suspend the sense of forward motion in time. The chorus is, in fact, still twelve bars long, but mm. 9 and 10 in the first chorus and 9–12 in the second seem to dissolve this regular time flow, momentarily.

FIGURE 6.1. "Blue Monk," John Coltrane and Thelonious Monk's Playing, mm. 9–12, First and Second Choruses

In the second chorus this allows the band to lead into Coltrane's solo without a clear punctuating end to the head.

Coltrane is the first soloist in this performance, and over a nearly three-minute, ten-chorus solo he interweaves ideas with his accompanists, suggesting a formal logic that coheres over time. The approach Coltrane uses works with three key parameters to structure the solo: regular versus irregular subdivision into phrases; alternation between rapid passagework and slower, melodic playing; and alternation between harmonic gestures that focus on consonances with the background harmony, particularly root tones, versus gestures that focus on harmonic dissonances. There are, on the largest scale, three sections to Coltrane's solo, each increasingly compact. The first section covers the first half of the solo, reaching a climax in choruses 4 and 5, and coming to a point of repose at the end of the fifth chorus. The second section, choruses 6 through 8, is both shorter and more intense than the first section, coming to the briefest of points of rest in m. 12 of the eighth chorus. Finally,

Coltrane plays a two-chorus section, which he uses to introduce a final set of climactic gestures and then signal a brief denouement.

The first section of the solo begins with largely sixteenth-note passagework and regular use of the tonic pitch, moving to a climax that comes in a burst of more melodic playing marked by longer notes in choruses 4 and 5 (Fig. 6.2). In the first chorus Coltrane sets the listener up to think in terms of relatively long time spans, making it comfortable to listen through the end of the fifth chorus as one long section. He does this in three ways: first by using little other than sixteenth-note figuration, second by avoiding regular four-measure subdivisions, and finally by carrying his phrasing over into the second chorus. The sixteenth notes provide long stretches without rhythmic stasis, and the irregular subdivision orients the ear to listen across the background harmony's short time structure to longer periods. Carrying the phrasing over the first chorus break immediately implies a form not defined by the short, twelve-bar structure; it is a gesture that indicates the potential of the solo being (as it is) relatively long. This section focuses substantially on the tonic note in the context of the B♭ Mixolydian scale over every I7 chord, and on E♭ in the context of its Mixolydian scale over the IV chords, which I hear as a way of producing a relative absence of harmonic tension. Since the alternation between dissonance and consonance is a common feature of jazz form, the opening focus on the tonic—the most consonant, "root-ed" tone of the piece—sets in place the expectation of listening over a relatively long time span for structural shifts from consonance to dissonance, and back.

The second and third choruses provide some contrast with Coltrane's first chorus, in terms of phrase structure, but continue to use primarily fast passagework, and to highlight harmonic consonance. Most notably, Coltrane subdivides both choruses into four-measure sections, in line with the blues form and more specifically the structure of the head. Shadow Wilson seems to recognize and support the more regular phrasing in these two choruses, playing substantial fills at the end of each chorus (Fig. 6.3). The second chorus continues to highlight the B♭ at the beginning, providing continuity with the first chorus. In the third chorus, Coltrane continues to use the B♭ Mixolydian scale with regular recurrences of the tonic pitch, but unlike with the first two choruses he does not come to rest on the B♭ at the beginning. Instead he builds through rapid passagework in mm. 1–8, pausing on B♭ in m. 9 where he uses it to emphasize the harmonic shift and then resumes the passagework, driving to a climactic B♭ in two octaves at the very end of the chorus, underscored by Wilson's drum fill. He then builds on this small climax by starting the fourth chorus with his first altissimo register playing, and with a more

FIGURE 6.2. "Blue Monk," John Coltrane's Solo, First Chorus, Including m. 1, Second Chorus

FIGURE 6.3. "Blue Monk," John Coltrane's Solo, Third Chorus, with Shadow Wilson's Fill in m. 12

FIGURE 6.4. "Blue Monk," John Coltrane's Solo, mm. 1–4 of Fourth and Fifth Choruses

melodic, prototypically bluesy passage. The rest of the chorus returns to sixteenth-note figuration, which carries over with no significant break at the end of the chorus (Fig. 6.4). Chorus 5 then repeats the basic structure of the fourth chorus, with bluesy melodic work at the beginning and a return to sixteenth-note figures from m. 5 through the end. The blues connotations of the two choruses are not motivically linked, but they share elements. In part it is Coltrane's use of slower passages in triplet eighth notes that links these two choruses together and makes them bluesy, and in part it is his use of an alternation between D♭ and D, the "blue" third of the B♭ dominant 7 chord. Coltrane concludes the section of the solo fairly decisively, coming to a strong break in m. 12 of the fifth chorus.

The second section of the solo begins in the sixth chorus and ratchets up the overall sense of intensity, a move that Coltrane nicely prepared with the long, steady buildup over the course of the first section. He immediately projects raised intensity in this section through structural harmonic dissonance, where the first section focused on structural consonance. The section's first chorus (number six) begins, after a pickup in the turnaround of chorus 5, with a series of sixteenth-note patterns that highlight C♮, the ninth of the pervading B♭ harmony, rather than the tonic pitch. This focus on dissonant chord extensions continues when, in m. 9, Coltrane holds a

D♮. The held note focusing attention on this spot is in line with Monk's approach to blues, in which m. 9 is the first appearance of the V7 chord, and therefore the point of maximal formal tension. Abdul-Malik's bass lines generally projected a V chord in m. 9 of each chorus, so it is best to hear this D♮ as a thirteenth against an F7 chord. Coltrane then returns to sixteenth-note passagework, which he carries over the end of the chorus, helping provide a sense of formal connection to the section. The second chorus of the section (number seven) has a less regular phrase structure than the previous chorus, as Coltrane largely erases the break from m. 4 into 5. He once again highlights C♮, particularly in mm. 2 and 3, creating continuity within this section of the solo. A descending figure in mm. 7 and 8 is striking and becomes motivic when he repeats it in the following chorus, again producing continuity within the section. After a long held F in m. 12, which serves as a transition into the third chorus of this section, Coltrane plays the most metrically complex material of the entire solo, creating another climax at the end of this section. Measures 1–4 and 9–11 of the chorus in particular are metrically unstable in comparison with the more straightforward sixteenth-note patterns Coltrane has used throughout the rest of the piece (Fig. 6.5). This climax leads to a moment of stability in m. 12, to mark the end of the section, as Coltrane lands on an F, the root of the V7 chord that serves as a turnaround in this measure.

FIGURE 6.5. "Blue Monk," John Coltrane's Solo, mm. 1–4 of Sixth and Seventh Choruses

The final section of the solo is the shortest, and the least like the first two, which shared a number of elements. Coltrane backs away from the peak of intensity in the previous section, grows to one last climax, and then prepares the way for Monk's solo. The opening gesture of the section, in mm. 1–4 of the first chorus, are unlike anything Coltrane has played up to this point in the solo. The measure-long riffs he plays here, which focus once again on the roots and sevenths of the chords (B♭, E♭, B♭, and B♭, respectively), reduce the level of intensity and prepare listeners for the end of the solo by returning not just to consonance but to root tones, and by reorienting the ear to short gestures that reinforce the background form, rather than cutting against it. Coltrane moves from this figure to new sixteenth-note passagework for the rest of the first chorus, steadily building up steam into the last chorus of the solo. The final chorus chugs along in primarily sixteenth-note figures, until the end of m. 10, at which point the phrase Coltrane has built reaches a final climax (Fig. 6.6). Having reached this point, he puts a period at the end of his solo, so to speak, playing stock blues phrases that signal ending in part by their return to the tonic, and in part by working their way gradually down from the top to the middle of the tenor saxophone's range.

Coltrane worked extensively with the blues form—and, of course, wrote a fair number of blues heads—and in a way his approach to the blues fit well with Monk's. As Lewis Porter says, "he usually liked a very down-home approach to the blues," and although his approach by the 1960s may have been "distinctive and nontraditional," it was still "powerful and basic in emotional impact" (2000, 116; 190). Perhaps the most important similarity to Monk's approach is that Coltrane tended to favor blues chord progressions without the ii–V substitutions that became common in bebop in the 1940s. Unlike Monk, who tended to write and

FIGURE 6.6.   "Blue Monk," John Coltrane's Solo, Ninth Chorus, mm. 1–4

play major-key blues, Coltrane was partial to minor blues, as can be heard in such pieces as "Blue Train" and "Equinox," among others. It is not hard to find blues recordings by Coltrane from around this time; he was quite busy, mostly as a sideman. In fact, "Blue Train" was recorded just about two months before the Carnegie Hall concert and "Bass Blues," which was released on the album *Traneing In*, about a month before that. Interestingly, aside from a certain sameness of harmonic and rhythmic language, "Blue Monk" is notably different from these two. He does remain down-home in a sense, with Monk, but he is if anything even more down-home in the other settings. The solos on "Blue Train" and "Bass Blues" show Coltrane playing more formulaic material, and material that more clearly references typical blues phrases. By contrast, in a later recording, like "Equinox," as Porter notes, Coltrane seems to be thinking more about the specificity of particular blues pieces, as he appears to be with Monk. Moreover, at least on "Equinox" Coltrane shows a level of attention to the shape of the solo as a whole—building gradually in both range and intensity to a climax in the ninth of his ten choruses (185–88). Porter describes how this puts Coltrane within the tradition, inasmuch as "many jazz artists liked to increase the intensity at the start of each succeeding chorus of a blues," but it also shows the impact of particular artists he worked with, notably Monk and Miles Davis (185).

Monk plays accompaniment parts throughout Coltrane's solo, in a way that was somewhat unusual for him at the time. Rather than get up from the piano, or simply lay out while Coltrane played the middle four or five choruses, Monk remains engaged, comping more or less actively the whole time (Fig. 6.7). His level of activity can be tied directly to Coltrane's formal logic, outlined above, but it becomes most notable in the final section. At the beginning of the ninth chorus, when Coltrane plays little motives that highlight the chord roots, Monk responds with chord hits that reinforce Coltrane's idea. As Coltrane raises the energy in the end of the ninth chorus and through the tenth, Monk plays his most active material of the whole solo, an intensely dissonant figure in sixteenth notes that bears at least a passing resemblance to the melody of his blues composition "Raise Four" (a reference to the figure's tritone melody). Monk carries this figure through bar 10 of the final chorus of Coltrane's solo, transposing it to fit the chord changes, and then he rests during mm. 11 and 12 of the solo as Coltrane plays his ending tag, creating some sonic space before he reenters as the soloist in the following chorus.

Monk treated "Blue Monk" as he often did blues tunes, working with each chorus as a self-contained block, and building a form out of the

FIGURE 6.7. "Blue Monk," Thelonious Monk's Comping, 3:31–3:47

relationship between those blocks. Over five choruses, his ideas span a fairly broad range, from stock phrases he used elsewhere, and a single dissonant interval, jabbed at in rhythmically odd moments, to licks borrowed from the head, and brief flourishes of passagework. Those five choruses follow a single trajectory, growing in tension through the first three, hitting a climactic point in the fourth, and then rounding out the form with a concluding fifth chorus. As in a number of Monk's solos—notably his long solo on "Bags' Groove," with Miles Davis and Milt Jackson from 1954—Monk appends a final chorus after the main multichorus form of his solo. At times it can be hard to know precisely what Monk intends with this sort of chorus, but in this case it is best heard as a transition chorus, from the solos back to the head. This sits well with a general understanding of Monk's penchant for transitional bits; he almost always played introductions to his pieces, and his solos routinely incorporate transitional moments, as palate cleansers between the previous solo and his own. Stand-alone choruses such as the sixth one in this solo similarly serve to transition from his solo to whatever comes next, either another solo or in this case the return of the head.

The five-chorus form Monk works out begins with a transitional opening chorus that uses primarily single-note melody lines. The material for this chorus is nondescript in a sense, inasmuch as it uses neither distinctly motivic material nor stock Monk formulas. Indeed, the generic, noodling quality of the melody here is responsible for creating the sense of transition. Monk breaks this chorus quite clearly into three four-measure sections, though he does not use the aa'b phrase patterning common to blues and characteristic of the head. Instead, each of the three sections has new material that flows primarily in eighth notes. A signal that the transitional phase is ending comes in m. 11 and the beginning of 12, when Monk plays a rising figure in parallel thirds, C♯–D and A–B♭, which is a clear reference to the head melody's closing figure. Monk moves into a second chorus, which begins building to the solo's climax (Fig. 6.8). He uses material that is similar to the first chorus but now more motivic in its melodic construction. The starting point for this chorus is a short, arch-shaped motive that outlines the root, fifth, and seventh of the B♭ chord in the first measure. The motive in its first iteration is one and a half measures long, which means that when he plays it a second time it is metrically shifted by two beats. In its second iteration Monk extends the motive to a full two measures, by keeping the same basic trajectory—from F up to C and down to A♭—but filling in more notes between these outer points. The third version of the motive, now foreshortened, ends with a C on the downbeat of m. 5, the start of the second section. Monk starts the second section (the a' phrase) with a version of the same motive, but now rather than making it arch-shaped he follows a pattern established with the third version, though using only the opening, rising line. Rather than stop at C, however, Monk expands the motive registrally, rising to an A♮ (or B♭♭), the flat fifth of the E♭7 chord in m. 6. This rise sets up a longer descending passage that ends the section, making it one large arch instead of a sequence of smaller ones. The final section returns to the higher register, and Monk plays a series of descending figures, ultimately playing one

FIGURE 6.8. "Blue Monk," Thelonious Monk's Solo, Second Chorus, mm. 1–5

long descent to return to the pitch level of the opening motive, and closing with a figure that aims at the tonic pitch, B♭.

The third chorus shifts away from the type of material that characterizes the first two choruses, into much less active melodic material, using longer time spans and a sense of melodic stasis to build tension. Monk begins with a rising fourth that is reminiscent of the opening figure in "Bemsha Swing," but then he continues into a two-note melody focusing on an A♮/B♭ pair, which is quite similar to the melody of "Thelonious." Monk uses this figure in irregular subphrase lengths, largely effacing the four-measure sectioning that characterized the previous choruses, but subtly marking the form with a rise to E♮ in mm. 8 and 12. The tension that built up over the third chorus—a kind of "potential energy" rising from the repetition of a static but dissonant motive—is released as kinetic energy in the climactic fourth chorus. Here Monk uses the comping figure he introduced in choruses 9 and 10 of Coltrane's solo as a melodic motive. In this chorus, Monk once again clearly subdivides into four-measure phrases, using a modified aa'b pattern (Fig. 6.9). The comping motive dominates the first four measures, and Monk uses it as the start to the a' section. He finishes the a' by moving away from it, using a whole-tone descending line. The b section connects to a' by starting with descending whole-tone material, and it ends with a striking gesture in whole notes in mm. 10–12, F–F–B♭ in the low register in octaves. The figure clearly orients the ear to a V–I cadence and suggests weight and gravity, but it also ties into one of the more iconic blues riffs, as a profoundly abstracted version of the rising fourth in Duke Ellington's

FIGURE 6.9. "Blue Monk," Thelonious Monk's Solo, Fourth Chorus

ABIDING FAVORITES

"C-Jam Blues." The fifth chorus completes the basic formal logic, as Monk provides a release from the climax of the fourth chorus and then a small push into the beginning of the next section. Here Monk obscures the four-measure subdivisions of the blues form, playing single-note melodies in mm. 1 and 2, followed by a gesture in parallel thirds that implies a relationship to the head in mm. 3–7, and rests in m. 8. In the last four bars, Monk once again strongly articulates the blues form, using the riff from his third chorus, with Fs in the bass for the entire four measures. This pedal tone creates an extended V, which, combined with the implication of odd meter in the top voice and increasingly active drumming by Wilson, builds tension that is finally released on the downbeat of the next chorus.

In the sixth, transitional, chorus Monk plays the head, this time as he played it in the introduction, with the opening figure in quarter notes and including the full melody of the last four bars. The relationship to the introduction may be obscured by the fact that this time he plays it with the band, rather than solo (since it is now serving as a transition between parts, rather than an introduction), but the key differences between his interpretation of the melody in this chorus and the head choruses that come afterward are unmistakable. After the transition, Coltrane enters for two final iterations of the head as a double out chorus. Once again he plays the lower of the parallel melody lines, and once again he and Monk trade off iterations of the melody from m. 9 instead of completing the tune. The concluding quality of these two choruses is amplified by Shadow Wilson's significantly increased use of the crash cymbal, which builds energy, and by Monk's more and more dissonant response figures in mm. 9–12 of the final chorus, which create a last climax for the end of the piece.

"EPISTROPHY"

Finally, both sets end with short versions of "Epistrophy," Monk's theme song. Only the first time is represented in its complete form on the album, but enough of both is there to say that the two versions differ. The most interesting question about these performances is how they place Monk within the models of artistry and entertainment in the jazz world at the time. Having a theme song, a musical nametag, in a sense, that the group plays at the end of most sets—not just on this night—would be normal for a pop swing band but is frankly a peculiar affectation for a modern jazz combo. In fact, "Epistrophy" has been the theme song not only for Monk but in at least two other contexts. It is one of Monk's earliest compositions, co-credited to Kenny Clarke, with whom Monk worked in the house band at Minton's, and the piece served as a theme song for that band.[4] According to Eddie "Lockjaw" Davis, it was also as a theme song for Cootie Williams's band in the early 1940s (Montgomery 1983, 14, cited in Ramsey 2003, 228 n. 49).

    What makes "Epistrophy" so compelling as a tune that Monk, Cootie Williams, and the assembled young modern jazz greats-to-be at Minton's treat it this way? Guthrie Ramsey, Jr., focuses on its potential as a medium for a paradigmatic Afro-Modern gesture in *Race Music*. In essence, it is possible to arrange the tune, which he describes as "an eccentric composition" that "seem[s] to satirize popular song, common-practice classical music, and the jazz tradition," in such a way as to highlight the contrast between materials (dissonant, modern, edgy) and performance (swinging, in the pocket; Ramsey 2003, 71). Ramsey's cogent interpretation makes particularly good sense of the Williams band's adoption of the song, but I would point to further elements of the piece that made it a clear choice for Monk and the crowd at Minton's, particularly as a piece to use to end live shows (as opposed to recordings). Ramsey rightly concentrates his analysis on the motivic repetitiveness of "Epistrophy," and the strangeness of its harmonic language—its use of dominant seventh chords a half-step apart in each measure of the A section—and what he calls its "seamless, 'looping around' quality" (71). However, as he says, the Williams band (with the exception of Joe Guy) largely ignores these elements, instead writing new background riffs for the band to play while Williams and other band members play "solid and expressive" solos (72).

    I do not necessarily hear "Epistrophy" as "satirical," in the way Ramsey does, but even though it is in a thirty-two-bar AABA form it certainly avoids the lyricism and functional, end-directed harmony of most standards. I think of it instead as a cyclical, riff-driven piece, ideally suited to open-ended, vamplike performances that build energy and can be extended or foreshortened in response to the energy in a room. In this sense, it is very much like certain swing showpieces, such as "Jumpin' at the Woodside" or "Sing, Sing, Sing (with a Swing)." The harmonic language of the A section in particular seems calculated to do little more than ratchet up energy. Half-step root movement between chords, such as characterizes this section, has essentially no tonal function, but it provides a churning sense of movement on the surface of an underlying harmonic stasis. It would become a common device in funk in particular, somewhat later, for precisely this reason; it builds energy without requiring that energy to have a particular trajectory or to be directed toward a particular goal. The harmonic move between mm. 4 and 5, transposition up a step, is similarly nonfunctional in common practice harmony, and yet commonplace in American popular music. It may not signal a tonal harmonic progression, but it does build intensity, primarily by virtue of making everything higher and concomitantly brighter. In pop music it is common to use this to highlight the last chorus of a song, but here Monk builds it into the piece's form. The large-scale inversion of this process, which comes from starting the second A section on E♭7–E7 and returning to D♭7–D7 in m. 5, does not so much satisfy long-term harmonic goals as reinforce the nonfunctional, stepwise logic of the harmony of the piece. The bridge, which presents a contrast with the A section by using more melodic, arch-shaped phrases, implies E major tonality, through a six-measure ii–V progression (four measures of F♯min7 followed by two measures of B7), but undercuts that implication by returning to D♭7 in m. 7 and D7 in m. 8. This move means that Monk recapitulates, in miniature, the D♭/D–E♭/E–D♭/D arc of the first two A sections to finish the piece. Since Monk routinely ends performances of "Epistrophy" with a G♭7 flat 5 chord, it is possible to hear the entire piece as a prolongation of D♭7 as V of G♭, with the G♭7 chord used as I, in the same way dominant seventh chords routinely serve as tonic harmonies in blues.

On the concert at Carnegie Hall, how Monk and the band play "Epistrophy" highlights its use as an energy builder, and going out on a high note. In the first set's version, the most important element is Shadow Wilson's shimmering ride cymbal patterns. Rather than play a standard time pattern, in the A sections Wilson plays a pattern in sixteenth notes, starting on the second half of beat 4, which is a key point of rest in the melody. Not only that, but for the only time on the set he plays on the center cone of the cymbal, rather than its rim, creating an exceptionally bright, bell-like sound. At the end of the second set the band plays "Epistrophy" even faster than it did the first time, and Wilson transforms the pattern he played during the first set into a less predictable, but still sixteenth-note-based mini-solo. Both times Coltrane solos in a way that anticipates his modal work, playing extended scalar passages over the static-yet-moving chords of the A sections. The band ends the first set's version with a substantially ornamented G♭7-flat 5 chord, and one has to assume they do the same for the second set, since the tape runs out, and the recording ends precipitously as Monk begins his solo.

With that the Thelonious Monk Quartet with John Coltrane finished their second set of the evening. That night was probably quite similar to other evenings the band had played together, in terms of repertoire and general sound concept. It was very, very good, but perhaps not better than some other nights. For a band that was playing together day in and day out, week after week, over the course of months there would have been lots of good nights, if also a few off ones. This one may have been exceptionally good, though, given the excitement of playing in Carnegie Hall, for a large and, by the sounds of it, appreciative audience, and knowing that it was being recorded for Voice of America's broadcast later on. Yet, as we know, Voice of America never did broadcast the concert, and instead the tapes sat on a shelf, gathering dust. That would have been the end of the story of this marvelous evening's concert, were it not for a Library of Congress archivist who happened upon a plain, manila folder containing the tapes nearly half a century later. The eventual release of the concert recording is in some ways a separate story, the subject of the next, and final, chapter.

CHAPTER 7

Together at Last, Together Forever
Monk and Coltrane on Record in 2005

THE ALBUM *THELONIOUS Monk Quartet with John Coltrane at Carnegie Hall* is, ultimately, more than the sounds of Monk, Coltrane, Abdul-Malik, and Wilson playing together, and more than a document of a concert in 1957. It is also, significantly, a recording released in 2005, circulating as part of the contemporary jazz scene. Unlike the moment of its creation, when Monk and Coltrane were playing six nights a week at the Five Spot, a small club, and when both toured regularly, in 2005 this recording had the value of scarcity. Moreover, as a "new release" from 1957, rather than repackaged, repurposed, reissued material, the album was really exceptional and much appreciated. It represents not only a bit of music by a band that was not otherwise substantially documented but also a window onto a time past, which has come to be seen as a golden age, with fewer surviving musicians every year. For this reason, as much as for the music itself, the album was greeted with great critical acclaim, finding its way into the American national and international media and topping most critics' "album of the year" lists.

This chapter situates the Carnegie Hall recording in its contexts, in the mid-2000s, to draw out what the changing shape of jazz over the last half century can tell us about the recording as a cultural artifact and what the artifact can tell us about its time. I look at the critical reception of the album to try to unearth responses to it in 2005, and then I consider it in relation to three aspects of contemporary jazz reception and production, to answer the big question: What does the presence of a historical recording at the top of critics' lists and sales charts mean for jazz in the 2000s? Is it a sign of lifelessness, of an unhealthy fixation on the past, or something more positive?

The heralding of the death of jazz is routine, and routinely spurious, used as a pretext to some other argument about the present and future of jazz, and yet it bears some attention in this context, if only because the success of albums like this one relates directly to such arguments.[1] Both Stuart Nicholson and Geoff Dyer have put forward strong cases that "Jazz," meaning "an American mainstream that dominates current jazz practice," is indeed dead (or no longer a site of important or creative new music); but that "jazz," meaning music that keeps its "lines of input open to appropriate whatever is around [it] today," is alive (Nicholson 2005, x–xi). Nicholson proposes that the living art has moved to Europe, where it is supported by government subsidy, and Dyer, writing rapturously about the avant-ambient trio the Necks tendentiously offers that "the new frontier of jazz is being forged in Australia" (Dyer 2011, 261).

Both authors' work is so full of unsupported claims and questionable argument as to hardly justify an extensive critique here; Nicholson, for instance, bases his whole proposition on the ludicrous Adornian grounds that "art and commerce seldom mix" (xi), and Dyer generalizes grandly about the future of jazz from the thinnest possible evidence. Yet the fundamental point they both rest on, summed up by Dyer in the pithy sound bite "jazz is history," points directly toward this album (2011, 254). As he says, "some of the best new jazz releases are actually old releases remastered and repackaged. Specialist publications aside, the only place where jazz commands extensive media attention is on the obituary pages, when living legends die" (ibid.). The life of the Carnegie Hall concert recording suggests otherwise, making this view of the relationship between past, present, and future, or between history and innovation, and between life and death in jazz seem intellectually lazy, at best.

To offer a vision of what this recording means, I start by expanding from the critical reception of the album to the larger discursive terrain that has characterized recent discussions of jazz's relationship to its own past, looking at the Carnegie Hall recording as a locus for the production of nostalgia. I then move to an analysis of two more concrete aspects of the contemporary jazz scene that supported the album's production, sales, and absorption in the early twenty-first century: first, the structure of the jazz recording industry and the Blue Note label's place in it, and second, the growing importance of the academy to the institutionalization of jazz. On the basis of these somewhat disparate elements, I propose that even though the relative lack of support for jazz recordings in the larger music industry may be unsettling to fans, and the anomalous success of this one recording may highlight the challenges jazz artists face in the new century, nevertheless this album is not a sign of a music whose best years are behind it. Rather, it signifies a mature, culturally enshrined music for which an interest in the past actually provides continuity between the current era and a historical legacy.

CRITICS' RESPONSES

If this recording had been released by Riverside in the 1950s, it would likely have been successful, both critically and economically, but it would have been a much smaller event with a notably shorter reach than was the case in 2005. Monk's recordings from the time were consistently well received by the jazz press, and he was successful enough that Columbia signed him to a major contract with mass distribution shortly thereafter.[2] In England Humphrey Lyttleton was writing about Monk as a "genius in a straw hat," and in the United States Nat Hentoff published a seminal article in *Down Beat*, arguing that despite his "enigmatic" qualities Monk was "a key figure in [jazz] development" (Lyttleton 1959, 13; Hentoff 1956, 15). The *Jazz Review* called *In Orbit*, with Clark Terry, "friendly" and "agreeable," noting however that "it may go undervalued" for these features (Coulter 1959, 37). Still, Monk was not at all universally lionized at the time. One reviewer, writing about an EP release of his trio recordings in 1955, noted the ambivalence in the air about Monk: "You never know how Monk is going to affect people," he wrote. "Modernists (of whom he is, to me, one of the most distinguished) sometimes fail to appreciate the logic and character of his hard, stark, yet entertaining harmonic and melodic conceptions. Traditionalists (who could be pardoned for not appreciating anyone so 'far out') have frequently told me how much they like him!" ("Thelonious Monk Trio" 1955, 16). Jack McKinney, writing in *Metronome* in 1959, observed a similar dynamic, saying, "Thelonious Monk is a musician who is either sworn by or at. He more than any other jazz musician...defies apathy. Many fans consider him a paramount voice, with a basic, rooted appeal that lies at the center of jazz. Others compare him and his group to a caterwaul...pointing out that his music is devoid of beauty, and churns ahead on one stark, turbid level, without subtlety or change" (McKinney, 1959, 21).

Even if Monk was mostly praised by the critics, he was discussed only in the fairly limited-circulation jazz press. *Down Beat* had the largest reach of any of the publications taking note of Monk's career and recordings in the late 1950s, but even its twenty thousand annual subscription was enough to make it only a successful niche magazine (Gennari 2006, 174). *The Jazz Review* published for just four years, and *Metronome* survived as a countercultural, beatnik culture outlet in the late 1950s solely because of the substantial personal investment of the family of the editor, Herb Snitzer. By the end of 1960 the family's support had dwindled and the magazine went out of print (Gennari 2006, 174). Monk would come to be covered more broadly in much more mainstream publications—famously on the cover of *Time* magazine (which by then had circulation that could be measured in the hundreds of thousands)—but not until the 1960s.

By contrast, the coverage of the Carnegie Hall recording when it was released in 2005 was extensive—and exclusively, overwhelmingly positive. Moreover, unlike Monk's work in the 1950s, this recording was covered not only in the jazz press—*Down Beat, Jazz Times, Jazziz*, and others all covered it, of course—but also in the mainstream media. National Public Radio (NPR) was particularly important in this process, as noted by Alan S. Bergman, then general counsel for the International Association of Jazz Educators, legal representation for the Monk estate, regular columnist on music and the law for *Down Beat*, and sometime drummer (2006). Terry Gross featured it on *Fresh Air*, with a review by Kevin Whitehead; *All Things Considered*, NPR's afternoon "news magazine," ran a story and review by Robert Siegel; and *News and Notes* carried an eight-minute piece by Roy Hurst.

The NPR pieces seemed to compete with one another to find praise sufficient to capture the importance of the discovery. "For the hardcore jazz fan, the tapes are something of a Holy Grail," said Hurst. The reviews generally agree on this point, calling the Monk/Coltrane band "one of the most important collaborations in all of jazz history" (Hurst 2005, 0:42). Whitehead noted that the Monk/Coltrane collaboration is familiar-sounding because it is similar in tone to what had been available to that point; but he describes Coltrane as more "happy" and "enthusiastic" than he sounds on any of the other recordings of this group. Whitehead closes his review with a perfect nod to the emotion this recording encouraged. Noting the rest of the bill on the Carnegie Hall concert, and the ticket price, he says, "Now you know what Steve Lacy meant when he spoke of New York in the '50s as 'paradise'" (Whitehead 2005, 5:58).

Coverage on NPR is indicative of the potential audience for this recording in 2005, and it may be compared with the potential audience in 1957. In 2005 NPR was a significant presence in American culture at large, boasting a weekly listenership of nearly twenty million people.[3] This, compared with *Down Beat's* readership in the tens of thousands in the mid-1950s, is striking, but the demographics of NPR's listenership are also interesting. The jazz audience base in the 1950s was still primarily young and perhaps bohemian, but it appears that the potential interest base for this recording in 2005 was not. NPR's audience at the time was disproportionately old—its average listener was fifty, while the median age of all Americans was thirty-six—and its audience was disproportionately well-to-do, earning $78,000 per year, well above the $46,000 national average.

Alan Bergman said of NPR's attention, "[it] immediately translated to a jump to number one on the Amazon chart where [the album] stayed for over a week. That's not the jazz album chart, where it was also number one," he continued, "but the pop album chart, outselling artists like Neil Young, Barbara Streisand, the Rolling Stones, Paul McCartney, and Sheryl Crow" (Bergman 2006, C31). Amazon's rankings are notoriously opaque—the company does not share its logarithm for determining sales rank—and it is nearly impossible to check the statistics for historical Amazon sales ranks, but even so, rising to number one in the pop album ranking suggests substantial success of a sort uncommon for instrumental jazz recordings in the 2000s. The artists Bergman highlights for comparison are particularly interesting, inasmuch as they all suggest a mature, largely white audience. The album also did well on *Billboard's* jazz charts, ending number eight for the year, on a list dominated by recordings of the era's crooners—two each by Harry Connick, Jr., and Diana Krall, and one each by Michael Bublé, Madeleine Peyroux, and Paul Anka—but it was not competitive with that year's pop hits, even in the album category. The sales figures for the album, which are not publicly available, were substantial. New jazz releases—even those by major figures such as Wynton Marsalis and Joe Lovano—are considered successful if they sell in the low tens of thousands, and this album has sold in the mid-hundreds of thousands, according to Blue Note's marketing department, literally an order of magnitude more. If its sales figures were small compared with major pop hits of the time, nevertheless it is quite likely that the Carnegie Hall concert was the top-selling new instrumental jazz release of the decade.

NPR was undoubtedly important, but it was not the only outlet to lavish such attention on the recording. A number of sources that did not traditionally cover jazz at the time produced pieces on this album, largely because of the novelty element of its archival discovery. CBS's morning show, for instance, aired a segment on the recording, and *Mother Jones* ran an encomiastic review (Young 2005). The jazz press also embraced the recording, with review after review noting the remarkable rapport between the players, picking out Wilson's unheralded mastery, and praising the excellent sound quality, particularly for a recording made in situ in the late 1950s (Ansell 2006; Cohen 2005; Corbett 2005; Medwin 2006). John Corbett, writing in *Down Beat*, began his review "Believe the hype" and called the album "an unearthing of such historic proportions as to constitute a major discovery" (2005, 65). Larry Blumenfeld capped off a review in *Jazziz* that called the album "a prize," with this advice: "My wife says that people shouldn't hold on to things; they should throw stuff away. I think not" (2005, 50).

Ben Ratliff's review of the album in the *New York Times* is among the most interesting of the discussions of the album from the year of its release. It goes beyond a simple statement of praise for the CD, engaging directly in the fundamental "golden era" discourse that surrounds not only this performance but discussions of the postwar era in the jazz community at large. The review begins with the ironic hook, "My favorite jazz record released this year, and one of my favorites of any year, was made in 1957" (2005, 1). After getting through the details of the recording and the circumstances of its release, Ratliff introduces a discussion of the much-heralded death of jazz. "There's a reason why these records stand out as the year's best," he says, "and I get the sense that many people feel they know the reason" (ibid.). He uses the idea that many feel Coltrane broke the mold, so to speak, leaving jazz "crinkled up and collapsed" in his wake, as a straw man, and pivots from it to a truly interesting argument about the importance of liveness in jazz, and in particular of long-standing engagements where working bands can get a feel for each other and engage in a reciprocal connection with audiences. Because of this, he says, "in jazz there is always the promise that the art's greatest examples—even by those long dead—may still be found" (ibid.). The irony is that although Ratliff rejects the simple argument that Coltrane was the last great jazz artist, he still sets this recording in a nostalgic view of a past that is always just on the edge of being lost to memory. Ratliff describes the 1950s and 1960s in New York as "a different time in many ways: it seems that anytime I meet someone who saw [Monk's band at the Five Spot in 1957 or Coltrane's band at the Half Note in 1964–65] they won't say they went once, as if to cross it off a list; they went twice or three times a week, as part of their lives. (No Internet. No TiVo. Cheap rent. No risk of being thought a loser if you liked to go to jazz clubs at night)" (ibid.).

NOSTALGIA

By the time the Carnegie Hall recording was released, jazz musicians had been wrestling with the question of how to deal with the growing weight of the music's past for at least twenty-five years. Wynton Marsalis came to be the figure most profoundly linked to "neoclassicism," which was a handy gloss for both the growth of repertory bands and a return to small-group acoustic jazz and the musical language of hard bop in the 1980s and 1990s, but as *Zeitgeist* historicism went much deeper. With musicians as distinct from Marsalis as the World Sax Quartet and the Art Ensemble of Chicago releasing projects exploring historical repertory, and with university jazz programs educating the new generation of musicians in unprecedented numbers, the historical canon came to be increasingly central to future development in the music.

I have written elsewhere about how memory came to dominate the discourses and practices of the jazz scene in the 1980s and 1990s, and David Ake has recently followed up on this thread, specifically exploring the prevalence and role of nostalgia in the racialization of jazz at the end of the twentieth century (Solis 2008; Ake 2010, 85–86, 99–101). I do not see all jazz memorial practice as nostalgia, but I agree with Ake that nostalgia was a normative mode for jazz journalism and for shaping jazz recordings in the past decade. Blue Note's activity and the release of the Carnegie Hall concert are paradigmatic in this regard. In fact, the label was a valuable asset to EMI precisely because of its past, having a cachet in the historical canon of jazz that few other active record companies could match. It had been a truly independent label in its heyday, developing a recognizable sound, and at least as importantly it had one of the most compelling graphic design looks in the history of American commerce. Blue Note's strong brand identity intimately tied it to the 1950s, a time that has come to be seen in retrospect as prelapsarian, the peak of popularity for modern jazz and the last glimpse of something like a unified musical language. Nostalgia is by no means the only explanation for the revival of Blue Note, nor for the success of the Carnegie Hall concert recording, but it has been undeniably important.

In all its many guises, nostalgia was a profound marketing tool for jazz in the 1990s and 2000s, as well as a source of no small amount of musical inspiration. Most visibly, the Lincoln Center jazz programs built significantly on the sense of a lost past. In the wake of these programs, and largely with the creative consultation of Jazz at Lincoln Center's guiding figures, Wynton Marsalis and Stanley Crouch, Ken Burns's *Jazz* documentary defined it as a historically minded art whose best years were most likely behind it, with the possible exception of Marsalis, its horn-blowing savior, riding in—almost literally—on a white horse.[4] I argue here that nostalgia in jazz is neither so new as a focus on Lincoln Center and the Burns documentary appears to suggest, nor limited to so-called new traditionalists or neoclassicists. In fact, nostalgia has had a place in jazz since at least the 1950s, and historicism in the music has been important even longer.

Svetlana Boym's work in *The Future of Nostalgia* is a good starting point for a theoretically informed discussion of nostalgia in recent jazz. David Ake sees one aspect of the emotion as Boym describes it—*nostos* (return home) and *algia* (longing) or, "a longing for a home that no longer exists or has never existed," and "a sentiment of loss and displacement, but . . . also a romance with one's own fantasy"—in Pat Metheny's pastoral recordings on ECM (Boym 2001, xiii; Ake 2010, 99–100). This is a white, suburban, middle-class nostalgia, he argues, a jazz that does not point to a longing for the urban landscape, but to a respite from it. For a post-Watergate American youth that came of age during an era of enormous crisis in the city, this nostalgia and the music that created it were enormously appealing.

It is not hard to understand why, in the face of this vision of "home"—a vision that at least incidentally erases the intimate connection among jazz, the American city, and African American communities—young, largely black musicians in the 1990s would have looked for a different memory of jazz. The "neoclassicists" are certainly some of American music's great nostalgics, but their work is driven not by a racial revisionist urge—a desire to figuratively whitewash jazz—but by a desire to celebrate and coincidentally benefit from the established legitimacy of African American cultural products. Theirs is a nostalgia for an urban, black archipelago—arguably a more reasonable vision of the place of jazz in American history than the one conjured up by Metheny's recordings. The "young lions" can be accused of shortsightedness and narrow-mindedness when it comes to thinking about jazz's relationship to the larger family of black musical vernaculars, but not of failing to grasp how enormous is the process that led to the music's recognition as a canonical African American art. The importance of canonical status for artists such as Monk and Coltrane in a music with a collective memory of struggling for recognition cannot be overestimated.

Boym goes on, in *The Future of Nostalgia*, to define nostalgia in terms that more closely follow commonplace uses of the word. "At first glance," she writes, "Nostalgia is a longing for a place, but actually it is a yearning for a different time—the time of our childhood, the slower rhythms of our dreams. In a broader sense, nostalgia is a rebellion against the modern idea of time, the time of history and progress. The nostalgic desires to obliterate history and turn it into private or collective mythology, to revisit time like space, refusing to surrender to the irreversibility of time that plagues the human condition" (Boym 2001, xv). This kind of nostalgia, the desire to "obliterate history," or in less spectacular terms to imagine a past that does not move inexorably to the present, to seek continuity or stasis in place of progressive change, and to recapture, even to dwell intimately in, a past that seems less alienating than the present was so commonplace in jazz throughout the last decades of the twentieth century and into the twenty-first as to be the mainstream *Zeitgeist* of the music, at least in the United States. It is the affect Blumenfeld taps into in his review of the Carnegie Hall concert CD when he says he thinks people should not throw away old things, and that Ratliff engages when he wistfully describes a time past, when there was no risk of seeming uncool for wanting to go to jazz shows in the evening.

It is hardly controversial to describe the most recent jazz era as one dominated by nostalgia, but for the sake of understanding the kind of nostalgia that is characteristic of the current time it is important to note that in fact ours is only the most recent nostalgic turn in jazz. Something similar can be found in jazz criticism at least as early as the 1950s. Ralph Ellison's article "The Golden Age, Time Past," first published in *Esquire* in 1959, and later included in the collection *Shadow and Act*, for instance, takes an unabashedly nostalgic position on the early 1940s (Ellison 1995). John Gennari places Ellison's nostalgia in the late 1950s in the context of the emerging jazz studies—the moment of publication of books by Winthrop Sargeant, Marshall Stearns, Rudi Blesh, Barry Ulanov, Sidney Finkelstein, and Leonard Feather. The historiographies these writers, and others, were working out generally took the form of either evolution or entropy, what Gennari calls "pro-modernist evolutionary" and "tragic decline" narratives (Gennari 2006, 120). What is interesting is the extent to which Ellison's work—more than any of the others, who were largely either East Coast natives or from outside the United States—fits Boym's sense of nostalgia as a longing for both the lost past and the lost home. The lost home, here, is the spaces uptown—Minton's and Monroe's—that offered bebop musicians (most of whom were not New Yorkers) a taste of "down home" in Manhattan. Moreover, Minton's and Monroe's were themselves, for Ellison, *already* nostalgic spaces where "those who shared in the noisy lostness of New York" could partake "of community, evocative of home, of South…, where in an atmosphere blended of nostalgia and a music-and-drink-lulled suspension of time they could retreat from the wartime tensions of the town" (Ellison 1995, 200–201).

It makes sense, following Boym, to see nostalgia as pervasive in the jazz world of the 1950s, for two reasons. First, as she says, "outbreaks of nostalgia often follow revolutions," because revolutions inevitably lead us to not a simple longing for the ancien regime or fallen empire (or for prior styles, I might add) but to a recognition of "the unrealized dreams of the past and visions of the future that became obsolete" (Boym 2001, xvi). This certainly is true of Ellison, who laments the waste that comes with revolution, in music as much as in politics, at least as he sees it. Gennari remarks on Ellison's cogent complaint that we do not fully grasp the pleasure potential in modern artistic discoveries; I would add that he is quick to make an explicit connection between domains of so-called progress: "Ours is the tempo of the motion picture, not that of the still camera, and we waste experience as we wasted the forest" (Gennari 2001; Ellison 1995, 201). Second, nostalgia is a specifically modern phenomenon as Boym describes it—"coeval with modernity itself," and "at the very core of the modern condition" (Boym 2001, xvi). Though jazz was arguably a modern art from the very beginning, the period after World War II was explicitly a period of self-conscious, critical reflection on and engagement with modernity and modernism in jazz and jazz criticism. The "Moldy Fig" critics, for instance, were classic modern nostalgics, longing for the past, the folk, and a rural space that existed as much in Manhattanites' or Parisians' imaginations as in reality (Gendron 1995, 38–40).

My point, then, is that this album comes into a world of jazz ripe with nostalgia, not only in the early twenty-first century but historically as well. The nostalgia of its moment, the nostalgia that it specifically fed, may be distinct from earlier nostalgias, however. Boym distinguishes between two kinds of nostalgia—"retrospective" and "prospective"—the first of which is a longing for an idealized past and the second a longing for "its many potentialities that have not been realized," that is, for alternative trajectories to the future (Boym 2001, 168).[5] The nostalgia that characterizes this album's promotion and reception is potentially distinct from that which Ake describes in relation to Metheny's 1980s recordings, for instance, or from much of the work of Jazz at Lincoln Center, as well as from Ellison's earlier perspective. Although Ake sees a retrospective nostalgia in Metheny's work, and Marsalis has been explicit in crafting retrospective nostalgia for the hard bop era, the Carnegie Hall concert can also be part of a more prospective nostalgia, because its production and reception does not explicitly reject the art produced between past and present. New York in the 1950s may not actually have been paradise, but remembering it with a bittersweet longing does not require seeing the paths jazz has followed since then as a kind of loss.

BLUE NOTE AND THE RECORD INDUSTRY

Jed Rasula has called recordings the "media of memory," and even though the same thing could probably be said of film and photography, there is something important about how sound recordings, especially in jazz, have come to be, in his words, "the actual historical medium, the style of telling, a vital component...of a people's culture" (1995, 156). Rasula's point, that recordings have a materiality and life in the jazz scenes that have embraced them, is well taken, relating directly to their ability to be so intimately connected to an era's nostalgia; yet he left the project of validating recordings for what they are unfinished in this article. With the exception of the *Smithsonian Collection of Classic Jazz*, he did not explicitly tie the sound of jazz recordings to those recordings' lives as commodities within an industry built to sell them. It is beyond the scope of this chapter to fully account for the jazz recording industry itself, and there is at present no single volume study of the subject, much less of the complex relationship between industrial production and musical creation, but I place this recording in relation to the recent history of Blue Note records because it is a key part of the recording's life in the 2000s.

Blue Note built heavily, and successfully, on the legacy of its image. As drummer T. S. Monk, Thelonious Monk's son, told me in an interview about his album *Monk on Monk*, the label's association with authentic, classic images of jazz in the 1960s was a motivating factor for musicians associating themselves with Blue Note in the 1990s as much as for fans. In his words, "I'll take [*Monk on Monk*] to Blue Note because...Monk is synonymous with Blue Note and Blue Note is synonymous with classic jazz."[6] And yet, this nostalgic legacy is by no means the only aspect of Blue Note that made it a good choice for the release of the Carnegie Hall concert, and that allowed it to make the album more than a collector's item. The label, in fact, maintains a fairly broad portfolio of artists; it has done so for most of its modern history, producing new jazz recordings by established artists, and by young luminaries, but deriving most of its revenue from reissues of its classic catalog and from a number of pop artists, most notably Norah Jones.

Blue Note, which was established by Alfred Lion and Max Margulis, with Francis Wolff joining them shortly thereafter, was one of the first organizations to take advantage of the major industry reorganization precipitated by the American Federation of Musicians recording ban in the early 1940s. It began to sell recordings in 1939 and was poised for success when the ban was lifted, becoming the paradigmatic independent jazz label in the late 1940s.[7] Throughout this period the major labels, among them Columbia, Capitol/EMI, and RCA, did continue to include jazz in their catalogs, but they did not support the development of new subgenres directly. Rather, they used the small labels at the time—many of which entered into distribution agreements with the majors—as a feeder system, allowing the small labels to invest in R&D, so to speak, and eventually skimming off the most successful acts. So, for instance, by the mid-1960s Thelonious Monk, who had been with Blue Note, Prestige, and Riverside in succession, was recording for Columbia, and John Coltrane, who had recorded extensively with Blue Note and Atlantic (which remained an independent label, if a fairly large one, until 1968), became the star of ABC-Paramount's new jazz subsidiary, Impulse! Records.

This industry structure was fairly stable until the end of the 1960s, when major conglomerates acquired most of the small jazz labels. This period of consolidation could have looked like a good thing for jazz; after all, if the majors were investing in jazz labels, it might have meant more opportunity to build distribution, visibility, and so on for musicians who had gotten by on much less for decades. However, with the American economy at large slowing and eventually entering a recession, the majors tended to promote the music they saw as the most economically viable, as might be expected. The growth of fusion—for better and for worse—can be seen as facilitated by this process, with Miles Davis, Herbie Hancock, Weather Report, Mahavishnu Orchestra, and Return to Forever all recording for Columbia during the 1970s.

Blue Note records' fate in this process is instructive and of particular significance here, since it was the label that ultimately released the Carnegie Hall concert worldwide. It had operated as an independent company until 1965, and been acquired by Liberty records (itself a small label). Liberty was bought by United Artists, which was then absorbed by EMI in 1979 (EMI was independent at the time, though it is now wholly owned by Citigroup). EMI phased out Blue Note shortly after taking over UA, reviving it a few years later principally to market reissues. In sum, once one of the biggest independent labels for modern jazz, Blue Note became a subsidiary of one of the oldest and largest media conglomerates and was quickly made obsolete, if only for a few years. Its revival was specifically linked to the opportunity to market the historical canon of jazz (if not to market nostalgia, pure and simple).

The Carnegie Hall concert recording was by no means the only new release of old material to be an important part of the jazz recording industry's—or even of Blue Note's—catalog in the 2000s. In fact, much of Rudy Van Gelder's work as an engineer was reissued in a special "RVG Edition" series, and many classic 1950s and 1960s albums that had been reissued early in the CD era were re-reissued with new mastering around the turn of the century. Michael Cuscuna, whose career has been particularly associated with the production of such albums, and who produced the Carnegie Hall concert release, described the albums in terms of musical interest, historical memory, and the production of a kind of intimacy with the music for listeners. In an interview tied to the release of the Monk and Coltrane album, he said, "Many titles that sell best are time-honored recordings that were bestsellers when they first came out and continue to be bestsellers. And as recording technology gets better, a lot more can be done, and things can be improved" (Kahn 2005, 29). He went on: "I believe that everything that continues to sell, that people have an interest in, deserves to be upgraded if it can be.... If you're someone who cares about [this music], you can't not upgrade it" (30). Ultimately, he singled out new issues, such as the Carnegie Hall concert, saying, "My main motivation is really not reissues, it's focusing on unissued material. Even if it deserves to come out, as long as it's unissued, it really doesn't exist.... Every label I've worked with, no matter how well organized and maintained their archive is, has lost tapes or had masters that were destroyed. And that was the biggest heartbreak of all" (ibid.). Cuscuna describes the loss of material that could be available to listeners, that could be part of our connection to the past, in such strong affective language that it is hard not to see his ideas in terms of the kind of sentiment-laden emotional territory Boym means when she talks about nostalgia.

The Carnegie Hall concert was not just another remastered reissue of well-known material—like the RVG editions—nor a collection of old tracks mixed with cutting-room floor marginalia—the outtakes and alternate takes that fill many re-releases of classic jazz. It had not been in Blue Note's catalog, and as a result had not been excerpted, anthologized, or otherwise bowdlerized over the years. Jazz fans have supported fairly extreme examples of these approaches, in the service of a completist mentality that sees a value in the false starts and flawed tries that were never intended for release, but the collectors' editions that feature such material—the stuff of Cuscuna's Mosaic releases, for instance—are off-putting to a more general audience. The appeal of the Carnegie Hall recording was that it was more than yesterday's roast augmented by table scraps. Beyond this, the fact that the recording was from a concert, not a studio date, made it appealing. Liveness is a complex proposition in musical recording, and its significance is problematically fetishized for a music that relies on critical reflection and revision as much as spontaneity and surprise; nonetheless, the fact that this recording was one nearly complete performance was vitally important to its success. For critics and fans, I think, it had the feel of something real, something pure and unsullied. Fred Kaplan says as much in an article for the online journal *Slate*, titled "Studio Jazz vs. Live Jazz," in which he describes the Carnegie Hall recording as "some of the most thrilling performances, by some of the greatest musicians, that have ever been preserved on disc" (2005). This prompts him to say, "maybe jazz musicians should record fewer albums in studios and more before live audiences, in nightclubs or concert halls, where the music naturally belongs" (ibid.).

JAZZ AND THE ACADEMY

Throughout the second half of the twentieth century, while jazz recording was undergoing massive changes—from a main commodity of the major labels to the centerpiece of a system of small, independent labels, and ultimately a small, much-manipulated, and only marginally profitable "prestige" niche of newly configured major labels—the music famously took up residence in America's (and soon many of the world's) university music programs. It is possible to see these trends as somehow causally linked—the growth of jazz education perhaps as a reaction to the loss of a jazz market—though it is hard to demonstrate more than a correlation. Nate Chinen made such a connection in a seminal *New York Times* article: "While jazz education is thriving, the business of jazz itself, as measured by things like marketshare and album sales, has been in a tailspin" (2007). A photograph accompanying the article bore a caption that went further, linking the rise in jazz education to a decline in "real" jazz: "Jazz in performance is withering, but jazz education is booming at both the high school and college levels." In contrast with the recent jazz recording industry, scholarly attention to which has been spotty, institutional jazz education has been the object of extended study. My argument builds on the work of Chinen, David Ake, and Kenneth Prouty, in particular, in order to articulate the connections among jazz education, the jazz industry, and the nostalgic and historicist impulses that ultimately made it possible for Thelonious Monk and John Coltrane to have a new hit record in 2005, decades after they both died.

The connection between jazz on university campuses and jazz at large, as Chinen goes on to say in his article and as David Ake has explored at more length in *Jazz Matters*, is complicated, at the very least. The two writers agree that "by nearly any measure, college-based programs have not only replaced the proverbial street as the primary training grounds for young jazz musicians, but they've also replaced urban nightclubs as the primary professional homes for hundreds of jazz performers and composers" (Ake 2010, 103). Rather than add to the argument about the relative value of jazz education, or the authenticity of "college jazz" versus "real jazz"—which Ake has nicely described as a distinction that is "blurry, even illusory"—it will be more useful here to follow up the question of how jazz education has helped shape the jazz industry into which the Monk and Coltrane Carnegie Hall concert recording was released (118). Chinen describes "the performance and business of jazz" as "anemic," and Ake also appears to take as given that the industry is worse off than it was in its halcyon years (Chinen 2007). Quoting Mark Gridley, Ake says, "With the exception of a few standouts, jazz had less exposure and fewer performance outlets during the 1990s and beginning of the twenty-first century than at any other time in its history. The number of nightclubs featuring jazz on a regular basis was smaller than ever before, and the fees paid to the musicians in them were lower" (Ake 2010, 106).

With a significant absence of quantitative studies of the industry, we are left to assess Gridley's, Ake's, and Chinen's arguments in something of a vacuum. Both Ake and Chinen suggest the possibility that collegiate, and even high school, jazz programs could produce jazz consumers and ultimately initiate functional music scenes. Chinen does not see this feeding a jazz industry per se; rather, he proposes that the performance of jazz in smaller settings, "where no club scene has ever thrived," creates a network that is impervious to "the implosion of the monolithic music industry." "In that sense," he says, "jazz has a shot of becoming a folk music again" (Chinen 2007). Ake, on the other hand, with substantially more sophistication, says, "those studying jazz at Berklee or the University of Kentucky or the University of Oregon...are not just waiting until they graduate to become part of a jazz scene. They *are* the jazz scene...." The shape of these jazz scenes, as Ake describes them, then, are thoroughly complex: "the roles of teacher, student, professional, performer, booking agent, colleague, festival adjudicator, friend, concert promoter, and audience member shift constantly" (Ake 2010, 118, emphasis in the original).[8] John Murphy views universities as key locations for the flowering of jazz scenes in recent history: "Young people who are drawn toward the music still benefit from the early influences of family and friends and still learn about the music directly from practitioners, from recordings, and on their own. But most of them first encounter jazz, or at least the opportunity to play it with others, in secondary schools, colleges and universities" (2009, 171).

I use the term *scenes* here as does Ake, and in the sense that Travis Jackson defines it quite broadly in *Blowin' the Blues Away* (2012), to mean social fields composed of musicians, audiences, industries and institutions through which "jazz performance occurs and is made possible" (67). Ken Prouty uses the similarly undertheorized and similarly difficult term *jazz community*, which he critiques extensively in *Knowing Jazz* (2012). Universities are part of "the jazz community," in Prouty's view, in addition to creating smaller, nested "jazz communities," which cohere as much through shared acts of listening (2012, 44–45). This aspect of Prouty's work is particularly appealing when thinking about jazz on university campuses and the Carnegie Hall recording, inasmuch as jazz communities' coalescence around listening to canonical recordings suggests a setting in which a new, previously unheard album by one of the legendary, but otherwise underdocumented bands of the 1950s would be deeply appreciated.

Collegiate jazz scenes have had a complex relationship with the recording industry, dramatically shifting the economics of jazz from a setting in which most musicians had to make whatever living they could from a combination of gigging and recording to one in which many (if not most) musicians derive a portion of their living (and get health insurance and retirement benefits) from professorships and university residencies. This means that the industry now has a large swath of recordings that can be made without concern for significant profits, often operating on a break-even model. The biggest names in jazz—the Marsalises and Lovanos, the Brad Mehldaus and Bad Pluses—still record with major labels and make some part of their earnings from albums, but many more do not. This means that the Carnegie Hall concert recording entered a jazz market that was, in the aggregate, much larger than it was in the 1950s, and that featured far more releases per year, but in which the scarcity and value of a truly massive, crossover "hit" recording of instrumental jazz was ironically even larger.

The most profound effect university jazz programs have had that bears directly on the sales and reception of the Carnegie Hall concert recording, however, is in supporting the orientation of contemporary musicians toward a historical canon for the music. Most of the discussion of institutional jazz education has focused on the role of the improvisation class in developing the language of young jazz soloists. Ake, in particular, has described it as a constraining force, focusing students' attention on one primary set of tools (essentially the harmonic language and pattern orientation of John Coltrane's work encapsulated in the recording *Giant Steps*; Ake 2001 122–27, 129–33). This, incidentally, establishes a kind of canonicity, though not a historicist one. Quite the opposite, in fact, inasmuch as Coltrane's language became canonized not as part of a jazz historical narrative but rather as an asynchronic, universally available (and in the worst case, "correct") approach to melodico-harmonic thinking (2001, 127–34). John Murphy has critiqued Ake's work, arguing that the improvisation class is usually only a starting point for jazz education, and that students routinely internalize a much wider range of ideas about playing from other sources—from each other, from private lessons with master musicians, from experience on the bandstand, and, I would add, from jazz history classes (Murphy 2009, 178–80).

The place of jazz history in the university curriculum has largely been ignored in these discussions, but I believe it is vital. Ken Prouty is the only scholar to look at it in detail, tying it to the larger question of how jazz education has built a particular vision of the canon. One of his key points is that although jazz history is routinely included in jazz curricula (and in fact is mandated by the National Association of Schools of Music, which provides accreditation to many jazz undergraduate and graduate degree programs), it has not been discussed in any depth in the pedagogical literature. Jazz historians and ethnomusicologists have been keenly attentive to questions of historiography (if not questions of pedagogy) in the past two decades, but the same has not been true of jazz educators. In particular, as he says, "the hegemony of canon is evidenced by its omission from the discussion. It is simply 'there'" (2012, 107). It is beyond the scope of this chapter to fully evaluate the range of historiographical positions encountered in the jazz history courses taught at universities across the United States and throughout the world, but Prouty's insistence on the prevalence of a hegemonic canon is intuitively reasonable. Though this may not be ideal in the view of most working jazz historians, it underscores my position that the expansion of university jazz programs created a world of jazz scenes that were primed by an inherently canonical outlook to embrace Monk and Coltrane's Carnegie Hall recording as the most important recording of its time, much as jazz critics did.

CONCLUSION

This album, the recording of the Thelonious Monk Quartet with John Coltrane's two sets benefiting the Morningside Community Center at Carnegie Hall on November 29, 1957, is a remarkable artifact. It is at once evidence of a historically significant moment, a compelling performance with some truly gripping music, and a window onto the state of jazz as a set of scenes, communities, or industries at the turn of this century. Unlike many other recordings, which were either in circulation continuously throughout the half century between the mid-1950s and the mid-2000s, or which were less unique as new discoveries, this album has the distinction of having been released to far more visibility years after its recording than it would have had when it was recorded. In a way, this goes against the consensus about jazz's relative importance in the new global music industries, and against arguments in particular about the decline in significance of jazz in the United States. It could be argued, of course, that its success is precisely evidence of the "museumification" of jazz that has given it the smell of mothballs, the kind of decline that has led to a current moment in which there is putatively so little new creativity that the most compelling release of 2005 was half a century old. This kind of argument typifies the "death of jazz" literature, but it is faulty, being built on half-truths and spurious reasoning. The excitement this album generated need not be seen as a sign that other releases from the same year were not creative and interesting, or that "real" jazz has been supplanted by "academic" jazz; in fact, its presence could easily be evidence of the opposite, that there is a deep pool of interest in jazz, which can only really be a result of a breadth of performers—across the United States and worldwide—who are pursuing the music in historically creative ways, and that such a contemporary jazz community sees the past as a source of enjoyment and inspiration, not anxiety and stultification.

This is not to say that the album sounds the same as it would have when it was recorded. Rather, the album sounds very different, and this is perhaps the strongest evidence for the remarkable ongoing creativity that the music has engendered in the past fifty years. Monk and Coltrane's shifting position between 1957 and 2005 is best thought of in terms of the shifting context for understanding what constitutes the mainstream and its outside in jazz over the period of time. The music on the recording itself is, of course, no different. Rather, how it could be heard has shifted. In the late 1950s Monk could still sound discomfitingly avant-garde, but by 2005 he was well within the tradition. The dissonances that shocked audiences in the 1950s had been "doubled-down" by a generation of artists who may even have abandoned the tonal underpinnings that Monk always used as a context for dissonance. The insistence on a personal conception of sound that audiences and critics alike occasionally mistook for a lack of technique had been taken to new heights by artists such as Ornette Coleman, who went so far as to record on violin—an instrument he had not studied—so as to avoid lapsing into habit. Even Monk's radical style—those hats and sunglasses, the goatee and penchant for obscure quips that delighted so many—had been rendered palatable to the middle of the road by the shifting mores of more than four decades. Likewise, Coltrane, who was just about to make the music for which he became canonical in the late 1950s and who would go on to make music in the later 1960s that pushed many of his admirers to the edge of their ability to accept musical extremes, and sometimes beyond, ultimately became a byword for all that is heroic in the jazz musician, if at the expense of his later work.

The opportunity to hear this change, and by this I mean to be struck by it viscerally, in the act of listening to a concrete musical utterance, captured on tape, is this album's most important quality today. It emerged by a happy accident—a result of Larry Appelbaum's curiosity, when faced with an unexpected manila envelope on the shelves of the Library of Congress marked only "Monk"—and was made widely available because of the marketability of the hard bop canon. One letter writer wondered in the pages of *Down Beat* what Monk and Coltrane would have thought about having a hit record so many years after they recorded it ("Buyer" 2006, 10). I suggest that they might not have been as surprised as the question supposes. Although this chapter has largely dealt with questions of criticism and marketing, it will be useful to point back to the music discussed in the previous chapters, to say that Monk and Coltrane, and Wilson and Abdul-Malik for that matter, sound as if they thought of that night in 1957 as something special, perhaps because of the venue, and perhaps because they knew it was being recorded for broadcast. They may well have felt they had recorded timeless music. No doubt there is something uncanny about the reappearance of an album like this—an ahistorical abruption in time—but perhaps it is enough to say that the pleasures such music brings are many and varied enough to satisfy many listenings in and out of its historical moments.

NOTES

INTRODUCTION

1. The discovery of the tapes was perhaps not quite as unexpected as the media coverage from 2005 suggests: Chris Sheridan mentions them as a "lost" item in *Brilliant Corners* (2001), for instance (79). Nevertheless, though there was some memory of their existence in the collector world, no one had heard them or even knew if they still existed until Appelbaum rediscovered them in the Library of Congress.
2. The word *zygon* is derived from Greek and means "yoke." Thus zygonic describes relationships in which two or more things are yoked together through modes of repetition.
3. Although I do not write about this in the language of Peircean semiotics, this is one of the central points of that theoretical framework. All of Peirce's sign types—indexical, iconic, and symbolic—rely in one way or another on repetition to become meaningful. Moreover, as Monson, Turino, and others have amply demonstrated, the repetition of figures in music creates meaning in ways that can easily be understood in terms of Peirce's semiotic theory (Monson 1996; Turino 2009). This is not to say that music "is like language," but rather that Peirce's semiotics is a theory of thought and communication and is thus applicable, at times in divergent ways, to both language and music.
4. Interestingly, just over forty years later, on a gig at New York's Birdland jazz club, I heard Griffin play a remarkably similar solo on "Evidence."
5. Perchard appears to have focused on Monk not only because this issue is so present in his work, but because it was something that the critic Jalard saw as a central fault line in Monk's career: the great break between a period of creativity, when he wasn't repeating himself, so to speak, and a period of stagnation, when he was (2011, 66–69).
6. A key difference between the recordings of "Evidence" that I discuss in my article "A Unique Chunk of Jazz Reality" (2004) and those Perchard discusses is that in the Five Spot recordings Monk made a clear, explicit choice between two similar, but not identical, takes for release, while in the live recordings from Europe Monk offered no similar judgment.

7. This in spite of the fact that, rather famously, the selection committee voted to give Duke Ellington the prize in 1965 but was overruled by the Pulitzer organization (Hentoff 1965, in Tucker 1993, 362).

CHAPTER 1

1. For biographical information about Monk, see Solis (2008) and Kelley (2009).
2. There is some lack of clarity in the literature concerning the cabaret card system. The cards were licenses, renewable every two years, to work in establishments that sold alcohol. Bartenders, wait staff, and others had to have them, as did musicians, and they functioned for the city primarily as a way to control a group of workers in a segment of New York's service sector who were seen as pro-labor, and potentially communist. Loss of the card did not entirely stop Monk from playing in the city, but it did limit his ability to play in the most visible (and potentially best-paying) clubs. Throughout the period, Monk traveled consistently, if not constantly, and recorded often.
3. Interview with the author, 1999.
4. For biographical information on John Coltrane, see Lewis Porter (2000) and Ben Ratliff (2008).
5. For an extended discussion of Coltrane's time with Monk, see Porter, op. cit., 107–13.
6. An earlier translation rendered this quote "The critics, at that time, were all appalled by what we were playing, but you know, for a musician, it's difficult to understand their position. . . ," but I think the translation above is more accurate. Coltrane seems to have been more flummoxed by the critics' fascination with the minutiae of his playing than upset by their negative judgments.

CHAPTER 2

1. See DeVeaux (1989) and Tackley (2012).
2. Even today, it should be noted, although jazz is by almost any measure likely to be seen as a highbrow music, fans often prefer nightclub performances to concert settings.
3. This concert was commonplace enough to warrant only a short, single-column notice in the *New York* Times, which focused primarily on Ray Charles's set ("Jazz Is Presented at Carnegie Hall," 1957: 12).
4. On the connections between various segments of the jazz scene and between jazz and other popular musics in the 1950s, 1960s, and today, see Monson (1996, 2007); Ake, Hiroshi Garrett, and Goldmark (2012); and Jackson (2012).
5. For a description of vaudeville and variety show act types, see Cullen, Hackman, and McNeilly (2007) and Rodger (2010).
6. For a representative sample of concert programs, see the Ann Arbor Michigan University Musical Society website, which reproduces historical programs going back to 1874 (http://ums.aadl.org/ums). In the nineteenth century, programs on the series, including those presented by major symphony orchestras, are quite varied, including songs, dance movements, solo and chamber works, individual symphonic movements and lots of Wagner excerpts. Chicago Symphony Orchestra programs begin to look more like contemporary ones, including only work for orchestra or orchestra

and soloist, programming complete symphonies, and presenting fewer works per program, in two halves separated by an intermission, starting around 1894: Boston Symphony Orchestra programs change around the same time, and Pittsburg Symphony Orchestra programs follow suit around 1898. The next decade appears transitional, with a range of program types, and by the early 1910s virtually all programs by all orchestras appearing on the UMS concert series follow a standard format.

7. Though, it should be noted, the inside front cover of the program for Hammond's *From Spirituals to Swing* concert included an appeal for donations to assist impoverished Spaniards, suffering from weather, famine, and violence as the country was rocked by civil war.

CHAPTER 3

1. An instance of Monk's general approach to programming (and a fairly standard approach, all in all) can be seen on his live album from the Blackhawk in San Francisco, recorded in two sets on April 29, 1960. Each set started with two medium-to-up-tempo pieces, followed by a ballad, and each ended with an up-tempo rendition of "Epistrophy." In the first set the pieces were similar in length, but in the second set an exceptionally long version of "Round Midnight" left time for only the briefest closing statement of the head of "Epistrophy."
2. With respect to my discussion of improvisation and composition in the Introduction, here is a kind of limit case for jazz that exposes the real distinctions jazz musicians make among composition, interpretation, and improvisation and that gives strength to Nettl's contention that these kinds of creative action are parts of a single process.
3. At least it appears Monk originally titled it "Feeling That Way Now," or perhaps "Y Don't U Try Now," or "Why Do You Evade the Facts" (Kelley, 2009, 113). The opening melody fits the words "That's the way I feel now" nicely, and he may have thought of the piece by that title at some point as well. Many of Monk's titles were fluid until he began recording regularly, at which point they tended to take on a fixed form.
4. Monk referred to the B section of his pieces in AABA song form as the "inside," rather than the "bridge," but for the sake of clarity I have followed the more standard terminology throughout this book.
5. My intention here is certainly not to demonstrate the universality of Schenkerian principles so much as to say that, as Henry Martin and others have suggested elsewhere, an analysis of at least some jazz melodies in terms of tonal voice leading and the projection of middle-ground melodies from more complicated foregrounds can be useful (Martin 1996, 13–20).
6. The recording on *Thelonious Himself* is slightly slow, so that everything sounds not quite a half step lower.
7. It is noteworthy that the kind of development between two performances by Monk with the same saxophonist—the intensification and growth of a specific concept in improvised aspects of a piece, whether it be solos, accompaniments, or, as here, ornamentation of the head melody—was not uncommon. As I have written elsewhere, two recordings of "Evidence" by Monk and Johnny Griffin, from a few

months apart in 1958 show a similar, though not precisely the same, process (Solis 2004, 317–27).
8. In fact, to highlight this change, the horns enter and play the first measure of the first A section in the second chorus of this take, but Monk plays the interjection in m. 2 solo, and the horns then come back in only at the bridge.
9. Defining a triplet rhythm does not seem like a substantial challenge, but for some reason this figure caused problems elsewhere as well. On the Town Hall concert recording, for instance, Hall Overton scored it for baritone sax, and Pepper Adams struggled with it.
10. Interview with author, 1999.

CHAPTER 4

1. Perhaps a reflection of his recent troubles with the legal system in New York, Monk seems to have gotten from the title "Just You, Just Me" to "Evidence" through the shift: "Just You, Just Me" = "Just Us" = "Justice." Evidence is, then, a fundamental requirement for justice (Kelly 2009, 114).
2. Interview with the author, 1999.

CHAPTER 5

1. "Bemsha," as Gary Mapp told Kelley, is a corruption of "Bimsha," which is itself derived from "Bimshire," a colloquial name for Barbados (Kelley 2009, 161).
2. Christopher Washburn has shown the presence of *clave* rhythms in Monk's compositions, but in most cases this seems as much to be a feature of jazz itself as a clear evocation of Afro-Caribbean styles (1997, 72–73).
3. For continuity of analysis between head and solos, I discuss the melodic and harmonic elements of the song in the transposed Eb key.

CHAPTER 6

1. Here we see the limits to using ontological models drawn from classical music to understand the creative process in Monk's work.
2. How this relates to Monk's life is hard to say with any certainty. Like most of the core modern jazz musicians, Monk was born outside New York—in Rocky Mount, North Carolina, specifically—but unlike many, he relocated to upper Manhattan with his parents as a small child. He came of age in New York's multicultural musical world, not the more intimate world "down South." Unlike Dizzy Gillespie, from Cheraw, South Carolina, or even Charlie Parker, for whom Kansas City may have seemed far from the real action, Monk had little to prove in terms of worldliness or cosmopolitan sophistication when he stepped onto the bandstand at Minton's.
3. All three sections are related and could be thought of as aaa', but I distinguish between the first two on the one hand, which start the same way, and the third, which starts differently.
4. The tune appears six times on Jerry Newman's recordings from Minton's in 1941 (originally part of the Columbia University Radio Club Broadcasts, and now in the WKCR archives), listed only as "Theme."

CHAPTER 7

1. The death of jazz discourse is also not new. In 1964, the magazine *Jazz* featured an installment of its "Jazz Forum" titled "Is Jazz Dead?" The editors apologetically prefaced the discussion this way: "What prompts this curt, unadorned query is the fact that we've been reading so much about the demise of jazz. For example, Frank Sinatra, in LIFE, asserted that jazz is dead" (59, original capitalization).
2. In 1963 Monk's star was bright enough for Columbia to select his second album with the label *Criss-Cross* as the "record of the month" for their mail-order sales program.
3. NPR's current audience statistics at the time of this writing are available on their website at http://www.npr.org/about/aboutnpr/audience.html.
4. There is, of course, more to Burns's documentary than this, and excellent reviews of it can be found elsewhere. John Gennari's assessment acknowledges the piece's failure to come to terms with new creativity in the music, while still arguing for its importance as an introduction to jazz for a generation who might not otherwise ever come to know the music; Robin Kelley's review highlights entirely different aspects of the documentary, lamenting its failure to situate jazz in its communities (Gennari 2006, 373–374; Kelley 2001).
5. This distinction, which Boym also connects to progressive and reactionary political goals, is similar to the one Dale Chapman makes between progressive and reactionary approaches to repertory jazz, although he does not articulate it in Boym's terms (Chapman 2003).
6. Interview with author 1999.
7. For an extended discussion of Blue Note from this period, see Richard Cook's *Blue Note Records: The Biography* (2004).
8. This has been relatively true about the jazz industry since at least the 1950s. Companies such as Riverside or Blue Note were not so large, nor the money to be made in any one facet of the industry so much, that these particular professional roles were clearly distinguished. Teo Macero, for instance, who is probably best remembered as the producer of Miles Davis's electric albums, was also a composer, tenor saxophonist of real skill, promoter, and friend to a number of musicians at various times. The change, if there has been one, is probably in degree, rather than kind.

REFERENCES

Ake, David. 2001. *Jazz Cultures*. Berkeley: University of California Press.
———. 2010. *Jazz Matters: Sound, Place, and Time Since Bebop*. Berkeley: University of California Press.
———, Charles Hiroshi Garrett, and Daniel Goldmark, eds. 2012. *Jazz/Not Jazz: The Music and Its Boundaries*. California: University of California Press.
Ansell, Derek. 2006. "Thelonious Monk Quartet with John Coltrane at Carnegie Hall." *Jazz Journal International* 59/1: 30–31.
Arnold, Denis. 1968. "Charity Music in Eighteenth-Century Dublin." *Galpin Society Journal* 21: 162–74.
Atre, Prabha. 2007. "Improvisation in Indian Classical Music." *Journal of the Indian Musicological Society* 38: 112–13.
Balliet, Whitney. 1957. "Musical Events." *New Yorker* (November 30): 201.
Bergman, Alan. 2006. "From Archive to Classic: The Story of the Epic Monk/Coltrane Carnegie Hall Recording." *Jazz Education Journal* 38/4: C30–C31.
Berliner, Paul. 1994. *Thinking in Jazz: The Ultimate Art of Improvisation*. Chicago: University of Chicago Press.
Blumenfeld, Larry. 2005. "Auditions: Seeds of Change, Unearthed." *Jazziz* (December): 50.
Boydell, Brian. 1992. *Rotunda Music in Eighteenth-Century Dublin*. Dublin: Irish Academic Press.
Boym, Svetlana. 2001. *The Future of Nostalgia*. New York: Basic Books.
Burlingame, Sandra. 2008. "Harry Tobias: Lyricist, Composer, Music Publisher (1895–1994)." *JazzBiographies.com*. http://www.jazzbiographies.com/Biography.aspx?ID=264, accessed October 21, 2012.
"Buyer." 2006. "Letters to the Editor." *Down Beat* 73/3: 10.
Chapman, Dale Edward. 2003. "Specters of Jazz: Style, Ideology, and Jazz as Postmodern Practice." Ph.D. dissertation, UCLA.

Chinen, Nate. 2007. "Jazz Is Alive and Well. In the Classroom, Anyway." *New York Times* (January 7): A1.

Cohen, Aaron. 2005. "Momentous 1957 Monk-Coltrane Carnegie Concert 'Discovered', Released." *Down Beat* 72/10: 16–17.

Compston, Christine. 2001. *Earl Warren: Justice for All*. New York: Oxford University Press.

Cook, Richard. 2003. *Blue Note Records: The Biography*. Boston: Justin, Charles.

Corbett, John. 2005. "At Carnegie Hall." *Down Beat* 72/10: 65.

Coulter, Glenn. 1959. "Clark Terry with Thelonious Monk—'In Orbit.'" *Jazz Review* 2/1: 37–38.

Cullen, Frank, with Florence Hackman and Donald McNeilly. 2007. *Vaudeville Old and New: An Encyclopedia of Variety Performers in America*, vol. 1. London: Routledge.

DeMichael, Don. 1960. "Coltrane on Coltrane." *Down Beat* 27/20: 26–27.

DeVeaux, Scott. 1989. "The Emergence of the Jazz Concert, 1935–1945." *American Music* 7/1: 6–29.

———. 1999. "*Nice Work If You Can Get It*: Thelonious Monk and Popular Song." *Black Music Research Journal* 19/2: 169–86.

DeVito, Chris. 2010. *Coltrane on Coltrane: The John Coltrane Interviews*. Chicago: Chicago Review Press.

De Wilde, Laurent. 1997. *Monk*. New York: Marlowe.

Dyer, Geoff. 2011. *Otherwise Known as the Human Condition: Selected Essays and Reviews*. Minneapolis: Greywolf Press.

Ellison, Ralph. 1995 [1964]. *Shadow and Act*. New York: Vintage Books.

Gabbard, Krin. 1995. "Introduction: The Jazz Canon and Its Consequences." In *Jazz Among the Discourses*, ed. Krin Gabbard, 1–30. Durham, NC: Duke University Press.

Garrett, Charles Hiroshi. 2008. *Struggling to Define a Nation: American Music and the Twentieth Century*. Berkeley: University of California Press.

Gendron, Bernard. 1995. "'Moldy Figs' and Modernists: Jazz at War (1942–46)." In *Jazz Among the Discourses*, ed. Krin Gabbard, 31–56. Durham, NC: Duke University Press.

Gennari, John. 2006. *Blowin' Hot and Cool: Jazz and Its Critics*. Chicago: University of Chicago Press.

Gillespie, Dizzy and Al Fraser. 1979. *To Be or Not . . . to Bop*. New York: Doubleday.

Gioia, Ted. 1998. *West Coast Jazz: Modern Jazz in California, 1945–1960*, rev. ed. Berkeley: University of California Press.

Gitler, Ira. 2005. *Thelonious Monk Quartet with John Coltrane at Carnegie Hall* Liner Notes. Blue Note Records 35173.

Goehr, Lydia. 1992. *The Imaginary Museum of Musical Works: An Essay in the Philosophy of Music*. New York: Oxford University Press.

Gracyk, Theodore. 1992. "Adorno, Jazz and the Aesthetics of Popular Music." *Musical Quarterly* 76/4: 526–42.

———. 1996. *Rhythm and Noise: An Aesthetics of Rock*. Durham, NC: Duke University Press.

Hentoff, Nat. 1965. "This Cat Needs No Pulitzer Prize." *New York Times Magazine* (September 12): 64–66ff.

———. 1956. "Just Call Him Thelonious." *Down Beat* 23/15: 15–16.

———. 1960. "The Private World of Thelonious Monk." *Esquire* (April): 133–37.
Howland, John. 2009. *"Ellington Uptown": Duke Ellington, James P. Johnson, and the Birth of Concert Jazz*. Ann Arbor: University of Michigan Press.
Hurst, Roy. 2005. "New Monk, Coltrane Recording Discovered." *News and Notes*. National Public Radio, http://www.npr.org/templates/story/story.php?storyId=4930231, accessed October 21, 2012.
Jackson, Travis. 2012. *Blowin' the Blues Away: Performance and Meaning on the New York Jazz Scene*. Berkeley: University of California Press.
Jasen, David. 2003. *Tin Pan Alley: An Encyclopedia of the Golden Age of American Song*. New York: Taylor & Francis.
"Jazz Forum: Is Jazz Dead?" 1964. *Jazz* v. 3–4: 59.
"Jazz Is Presented at Carnegie Hall." 1957. *New York Times* (November 30): 12.
Jones, Malcolm. 2005. "Monk and 'Trane—Together at Last." *Newsweek* (September 25).
Kahn, Ashley. 2005. "The Art of the Reissue: Michael Cuscuna Has His Hands in a Mosaic of Releases." *Jazz Times* 35/7: 29–31.
Kaplan, Fred. 2005. "Fresh Tracks: Jazz in the Studio vs. Jazz Recorded Live." *Slate* (October 18). http://www.slate.com/articles/arts/music_box/2005/10/fresh_tracks.html, accessed 7/3/2013.
Keepnews, Peter. 2000. *The Complete Prestige Recordings*, liner notes. Berkeley: Prestige Records DIDX-71913–DIDX-71915.
Keil, Charles. 1987. "Participatory Discrepancies and the Power of Music." *Cultural Anthropology* 2/3: 275–83.
Kelley, Robin D. G. 2001. "In a Mist: Thoughts on Ken Burns's *Jazz*." *ISAM Newsletter* 30/2: 8–10.
———. 2009. *Thelonious Monk: The Life and Times of an American Original*. New York: Free Press.
Kinderman, William. 2009. "Improvisation in Beethoven's Creative Process." In *Musical Improvisation: Art, Education, and Society*, ed. Gabriel Solis and Bruno Nettl, 296–312. Urbana: University of Illinois Press.
Lyttleton, Humphrie. 1959. "Monk: Genius in a Straw Hat." *Melody Maker* (October 10): 13.
Martin, Henry. 1996. *Charlie Parker and Thematic Improvisation*. Newark, NJ: Institute of Jazz Studies, Rutgers.
McDonough, John. 2006. "Benny Goodman at Carnegie Hall: The Story of the Session." *IAJRC Journal* 39/4: 29–40.
McKinney, Jack. 1959. "Giants in Jazz: Thelonious Monk." *Metronome* 76/1: 21ff.
Medwin, Marc. 2006. "At Carnegie Hall." *Cadence* 32/2: 120–21.
Monk, Thelonious. 2002. "Thelonious Monk Fake Book." New York: Hal Leonard.
Monson, Ingrid. 1996. *Saying Something: Jazz Improvisation and Interaction*. Chicago: University of Chicago Press.
———. 1999. "Riffs, Repetition, and Theories of Globalization." *Ethnomusicology* 43/1: 31–65.
———. 2007. *Freedom Sounds: Civil Rights Call out to Jazz and Africa*. New York: Oxford University Press.
———. 2008. "Hearing, Seeing, and Perceptual Agency." *Critical Inquiry* 34/S2: 36–58.

———. 2009. "Jazz as Political and Musical Practice." In *Musical Improvisation: Art, Education, and Society*, ed. Gabriel Solis and Bruno Nettl, 21–37. Urbana: University of Illinois Press.

Montgomery, Vern. 1983. "Jaws Unlocks." *Jazz Journal International* 36: 14.

Murphy, John P. 2009. "Beyond the Improvisation Class: Learning to Improvise in a University Jazz Studies Program." In *Musical Improvisation: Art, Education, and Society*, ed. Gabriel Solis and Bruno Nettl, 171–84. Urbana: University of Illinois Press.

Narmour, Eugene. 2000. "Music Expectation by Cognitive Rule-Mapping." *Music Perception* 17/3: 329–98.

Nettl, Bruno. 1974. "Thoughts on Improvisation: A Comparative Approach." *Musical Quarterly* 60/1: 1–19.

Nicholson, Stuart. 2005. *Is Jazz Dead: Or Has It Moved to a New Address?* London: Routledge.

Nooshin, Laudan. 2003. "Improvisation as 'Other': Creativity, Knowledge, and Power—the Case of Iranian Classical Music." *Journal of the Royal Musical Association* 128/2: 242–96.

Ockelford, Adam. 2005. *Repetition in Music: Theoretical and Metatheoretical Perspectives*. Aldershot, UK: Ashgate.

Owens, Thomas. 1974. "Charlie Parker: Techniques of Improvisation." Ph.D. dissertation, Music Department, UCLA.

"Orrin Keepnews, Producer: Monk at Town Hall, pt. 1." Concord Music Group, podcast February 24, 2008, http://www.concordmusicgroup.com/media/podcast.php?Channel List_Slug=podcasts-default, accessed October 21, 2012.

"Orrin Keepnews, Producer: Monk at Town Hall, pt. 2." Concord Music Group, podcast March 9, 2008, http://www.concordmusicgroup.com/media/podcast.php?Channel List_Slug=podcasts-default, accessed October 21, 2012.

Paddison, Max. 1982. "The Critique Criticized: Adorno and Popular Music." *Popular Music* v. 2: 201–18.

Parikh, Arvind. 2007. "Can Improvisation Be Taught?" *Journal of the Indian Musicological Society* 38: 105–11.

Perchard, Tom. 2011. "Thelonious Monk Meets the French Critics: Art and Entertainment, Improvisation, and Its Simulacrum." *Jazz Perspectives* 5/1: 61–94.

Porter, Eric. 2012. "Incorporation and Distinction in Jazz History and Jazz Historiography." In *Jazz/Not Jazz: The Music and Its Boundaries*, ed. David Ake, Charles Hiroshi Garrett, and Daniel Goldmark, 13–30. Berkeley: University of California Press.

Porter, Lewis. 2000. *John Coltrane: His Life and Music*. Ann Arbor: University of Michigan Press.

Prouty, Kenneth. 2012. *Knowing Jazz: Community, Pedagogy, and Canon in the Information Age*. Jackson: University Press of Mississippi.

Ramsey, Guthrie Jr. 2003. *Race Music: Black Cultures from Bebop to Hip Hop*. Berkeley: University of California Press.

Rasula, Jed. 1995. "The Media of Memory: The Seductive Menace of Recordings in Jazz History." In *Jazz Among the Discourses*, ed. Krin Gabbard, 134–64. Durham, NC: Duke University Press.

Ratliff, Ben. 2008. *Coltrane: The Story of a Sound*. New York: Farrar, Straus & Giroux.

———. 2005. "Jazz Gem Made in '57 Is a Favorite of 2005." *New York Times* December 21: Section E, Column 1, p. 1.

Ravikiran, Chitravina N. 2007. "Improvisation in Carnatic Music." *Journal of the Indian Musicological Society* 38: 125–28.

Rodger, Gillian. 2010. *Champagne Charlie and Pretty Jemima: Variety Theater in the Nineteenth Century*. Urbana: University of Illinois Press.

Rosenthal, David. 1992. *Hard Bop: Jazz and Black Music 1955–1965*. New York: Oxford University Press.

Sarkella, Sandra, and Patrick Mazzeo. 2006. "Reverend James H. Robinson and American Support for African Democracy and Nation-Building, 1950s–1970s." In *Freedom's Distant Shores: American Protestants and Postcolonial Alliances with Africa*, ed. R. Drew Smith, 37–52. Waco, TX: Baylor University Press.

Schudel, Matt. 2005. "When Trane Met Thelonious." *Washington Post* October 16: Sunday Arts No1.

Severo, Richard. 2001. "Norman Granz, Who Took Jazz out of Smoky Clubs and Put It in Concert Halls, Dies at 83." *New York Times*, November 27: D7.

Sheridan, Chris. 2001. *Brilliant Corners: A Bio-Discography of Thelonious Monk*. Westport, CT: Greenwood Press.

Solis, Gabriel. 2009. "Genius, Improvisation, and the Narratives of Jazz History." In *Musical Improvisation: Art, Education, and Society*, ed. Gabriel Solis and Bruno Nettl, 90–102. Urbana: University of Illinois Press.

———. 2008. *Monk's Music: Thelonious Monk and Jazz History in the Making*. Berkeley: University of California Press.

———. 2004. "'A Unique Chunk of Jazz Reality': Authorship, Musical Work Concepts, and Thelonious Monk's Live Recordings from the Five Spot, 1958." *Ethnomusicology* 48/3: 315–47.

Sutton, R. Anderson. 1998. "Do Javanese Gamelan Musicians Really Improvise?" In *In the Course of Performance: Studies in the World of Musical Improvisation*, ed. Bruno Nettl with Melinda Russell. Chicago: University of Chicago Press.

Tackley, Catherine. 2012. *Benny Goodman's Famous 1938 Carnegie Hall Concert*. New York: Oxford University Press.

Tenzer, Michael. 2006. "Introduction: Analysis, Categorization, and Theory of World Music." In *Analytical Studies in World Music*, ed. Michael Tenzer, pp. 3–38. New York: Oxford University Press.

Tucker, Mark, ed. 1993. *The Duke Ellington Reader*. New York: Oxford University Press.

Turino, Thomas. 2009. *Music as Social Life: The Politics of Participation*. Chicago: University of Chicago Press.

Vail, Ken. 1999. *Duke's Diary: The Life of Duke Ellington, 1950–1974*. Metuchen, NJ: Scarecrow Press.

Vosburgh, Dick. 1995. "Obituaries: Harry Tobias." *Independent* (January 2): Gazette Section, p. 16.

Washburn, Christopher. 1997. "The Clave of Jazz: A Caribbean Contribution to the Rhythmic Foundation of an African-American Music." *Black Music Research Journal* 17/1: 59–80.

Whitehead, Kevin. 2005. "Hearing New Music from Monk and Coltrane." *Fresh Air*, National Public Radio. http://www.npr.org/templates/story/story.php?storyId=4949427, accessed October 21, 2012.

Young, Jon. 2005. "At Carnegie Hall: Thelonious Monk Quartet with John Coltrane." *Mother Jones* (November). http://www.motherjones.com/media/2005/11/carnegie-hall, accessed July 3, 2012.

Zak, Albin. 2001. *The Poetics of Rock: Cutting Tracks, Making Records*. Berkeley: University of California Press.

INDEX

ABC-Paramount Records 157
Abdul-Malik, Ahmed 3, 21, 30, 67, 82, 117–118, 119, 135
Adams, Pepper 168n9
Adorno, Theodor 147
Aeolian Hall see "Experiment in Modern Music"
aesthetic ontology 18, 168n1
　see also work concept, musical
aesthetics, black 12–13
African American music 31, 153
African diaspora 14
African music 43, 95
Afrocentrism 94–95
Afro-modern 12–13, 143
allographic/autographic distinction 18
Amazon 150
American Federation of Musicians 157
Ammons, Albert 25, 43
analysis, harmonic 58–59, 63–65, 72, 83, 98
　melodic 57–58, 61–63, 82–83, 97–98, 127–28
　Schenkerian 58, 167n5
Apollo Theater 49
Appelbaum, Larry 4, 164, 165n1
Armstrong, Louis 16
Arnheim, Gus 108

arrangement, musical 56, 65, 107, 111–12
Art Ensemble of Chicago 152
Atlantic Records 157
"Au Privave" 127
audience expectations, live jazz 45–46, 70–71
audience for the Morningside Heights Community Center benefit concert 50, 82
Australia 147
avant garde jazz 39

Bad Plus, the 161
"Bags' Groove" 138
Baker, Chet 48, 50
Baker, Houston A. 12
Balliet, Whitney 50, 124
Basie, Count 127
　orchestra 43
"Bass Blues" 137
Bebop 84, 107
Bechet, Sydney 25, 43
"Bemsha Swing" 94–95, 140
　title 168n1
Benedetti, Dean 34
Bergman, Alan S. 149, 150

Berliner, Paul 13
Best, Denzil 94
Billboard (magazine) 50, 150
"Billie's Bounce" 127
Birdland jazz club 165n4
Black, Brown and Beige 43–44, 95
Blakey, Art 5, 25, 26, 27, 30, 81, 109
    approach to comping 28, 66–67
    approach to tempo 129
Blesh, Rudi 154
"Blue Monk" 26, 81, 126–42
    compared with "Nutty" 128
    Prestige recording 26–28
Blue Note record label 4, 24–26, 150, 152, 156–58
"Blue Trane" 137
blues
    form 10, 28, 126–27
    in modern jazz 126
"Blues for Alice" 127
Blume, August 34
Blumenfeld, Larry 151, 153
boogie-woogie 25, 43
"Bolivar Ba-Lues-Are" 127
bop, *see* bebop
Boym, Svetlana 153–54, 155, 158
Brown, Ray 46
burlesque (American theatrical tradition) 49
Burns, Ken 153
"Bye-Ya" 94–107
    compared with "Sweet and Lovely" 109, 112
    title 94

cabaret card system 25, 30, 49, 166n1
calypso 94–95
canon, musical 162
Capitol records 157
Carnegie Hall Concert (Benny Goodman) 39, 42–43
Carter, Benny 42
CBS television 151
Chambers, Paul 32
Chapman, Dale 169n5

Charles, Ray 48, 50, 166n3
Charles Mingus Presents Charles Mingus 51
Chinen, Nate 159–60
Chopin, Frederic 62
chorus forms 10–11
Clarke, Kenny 28, 143
Clef Club 41
Cole, Nat "King" 46
Coleman, Ornette 164
collaboration, musical 24, 29
"college jazz" 160
Coltrane, Naima 3, 33, 34
Coltrane, John
    as composer of blues 136–37
    musical growth 34, 35–36
Columbia records 157
Columbo, Russ 108
commodification 156
composition, musical 14, 15–16, 17, 24, 55, 61
    oral-formulaic 17
comprovisation 11, 13, 119
concerts, benefit 47
Congress on Racial Equality (CORE) 47
convention, musical 55, 72, 93
Cookin' 32
Copland, Ray 24, 28, 29, 62
Corbett, John 151
creativity, musical 24
"Crepuscule with Nellie" 51, 61–68
    compared with nineteenth-century classical works 62
    compared with "Nutty" 70
    version on *Monk's Music* 62, 65, 66–68
    version on *Thelonious Monk in Italy* 65
    version on *The Thelonious Monk Orchestra at Town Hall* 65
Criss Cross 169n2
criticism, jazz 39–40
Cromer, Austin 48
Crouch, Stanley 153
Crosby, Bing 108
Cubop 95
Cuscuna, Michael 158–59

Daniels, Charles 108
Davis, Eddie "Lockjaw" 143
Davis, Miles 3, 19, 26, 28, 32, 35, 49, 51, 138
    and fusion 157
    impact on John Coltrane 137
    Prestige recordings 5
    Columbia recordings 5
Davis, Sammy Jr. 49
Debussy, Claude 62
DeMichael, Don 35, 36
"Don't Get Around Much Anymore" 44
Down Beat 148, 149, 150
Drew, Kenny 33
Dyer, Geoff 147

East Coast jazz 39
Ebony 48
ECM 153
economy, political 7, 19, 52
Eldridge, Roy 46
Ellington, Duke 14, 19, 42
    Carnegie hall concert 143–44
    Morningside Community Center benefit 48
    Pulitzer Prize 166n7
Ellison, Ralph 154–55
EMI 152, 157
"Epistrophy" 51, 92, 142–45, 167n1
"Equinox" 137
Esquire 154
Europe, James Reese 41
"Everything Happens to Me" 70, 109
"Evidence" 71–81, 165n4, 165n6, 167n7
    melody found in accompaniment to "Groovin' High" 72
Experiment in Modern Music 39, 42

Feather, Leonard 154
"Feeling that Way Now" *see* "Monk's Mood"
Finkelstein, Sidney 154
Fitzgerald, Ella 46
Five Spot Café 3, 16, 30–31, 33, 34, 36, 38, 49–50, 151
form, musical 35–36

Foster, Frank 28, 29
Freedom Now Suite 47
Fresh Aire (radio program) 149
From Spirituals to Swing 42, 43, 167n7
Fuller, Gil 56
funk 143
fusion jazz 157
The Future of Nostalgia 153–54

gamelan 15
Garland, Red 32, 33
Garrett, Charles H. 16
Genius concept 31
Genius of Modern Music 71
Genius Plus Soul Equals Jazz 48
The Gentle Side of John Coltrane 68
Getz, Stan 46
"Giant Steps" 24
Giant Steps 102
Gillespie, Dizzy 5, 19, 32, 46, 48, 50
    and Latin jazz 95
    big band 95
    "Monk's Mood" 56
Gitler, Ira 49
Giuffre, Jimmy 47
Goehr, Lydia 14, 17–18
Golson, Benny 5
Gordon, Dexter 108, 111
gospel 126
Gracyk, Theodore 18
Granz, Norman 45
Gray, Wardell 108, 111
Greer, Jesse 72
Gridley, Mark 160
Griffin, Johnny 7, 11–12, 31, 82, 96, 126, 128, 165n4
groove 9
Gross, Terri 149
Gryce, Gigi 24, 33, 62, 66
"Gully Low Blues" 16
Guerra, Mike 31
Guy, Joe 143

Half Note (jazz club) 151
Hancock, Herbie 157

Handy, W.C. 42, 63
Hanes, Roy 82
hard bop 32, 95, 108, 119
    era 5–6
Hardman, Bill 128
Hawkins, Coleman 24–25, 33–34, 62
Heath, Jimmy 31
Heath, Percy 25, 26, 27, 28, 81
Henderson, Bill 47
Hentoff, Nat 47, 55, 148
heterophony 81
Hill, Andrew 6
hip hop 25
historiography 162
Holiday, Billie 48, 50, 51
homophony 91
Horowitz, Vladimir 62
Howland, John 41
Humes, Helen 43
Hurst, Roy 149
Hurt, Mississippi John 128

"I Mean You" 25, 81
improvisation 11, 14–15, 24
Impulse! records 157
"In Orbit" 148
Indian classical music 15
influence, musical 60–61
intensity, as analytical feature 28, 66, 124, 134–37, 143–44
interpretation, musical 17, 55, 65–68, 92, 112–13
intertextuality 11, 13

Jackson, Milt 24, 26, 28, 108, 138
Jackson, Travis 161
Jacquet, Illinois 46
Jalard, Michel-Claude 11–12
jam session 109
jazz, compared with Western classical music 46
    death of 147–151, 163, 169n1
    education 159–62
    industry 156–58, 161–62
    live compared with recorded 40, 53, 159

jazz concerts, and compensation 52
    common in the 1950s 39
    prestige of 41–42
Jazz (magazine) 169n1
Jazz (documentary) 153
Jazz at the Philharmonic 39, 45–46
Jazz for Moderns 51
Jazz Messengers 111, 126, 128–29
The Jazz Review 148, 149
Jazziz 149, 151
Jet 48
John Coltrane and Johnny Hartman 68
Johnson, James P. 42
Jones, Norah 156
Jones, Philly Joe 32
Jones, Sam 30
"Jumpin' at the Woodside" 143
"Just a Gigolo" 26, 70, 109
"Just You, Just Me" 72–73

Kaplan, Fred 159
Keil, Charles 9
Keepnews, Orrin 30
Kelley, Robin D.G. 36, 62, 128–29
    on Caribbean rhythms in "Bye-Ya" 94
    on origins of "Evidence" 71–72
    review of *Jazz* (documentary) 169n4
Kennedy, Robert F. 48
Kenton, Stan 45
Kinderman, William 17–18
Koeningswarter, Pannonica de 32
Kolax, King 31
Krebs, Maynard G. 49
Krupa, Gene 42

Lacy, Steve 37, 150
Latin jazz 94
Lemare, Jules *see* Daniels, Charles
Lewis, Meade Lux 25, 43
Liberty Records 157
Library of Congress 37, 165n1
Lincoln Center 153, 155
Lion, Alfred 25, 157
Live at the Blackhawk 167n1
Live at the Five Spot: Discovery! 4, 33

"Liza" 109
"Locomotive" 29
A Love Supreme 36
long playing (LP) records 45
Lovano, Joe 150, 161
"Lulu's Back in Town" 11
lyrics 70, 72, 109–11
Lyttleton, Humphrey 148

Macero, Teo 169n8
McGhee, Howard 108
McKibbon, Al 25
McKinney, Jack 148
Mahvishnu Orchestra 157
"Manhattan Moods" *see* "Ruby, My Dear"
Many Loves of Doby Gillis 49
Mapp, Gary 26, 109
Margulis, Max 157
Marsalis, Wynton 19, 150, 152, 153, 155–56
Martin, Henry 17, 167n5
Mehldau, Brad 161
memory 156
Metheny, Pat 153, 155–56
Metronome 149
Mingus, Charles 14, 51
Minton's 28, 34, 126–27, 143, 154–55
"Misterioso" 126
Misterioso 82
Mobley, Hank 5
Modern Sounds in Country and Western 48
modernity 155
Monk, Nellie 61–62
Monk, Thelonious, as accompanist 33, 35, 38, 78–79, 100, 137
 as bandleader 31, 36–37
 as composer of blues 126–27, 136–37
 compared with Art Tatum 60
 use of transitions 27–28, 79, 88, 91, 111
 youth in New York 95
Monk, Thelonious (T.S.) 156
Monk and Coltrane 33
"Monk's Dream" 125

"Monk's Mood" 32, 33, 56–61, 70, 95, 125
 compared with "Crepuscule with Nellie" 62
 compared with "Evidence" 70
 version on *Thelonious Himself* 59–60
 version on *The Thelonious Monk Orchestra at Town Hall* 60–61
Monk's Music (album) 24, 33, 35–36, 62
Monk on Monk 156
Monroe's 154–55
Monson, Ingrid 8–9, 13, 47, 49, 52, 165n3
"Mood Indigo" 44
Morgenstern, Dan 49–50
Morningside Heights Community Center 48
 benefit concert 4, 11
Mother Jones 150
Mulligan, Gerry 5, 51
Murphy, John 160–61, 162

Narmour, Eugene 8
National Association for the Advancement of Colored People (NAACP) 47
National Public Radio (NPR) 149–51
neoclassicism 152, 153
Nettl, Bruno 14–15, 18, 167n2
New York Times 50, 151
New Yorker 50
Newman, Jerry 34, 168n4
News and Notes 149
"Nica's Dream" 94
"Nice Work (If You Can Get It)" 109
Nicholson, Stuart 147
"A Night in Tunisia" 94
nostalgia 7, 152–56, 158
"Nutty" 34, 41, 81–92, 101
 compared with "Blue Monk" 128
 version on *Thelonious Monk and John Coltrane* 83, 87–88
 version on *Work* 81

"Off Minor" 101
Ockelford, Adam 8
"Original Faubus Fables" 51

Overton, Hall 41, 168n9
Owens, Thomas 16–17

Parker, Charlie 16–17, 19, 34, 46
    and blues 127
participatory discrepancies 9
Peirce, Charles 165n3
Perchard, Tom 11–13, 165n5, 165n6
Persian classical music 15
Peterson, Oscar 42
Philips, Flip 108
pianism 62
"Playhouse," see "Bye-Ya"
polyrhythm 28
Porter, Lewis 31, 136–37
Postif, François 34
pop music 39, 49, 150, 166n4
Pozo, Chano 95
Preludes, see Debussy, Claude and Chopin, Frederic
Prestige records 25–26, 29, 32, 82, 157
Prouty, Kenneth 159, 161, 162
Pulitzer prize 19, 166n7

R&B 31, 39, 48
race 19, 153
Race Music 143
Ramsey, Guthrie Jr 143
"Raise Four" 74, 137
Rasula, Jed 156
Ratliff, Ben 35, 151, 153
RCA 157
Reagon, Bernice Johnson 47
Reception, critical 35
    of Morningside Heights Community Center benefit concert 50–51
    of Thelonious Monk 148–49
    of *Thelonious Monk Quartet Featuring John Coltrane at Carnegie Hall* 4, 149–52
recording, *in situ* 34
    live 6
Relaxin' 37
repetition, and cognition 8
    and cyclicity 9
    and periodicity 8

and zygonic theory 8
incorporation at multiple formal levels 9
motivic 11
Return to Forever 157
Rhapsody in Blue 42
rhythm, and musical form 76, 94, 96–97, 112–113, 119, 124
    as element of style 68, 74
    Latin 95, 107, 168n2
Riley, Ben 27, 82
Riverside records 24, 30, 82, 157
Roach, Max 5, 26, 47
Robinson, Bill "Bojangles" 44
Robinson, James 48
Rollins, Sonny 3, 25, 26, 48, 50, 94
Rosenthal, David 5–6
Round About Midnight 5
"Round Midnight" 81, 125, 167n1
Rouse, Charlie 7, 31, 34, 67
"Ruby, My Dear" 34, 61, 70
Rushing, Jimmy 43
Russel, Curly 28

"S. O. L. Blues" 16
sales of jazz albums 150
San Juan Hill neighborhood 95
Sandole, Dennis 31
Sargent, Winthrop 154
Saturday Review 50
scene, musical 160
semiotics 165n3
Shadow and Act 154–55
sheets of sound 60, 74, 98–99
Sheridan, Chris 34, 165n1
Shihab, Sahib 24
Sickler, Don 68
Sigel, Robert 149
Silver, Horace 5, 26, 32
Sims, Zoot 46, 48, 50
Sinatra, Frank 49, 169n1
"Sing, Sing, Sing (with a Swing)" 143
Smith, Benetta 62
Smith, Bessie 128
Smithsonian Collection of Classic Jazz 156
Snitzer, Herb 149

sociology of music 40
Sony Music co. 25
"St. Thomas" 94
standards 10, 109, 143
Steamin' 32
Stearns, Marshall 154
Stewart, Rex 41
"Stickball," *see* "I Mean You"
Stitt, Sonny 5
"Straight, No Chaser" 126, 127
Student Non-Violent Coordinating Committee (SNCC) 47
Sulieman, Idrees 24
"Sweet and Lovely" 26, 107–24
    connection to "Bye-Ya"
    version on *Mulligan meets Monk*
    versions with Charlie Rouse

"Take the A Train" 91
Taylor, Art 30
Tempo 26–27, 82, 112, 124, 128–29
Tenor Sax 25, 32, 99
Tenzer, Michael 8
Terry, Clark 47, 148
Terry, Sonny 43
Tharpe, Sister Rosetta 43
"That's the Way I Feel Now," *see* "Monk's Mood"
"Thelonious" 140
Thelonious Himself 32, 33, 71, 167n6
Thelonious Monk Trio 26
theme song 142–43
"These Foolish Things" 26
third stream 44
Time (magazine) 49, 149
Time, in music 9
Tobias, Harry 108
Town Hall concert, Monk 39, 41, 49–50
trad (traditional) jazz 25
Traneing In 137
"Trinkle Tinkle" 34
Tristano, Lennie 5
Turino, Thomas 165n3
Turner, Joe 43

Two Girls and a Sailor 108

Ulanov, Barry 154
United Artists 157
unity, musical

Van Gelder, Rudy 25, 158
variety show 42, 49
Voice of America 4, 22, 37, 45

Watkins, Julius 28
Ware, Wilbur 3, 30, 67
Way Out West 5
Weather Report 157
Weinstock, Bob 26, 29, 126
"Well, You Needn't" 79, 107
Werkbegriff, *see* work concept, musical
West, Danny Quebec 24
West Coast jazz 39
Whitehead, Kevin 149–50
Whiteman, Paul 39
"Why Do You Evade the Facts," *see* "Monk's Mood"
Wild, Laurent de 9
Williams, Bert 49
Williams, Clarence 63
Williams, Cootie 143
Wilson, John S. 50
Wilson, Shadow 3, 20, 30, 67, 74, 94. 144
    as accompanist 106, 118, 121–23, 131, 142
    on *Genius of Modern Music* 71
Wolff, Francis 26, 157
Work 71, 126
Workin' 32
World Sax Quartet 152
work concept, musical 13, 14, 17, 24, 26, 92, 93

"Y Don't U Try Now," *see* "Monk's Mood"
Yamekraw: A Negro Rhapsody 42
Young, Lester 46

Zak, Albin 18
Zygonic relationships 165n2